Rewriting the History of the Judiciary Act of 1789

Rewriting the History of the Judiciary Act of 1789

Exposing Myths, Challenging Premises, and Using New Evidence

By
Wilfred J. Ritz

Edited by
Wythe Holt
and
L. H. LaRue

University of Oklahoma Press : Norman and London

Library of Congress Cataloging-in-Publication Data

Ritz, Wilfred J.
   Rewriting the history of the Judiciary Act of 1789 : exposing myths, challeng-
ing premises, and using new evidence / by Wilfred J. Ritz ; edited by Wythe
Holt and L. H. LaRue.
      p.   cm.
   Includes bibliographical references.
   ISBN 0–8061–2239–0 (alk. paper)
   1. United States.   Judiciary Act of 1789.   2. Courts—United
States.   3. Jurisdiction—United States.   I. Holt, Wythe, 1942–
II. LaRue, Lewis H.   III. Title.
KF8714.52.A16R57   1989
347.73′1—dc20
[347.3071]   89–37863

The paper in this book meets the guidelines for permanence and durability of
the Committee on Production Guidelines for Book Longevity of the Council on
Library Resources, Inc. ∞

Contents

Acknowledgments

THE EDITORS would like to acknowledge the gracious aid of the following: Thomas Radko, who encouraged us to complete our colleague's manuscript, and gave us wise counsel; Sue Ritz, who had confidence in us, and gave us permission to edit her husband's opus; the anonymous readers, who were extraordinarily careful and acute in their reading, and whose suggestions were always helpful; William Wiecek and Kathryn Preyer, who took the time to give us a last-minute read; and Margaret Williams, who undertook a herculean task of typing and retyping, and who kept our spirits high by her unflagging belief in the value of our labor and of her own.

Editorial Statement *by Wythe Holt and L. H. LaRue*

IN FEBRUARY, 1986, Wilfred Julius Ritz had a stroke; he is now disabled, confined to a wheelchair, and can no longer do scholarly work. At the time of the stroke, Bill left uncompleted a book-length manuscript on the history of the First Judiciary Act. We have prepared it for publication with his permission.

A year before his stroke he had submitted the manuscript to the University of Oklahoma Press. The readers for the press had said: "Yes, but," that is, *yes* the manuscript should be published, *but* revisions were needed. Six months before his stroke, Bill began revising the manuscript for publication, but the stroke cut short his work.

Those who know him well saw the frustration of this project as a tragedy. This book is not merely a major work; it represents the better part of more than thirty years of research. From the beginning of his teaching career in 1952, he taught a course in conflict of laws, in which one studies the legal complexities of transactions that involve citizens of several states or nations. The intellectual challenge of this topic is formidable. It is not easy to decide which state's law should govern when a transaction spans several states. Early on, he began to do research into the relevance of the Constitution and the First Judiciary Act to the questions that lay behind the issues in conflicts. He gathered an enormous quantity of primary sources that illuminate the historical issues, and he asked original and fresh questions about those issues. The conclusions he reached are both unorthodox and persuasive. This is not the place to anticipate Bill's theses (see the introduction), but we would say at this point that his greatest achievement was to see the problem through eighteenth-century eyes, not our own. Bill honored the historian's first maxim; he reconstructed the intellectual world of those who enacted the First Judiciary Act, thus enabling us to escape the limitations of our own categories.

There is no doubt that Bill would have finished this book years earlier had he not, in the prime of his career, sharply changed his teaching. In the late sixties he introduced a new course that dealt with sentencing, and he altered the direction of his research and teaching in criminal law. In the midseventies he told one of us that he had come to think that all that he had taught in criminal law for the previous two decades was irrelevant nonsense, and so he did something about it.

One form that this radical reorientation took was his initiative in organizing an innovative legal aid program; he set up a program to provide legal assistance to the prisoners in the Federal Reformatory for Women in Alderson, West Virginia. In supervising this program, Bill devoted countless hours to educating students and to assisting women who were in need of help. Several deans tried to ease his burdens by relieving him of responsibility for teaching certain courses, but Bill would never agree to a reduction in teaching load, and so the decanal solicitude was frustrated.

We must all admire the human decency of his choices, but we regret deeply that it entailed the loss of precious time that could have been used to complete this book.

As we began the task of revision, we started, naturally enough, with the criticisms of the readers for the University of Oklahoma Press. They were enthusiastic about the substance of the book; they asserted in strong terms that Bill's thesis was new, that his use of evidence in support of it was convincing, and that it was a scholarly work that had no competition. However, they found its organization confusing, and they entered a strong plea for its reorganization. Our first job was to unearth the source of the confusion.

In our judgment, the readers were correct in stating that Bill's book would be opaque, in several crucial places, to the average reader. In reconstructing and rewriting the history of the Judiciary Act of 1789, Bill saw the puzzle as a whole, but he wrote with reference to pieces of the puzzle, attempting to lay them out and fit them together. Unfortunately, the assembly of pieces into a whole is difficult to comprehend unless one has the range of knowledge that Bill possessed. Throughout the manuscript, Bill flattered his readers unjustly by assuming knowledge on their part, and this assumption was surely erroneous.

Furthermore, the order in which Bill presented the several pieces to the reader proved to be daunting, even to those who were knowledgeable about the topic. Bill started the book with a chapter titled "Sources," in which he gave a careful description of the evidence from which all inferences must be constructed. To start with the evidence is surely the most careful way to begin, but it taxes the powers of those who do not have a good grasp of the context for the evidence. Having discussed the evidence, Bill then moved to a description of the scholarly work that had used the sources; he stated what his predecessors had done and condemned their errors. Once again, this is an orderly way to proceed; responsible scholars always confront what their predecessors have done; and there is no need to publish unless one can add new truths or refute old errors. But of course, it is baffling for most readers to be plunged into a scholarly debate without adequate preparation.

There are other sources for confusion in the manuscript. Since Bill approached the question as a difficult intellectual puzzle, he never cast his conclusions into a narrative form. Most of us find stories easy to understand, but Bill made no concession to our desire for a narrative. Furthermore, he was saying something new, and although at times his choice of metaphor is clear and dazzling, in other places there is a struggle to find a vocabulary that will articulate his thought. Throughout his research, Bill tended to work alone, and he shared his manuscripts with only a few people, people who generally understood what he was driving at. Bill never anticipated the problems of understanding that others would have and have had.

Consequently, our editorial task has been both difficult and extensive. We have altered the text that Bill left uncompleted in the following ways:

First, we have written a short introduction in which we try to orient the reader by indicating the direction in which Bill was proceeding. We do this by bringing forward material that had appeared later in the manuscript. Our hope here is that by showing the general direction of his thought, we are aiding the reader in seeing the overall shape of this book.

Second, we have added a chronology, or narrative, of the progress of the Judiciary Act through the First Congress. We are convinced that this narrative is absolutely essential to aid those who do not have the easy command of the sources that Bill Ritz so handily had, and so we have consolidated into a single chronology items that Bill had scattered throughout his manuscript.

Third, we have reorganized the book. We have moved Bill's opening chapters, in which he discussed the evidence and the work of his scholarly predecessors, to the end of the book, and we have put these chapters into several appendices. This reorganization brings forward the principal substantive chapters of the book; we believe that most readers would prefer this reordering of the material. Furthermore, we have reorganized several of the substantive chapters by bringing forward to the beginning of each chapter the theses that Bill advances. Bill tended to work through the details and to present conclusions only at the end; in other words, he replicated in the order of his presentation the order of his discovery. By altering the order of presentation, we believe that we have improved the clarity of these chapters; the reader is able to see the relevance of the details.

Unfortunately, this reorganization of the sequence of presentation has required some rewriting. It was not feasible simply to cut and paste so as to move sentences forward while leaving other sentences unaltered. However, as far as possible we have preserved the wording and the style of the text that Bill left uncompleted. Where we were forced to rewrite, we have altered the letter, but we believe that we have preserved the spirit.

Our fourth editorial contribution is more controversial, yet we think necessary. We have stated explicitly matters that Bill assumed without stating. Throughout the manuscript, there are places where Bill presents evidence, assuming that all will see its relevance, whereas its relevance is opaque to those who do not already understand the overall thrust of his thought. Filling in the gaps has required some informed guesswork on our part, and we have surely erred in places. However, we can see no reasonable alternative to our course, and so we have taken the risk of error.

Fifth, there are some minor mistakes. One of us has encountered some documents and materials that Bill did not have a chance to read. Here the editor must correct where there is error, and note ambiguities where the new information has raised them. We have indicated by way of note these minor corrections and left the text itself unaltered.

Sixth, there are a few places where we have had to confront the problem of our disagreement with an interpretation. Like all of us, Bill Ritz is human, and he too would at times get caught up in an argument and carry it too far. With reference to these issues, we present both his interpretation and our disagreement. We hasten to add that we do agree with the large burden of his argument. Only in a few details have we found it necessary to record (as unobtrusively as possible) an alternative interpretation.

Seventh, we agree with the University of Oklahoma Press readers that Bill's criticism of the work of Julius Goebel and particularly of Charles Warren is sometimes expressed too acutely, perhaps too fulsomely. We have taken the liberty of muting the tone of this critique, though we agree with Bill in the thrust of its substance. Furthermore, it was especially unfortunate that Bill began his manuscript with a criticism of Warren's theses. To begin with the negative of another's views, instead of the affirmative of one's own, will inevitably confuse the reader; unless the reader already knows (and remembers) the substance of Warren's thesis, the relevance of the refutation is opaque. Consequently, as stated above, we have moved this material into an appendix.

We have undertaken this editorial labor because of our judgment that Bill's manuscript is a brilliant achievement. He has done what other scholars, excellent scholars, were unable to do, and we believe that his book is one of the foundations upon which any future work in this area must build. He has reconstructed in a fresh and illuminating way the legal and political culture of the early Republic and he has shown how and why they are inextricably intertwined. He has placed the Judiciary Act of 1789 into the context of this web of legal and political culture, and he has advanced scrupulous interpretations of the details of its language in light of this larger context. Those who come after and write on law and politics in the early Republic will have to reckon with his achievement.

We ourselves have learned much from him, both his work and his example, and since we regard ourselves as his friends and colleagues, we also judge ourselves to be privileged to have his consent to complete this work. We edit in the spirit of scholarly piety.

Rewriting the History of the Judiciary Act of 1789

CHAPTER I

Introduction

In 1789 the First Congress enacted a law that established the national courts. Understanding what the members of the First Congress did is difficult, and the main source of the difficulty is that we read back into the history of this legislation our own ideas and disputes, instead of seeing it as they saw it, in terms of the conflicts and principles with which they were preoccupied. A small but illuminating example of our inveterate anachronism is the title by which we designate this statute. We customarily refer to it as "The Judiciary Act of 1789," or in more honorific terms, as the "First Judiciary Act."

The phrase "Judiciary Act" is modern usage; the term was not used then by either Congress or the public, so far as we can determine. The modern use of the term reflects the course of subsequent events; there now exists a powerful and functioning institution, the national judiciary, and so we refer to several important statutes as "judiciary acts." When the First Congress acted, what we now know was in the future. The actual title of the act was more prosaic than our customary designation; it was titled, "An Act to establish the Judicial Courts of the United States." To a modern eye, the phrase "the Judicial Courts" is redundant, but this modern perspective is an anachronism. In 1789 judiciaries were becoming distinct, but were not yet distinct, from the legislative and executive branches of government. It was a novel and somewhat inscrutable project to imagine how judges might form a third and separate branch of government. The first step in avoiding the modern perspective, so as to see the act in its own historical context, is to recognize the fact of novelty.

We shall follow customary usage and refer to the act as the Judiciary Act of 1789, but we start by noting that this usage reflects a subsequent historical achievement, which of course must be honored; however, the actual legislative history of the act is another matter. Reconstructing the legislative history of the act is worth doing since the current scholarly consensus about the history of the act is erroneous. The currently accepted legislative history of the Judiciary Act of 1789 is mythic in content, based on questionable premises, and subject to large-scale revision.

The task of explaining the process by which the Judiciary Act of 1789 was drafted and enacted must begin by noting a fact that is well known but sometimes forgotten—some sort of legislative act was necessary, since the constitution left many questions open. The Constitution itself establishes the Congress and the presidency, but the drafters of the Constitution left the job of establishing a judiciary to the Congress. Moreover, the language of Article III of the Constitution—the judiciary article—is extremely open-ended and provides an umbrella under which virtually any type of judicial system can be organized. To be sure, Article III does contain some significant provisions on how the judiciary may do its business, but there is precious little in the text on the structure of the judiciary. The only *structural* statement in the constitutional text about the sort of institution that the judiciary should be is the statement that there should be one (and presumably only one) "supreme Court." There is nothing in the Constitution about how many judges should sit on the "supreme Court." Furthermore, the text does not decide the question of whether this "supreme Court" is to be the only national court; instead, the text provides that there are to be "such inferior Courts as the Congress may from time to time ordain and establish."

The second important fact (and again, it is both obvious and crucial) is that establishing a court system was a politically controversial matter. The controversy centered around questions of power, that is, on the divisions of power that we know as the federal system. Under the previous constitution of the United States, the Articles of Confederation, there was no national judiciary, nor was there a national executive. Consequently, there were no national institutions that the Congress could use to enforce its will. The new Constitution not only transferred important powers to the central government, so that the new Congress would be more powerful than the old; new institutions were available to execute these powers. Although the passage of the new Constitution consolidated the fact that there was to be a change, there was no consensus about the details of the change. In passing the Judiciary Act of 1789, the Congress had to adjust the details, and so the drafting and enacting of the act was a politically controversial affair. Of course, the First Congress did not address all of the relevant details, nor did they act with perfect clarity in doing what they did. Politicians never do such things. Nevertheless, certain choices were

4

made, and in order to understand what was done, we need to understand some of the political context in which they acted.

Part of that context was established by the controversies that had surfaced during the ratification process. Considerable opposition to the Constitution became evident among those who thought that the proposed new national governmental structure was too undemocratic, too strong, too centralized, and took or threatened to take too much power away from the states. The Anti-Federalists, as these opponents confusingly became known, focused much of their attack on the vagueness of the proposed judiciary article and the potentially enormous power that might thereby be given to the novel national judicial system. Their strength forced the ratification conventions to propose numerous amendments to the Constitution, as is well known. The First Congress, although it was peopled almost entirely by Federalists, as the supporters of the Constitution became known, found it politically advisable to respond. We are all familiar with the fact that these proposals led to the ten amendments that we refer to as the Bill of Rights.

However, the relevance of the Judiciary Act to these proposals is not well known. Several important amendments were proposed that would have drastically altered and limited the national judiciary. One thesis of this book is that the Judiciary Act of 1789 was a compromise that addressed several of the demands and quieted some of the controversy over the nature of the national judicial system. In order to quiet controversy, the drafters of the act had to strike out in new directions.

The most striking fact about the new national judicial system is that it was in fact new. We have grown so accustomed to the current shape of the national courts, which is a hierarchical three-tiered system, comprising trial courts, intermediate courts, and a supreme court, that we have come to think of it as a natural and inevitable system. However, it must be emphasized that the state judiciaries that existed at the end of the eighteenth century were not organized in this fashion, and that part of the controversy surrounding Article III arose on this historical fact. Consequently, it is desirable to say a few things about the then-existing state judiciaries. Only in this way can one appreciate the nature of the achievement of the First Congress. Another thesis of this book is that the national judicial system established in 1789 was a historical novelty. It was not modeled on the state systems; instead, the state systems have subsequently been modeled on it.

If one examines closely the then-existing state judiciaries, they might be described in the following way: Most states had a corps of judges who sometimes went singly into the field to try cases, and who at other times assembled together in the capital to try cases and consider "appeals." In other words, even when there existed the formality of designation that distinguished "inferior" courts from "superior" courts, there was no distinction in judicial personnel. The same group of judges sat at different times in the different "courts." Furthermore, the "superior" or "supreme" courts were all "trial" courts as well as "appellate" courts, and the "review" of an inferior court by a superior court was commonly a retrial, with a new jury. Finally, the courts of last resort were commonly a branch of the legislature, or a body amalgamating judges, legislators, and members of the executive. Distinctness and hierarchy did not characterize the court structures, and "superior" usually meant only that a reviewing court had more judges sitting on it. To us this may seem strange; in those days, it was the routine. (Of course, these generalizations must be qualified, and the details of the state systems that then existed are set out in the course of this book. However, these generalizations are accurate enough for purposes of this introduction.)

Once we understand that the existing state judiciaries did not have the sort of distinction between trial courts and appellate courts with which we are familiar, then we can understand the controversies that were generated by the original text of Article III. One of the provisions in Article III states that "the supreme Court shall have appellate Jurisdiction, both as to Law and Fact." The opponents of the Constitution, and even some of its friends, were alarmed by this provision, since they read it in the context of the then-existing state courts.

In the state court systems as they then existed, there was no clear distinction between the *functions* of an "appellate" court and a "trial" court, and indeed, these very terms, "appellate" and "trial," were not routinely used in those days. Since the functions were not sharply distinguished, the terminology had different overtones. The statement in Article III that the Supreme Court was to have "appellate Jurisdiction, both as to Law and Fact" seemed to the opponents to describe the same sort of system that they then knew in the states. If this were so, it followed that a litigant might have to travel to the national capital and retry a case. At the very least, this would prove burdensome; at the worst, it would enable the rich litigant to abuse the poor litigant. Furthermore, it would deprive litigants of trial before a jury drawn from the same locality as the commission of the crime.

The provisions as to "appellate Jurisdiction" alarmed opponents in a second way. Although the designation of superior courts as appellate courts was not customary, the form of procedure called an "appeal" was well known. This form of procedure was associated with the civil law, not the British common law in place throughout the colonies, and it was used in admiralty and equity. It was understood to permit judicial consideration of a case without the aid of a jury. In this context, the language of Article III seemed ominous. The language granting "appellate Jurisdiction, both as to Law and Fact" seemed to threaten the time-honored way of the common law, and especially the autonomy of the jury.

Consequently, it was politic to construct a national judicial system that differed sharply from that of the states. Under the innovation embodied in the Judiciary Act, the system of appeals would work differently. When a case was appealed to the Supreme Court, it was to go by way of the procedure that was denominated as a "writ of error." Under this procedure, which was not widely used in 1789, the Supreme Court would be limited to questions of law on the appeals that were brought before it. Facts could not be retried. This compromise pacified some of the opposition, and it limited any effective changes to the national judiciary by the Bill of Rights; numerous changes were proposed, but the only important ones that passed were the provisions of the Sixth Amendment, which guaranteed "an impartial jury of the state and district wherein the crime shall have been committed," and of the Seventh Amendment, which stated that "no fact tried by a jury shall be otherwise re-examined in any Court of the United States, than according to the rules of common law."

Lurking behind these issues, which involved the finality of jury decisions and potential abuse of litigants, was another set of issues on the deep questions of political power that are generated by a federal system. What are the relationships between the national court system and the state court systems? And what will be the relationship of national law and state law? These questions may sound like abstract legal issues, but when they are pursued, the questions raise fundamental issues of power. Let us give an example.

One of the fundamental decisions made by the First Congress was its decision to implement Article III's authorization of "diversity jurisdiction." The phrase "diversity jurisdiction" is a lawyer's term of art, and it is used to denominate that class of lawsuits over which the national courts have jurisdiction for the sole reason that the parties to the lawsuit are citizens of different (diverse) states. If a citizen of Virginia has a civil controversy with a citizen of New York, it is possible under the scheme for the

Virginian to sue the New Yorker in the New York state courts, or else in the national court that was sitting in New York. (A technical aside: in the eighteenth century, limitations on making a lawful service of process would probably limit the Virginia plaintiff to these two alternatives, but in modern times, the Virginia plaintiff might also have two other choices, the state courts in Virginia or the national courts in Virginia.)

This privilege of going into a national court has traditionally been regarded as one of the fundamental features of our federal system. It was authorized by the Constitution, put into execution by the First Congress, and survives in the statutes as they exist today. However, there are numerous details for the management of such lawsuits that must be addressed in order to give life to this privilege. For example, how should a national court go about deciding diversity cases? Should it feel free to reach results that would be radically different from those that the state court would have reached? Presumably the national trial court is a more fair forum for the resolution of diversity cases, but what sort of fairness is called for? Is the national court more fair because its personnel are supposedly more dispassionate, more free from local prejudice, or is it to apply a substantive law that is itself less locally biased? Furthermore, are there any provisions in the First Judiciary Act that speak to the question?

The current scholarly consensus is that the Judiciary Act does speak, and that the relevant section is Section 34. If Section 34 does speak to such a fundamental question, it is perhaps surprisingly placed in the act, since it is the next-to-the-last section of the act. (It also gets another second-place award; it is the second shortest section in the act.) The language of Section 34 is as follows:

> That the laws of the several states, except where the constitution, treaties or statutes of the United States shall otherwise require or provide, shall be regarded as rules of decision in the Courts of the United States in cases where they apply.

By tradition, this provision is said to speak to the issue of diversity cases, although there is reason to doubt. However, before beginning with the doubts, let us review the history of Section 34's subsequent interpretation.

One of the main curiosities of Section 34 is the phrase, "the laws of the several states." The first major interpretation of this phrase was offered in 1842—fifty-three years after its adoption—by Justice Joseph Story in the famous case of *Swift v. Tyson*. A careful reading of that case reveals that Story did not regard the interpretation of Section 34 as crucial to his decision, but in an aside, he made some remarks that were embraced by his successors. In dictum, Story said that "laws" refers only to the statutes of the several states, and not to their judicial decisions.

Twentieth-century legal historian Charles Warren, recognizing that something seemed wrong with Story's reading, set out to discover more about the legislative history of the Judiciary Act of 1789. Warren discovered in the attic of the Senate the original manuscript draft of the Judicial Bill, and on the basis of this manuscript, he concluded that Story was in error. Much of what Warren wrote about the act is sound, including his criticisms of Story; however, an egregious error pervades the article he wrote on the subject. Warren assumed that the Senate used the manuscript bill during its deliberation, whereas in fact the bill was printed and the Senate used the printed bill. A third thesis of this book is that the Senate actually used the printed version. The pagination of the two versions is quite different, and (as will be seen in detail) Warren's most important conclusions are based upon the pagination. Consequently, the details of the legislative history that Warren constructed are wholly illusory.

In the famous case of *Erie Railroad Co. v. Tompkins,* Justice Louis Brandeis wrote an opinion overruling *Swift,* and in this opinion, Brandeis cited Warren's research approvingly. On the basis of Warren's research, Brandeis opined that: "The purpose of the section [34] was merely to make certain that, in all matters except those in which some federal law is controlling, the federal courts exercising jurisdiction in diversity of citizenship cases would apply as their rules of decision the law of the state, unwritten as well as written." Unfortunately, this interpretation of Section 34 is as erroneous as was Story's.

The errors have been compounded in the latest scholarly work on the Judiciary Act, as written by Professor Julius Goebel, Jr. Goebel was astute enough to discover that the manuscript draft was not the bill that was used during the Senate deliberations, and so he duly (if quietly) corrected this error. However, in constructing his own version of the legislative history, Goebel himself used an erroneous premise. Goebel assumed that the federal judicial system was modeled after the then-existing state judicial systems, which is a demonstrably false premise, and this false premise led him to create his own illusory history.

It shall be the burden of this book to explain exactly why the distinguished quartet of Story, Warren, Brandeis, and Goebel were wrong. However, in order to demonstrate this error, it is necessary to examine the act as a whole, attending to a wide range of questions, including details as to wording as well as the general historical context of the act. In this investigation, it will be relatively easy to prove that the First Congress could not have had the intent attributed to it by *Erie,* even though this is the modern orthodoxy. However, it will be far more difficult to establish with certainty an alternative conclusion.

In order to understand why the modern interpretation is wrong, it is necessary to recur to the historical context of the 1789 act. As has already been said, the state systems were at that time not "hierarchical" in their structure. Instead, they were organized in what might be called a "horizontal" structure. There was a single corps of judges, who sat now in one court, now in another, and although one of these courts could have the final say in a particular lawsuit, it was not empowered to hand down authoritative common-law decisions in our sense of what that power entails nowadays. Judges were not empowered to make authoritarian common-law decisions because the jury had the final say, in both "inferior" and "superior" courts. One must remember that in the era of the early Republic, the jury was often instructed that it had the final say, not only as to facts, but also as to the law. (One should also recall that multijudge trials were common, and that in such trials, each judge could advise the jury about his view of the law, and the several instructions were not necessarily consistent.)

Furthermore, at the time the act was passed, there were no common-law decisions in print; the first American law reports postdate the act, and thus the publishing of judicial decisions as we know it today did not then exist. To make matters worse, state statutes were not generally collected and printed, and even where the statutes had been printed, the published versions were many years out of date. These facts were well known to those who drafted the act, and so interpretation of the Judiciary Act must begin with such facts. No rational Congress would have required federal courts to apply a nonexistent state common law, nor a virtually inaccessible state statute law.

To us, these facts are almost unimaginable. We find it hard to imagine a world in which there is no single highest court that can authoritatively declare the law, and we also find it hard to imagine a world in which the decisions of courts and the acts of legislatures are not printed and distributed. However, we will be unable to understand the Judiciary Act until we can understand the existence of such a world, and furthermore, can understand how it could have a perfectly rational and well-functioning legal system.

In short, one ought not read Section 34 as doing what to moderns it seems perfectly obvious that it does and should do, that is, to instruct national judges to look at state statutes and state decisions and follow their lead. It could not mean this, since doing so in 1789 would have been flatly impossible. But if it doesn't mean that, what does it mean? There are at least two alternatives, although neither of them can be established with certainty.

One might conclude that Section 34 was not meant to be a major and fundamental section, but rather, that its position as next-to-last is in some way indicative of its overall importance. As thus downgraded, the section's reference to "the laws of the several states" probably was meant to say nothing more remarkable than that the national courts should use American law, and not British law. Prior to the Revolution, British common law had prevailed, at least in theory, if not in practice. But American law was moving away from its British roots, and so Section 34 might have been nothing more than a ratification of what was already the practice. On this alternative, one can understand the phrase "the several states" as referring to the states collectively and thus as a compendious way of distinguishing American from British law.

A more complex alternative is that Section 34 deals with the use of American law in criminal cases, and was intended only as a stopgap measure until a new national criminal code could be prepared. It appears that the First Congress accepted the notion that there was to be a national common law of crimes, at least until matters were fixed up by statute. And so the second alternative is that Section 34 authorized the judiciary to use an American common law of crimes as an interim measure. This more complex interpretation is far more radical in its consequences than is the simpler alternative advanced above, but rather surprisingly, it seems more plausible on the evidence.

As historians, we should start from the position that those who enacted the First Judiciary Act were not interested in our problems and did not make modern assumptions about the nature of law and the organization of the judicial process. Instead, their own political problems were foremost on the agenda. The political problems that had to be addressed, and resolved, were the numerous demands for constitutional amendments that would have modified Article III and thus (in the judgment of the Federalists) would have crippled the national judiciary.

The solution to this political challenge was to innovate by establishing a hierarchical judicial structure that differed sharply from the horizontal form of organization that characterized the then-existing state judiciaries. This new form of organization limited the higher national courts, and especially the Supreme Court, to questions of law. Limiting the higher courts to questions of law was politically attractive in the context of the time. The limitation protected the autonomy of local juries, and it meant that litigants and their witnesses could not be dragged to the capital to testify for a second time. In general, we ought to understand the organizational and jurisdictional provisions of the First Judiciary Act as directed toward solving contemporary political problems.

Understanding the political context of the act has a converse, which is, avoiding the use of our own political categories. For modern scholars, the problem of "choice of law," that is, choosing between using state law or national law to decide a case, is one of the fundamental problems generated by a federal system. Consequently, it seems natural to assume that the drafters of the First Judiciary Act must have agreed that this was a fundamental problem, and further, that they must have written into the act a solution to this problem. Having made these two assumptions, it follows, on this line of thought, that Section 34 was drafted to solve the problem. However, this entire line of thought is anachronistic, and further, it is erroneous. To be sure, modern scholars are correct in saying that choice of law (deciding how to weave together state and national law) is a fundamental problem in a federal system. But it does not follow that the members of the First Congress thought that choice of law was a fundamental problem. The historical evidence indicates that they worried about a different set of fundamental problems.

CHAPTER II

Chronology and Description

INTRODUCTION

THE SECOND CONSTITUTION of the United States was ratified by a ninth state—New Hampshire—on June 21, 1788, thereby putting the document into effect as the blueprint for a revised national government. By resolution of September 13, 1788, the Continental Congress (operating under the first constitution of the United States, the Articles of Confederation) fixed the place and date for the commencement of the new national government to be New York on March 4, 1789.[1]

Quorums of the two houses of Congress did not exist on the appointed day in March. The appearance of Senator Richard Henry Lee of Virginia made a quorum of the Senate on April 6; the House of Representatives had managed a quorum several days before, and so the new Congress could begin.[2] Their achievement was extraordinary; they established, quite literally from scratch, the whole framework of the new national government in only twenty-seven separate acts and four resolutions. Legislation was developed simultaneously by the two houses of the Congress, and so one must often attend to the overall context in order to understand a single act, such as the First Judiciary Act.

By a decision process that is unknown, the new Senate undertook as its first order of business the formidable task of constructing an act that would establish the third branch of government, the judiciary. This division of labor was apparently agreeable to the House of Representatives, but we do not know how this agreement was negotiated. At any rate, on April 7, the day after a quorum was achieved, a committee was chosen by the Senate to draft an act.[3] The committee consisted of one senator from each state then represented in the Senate; soon thereafter, a committee was established to draft a bill defining crimes and punishments, and its membership consisted of the other senator from each state.[4] As tardy senators arrived, they were placed on one or the other of the two committees.

SCOPE OF CONGRESSIONAL AUTHORITY

In the introduction, we stated that the Congress had a wide array of choices in establishing the new judiciary. No national judiciary had existed under the Articles, and the new Constitution left almost everything to the political imagination of the First Congress. Let us now give further details on the amount of discretion that the Congress had.

Article III of the Constitution, which is devoted to the judiciary, is about one-half the length of Article II, which established the presidency, and it is about one-fifth the length of Article I, which established the Congress. In addition to its brevity, its language is mostly general and open-ended, a trait it shares with the rest of the text. Section 1, which is the basic "organizational" section, has only four mandatory provisions: there is to be "one" (and presumably only one) "supreme Court"; the judges are to hold office "during good Behaviour"; they are to be paid "at stated Times"; and their pay "shall not be diminished during their Continuance in Office." The last three of these provisions, which relate to tenure and pay, were meant to isolate the judges from certain forms of partisan politics, but obviously, these three provisions do not limit the form of any judiciary that might be created. Only the first provision, which mandates "one supreme Court," has major structural implications.

Section 2 of Article III is the longest section of that article. It is important in that the first paragraph of that section outlines the kinds of jurisdiction that the national courts might entertain. Although these provisions are obviously crucial, a close inspection of the language reveals a significant silence. The constitutional text does not say whether this jurisdiction is mandatory, that is, the Constitution does not say whether this jurisdiction must be exercised by the national courts. Moreover, even if the constitutional list of jurisdiction is exercised by the national courts, nothing is said about whether any of this jurisdiction is to be exclusive of the state courts. Consequently, the Congress appears to have a free hand in adjusting these matters of jurisdiction. The remainder of the article has some procedural details that appear to be mandatory (dealing with the Supreme Court's original jurisdiction, with jury trials, and with trials for treason), but these provisions are neither central nor decisive with respect to the judicial structure.

Consequently, the most important details were left to the discretion of the Congress. For example, the number of judges who were to sit on the Supreme Court was not stated in the Constitution. More important, there is no requirement that there be inferior national courts; instead the text states that there would be "such inferior Courts as the Congress may from time to time ordain and establish." In fact, the Congress did choose to establish inferior courts, and by this choice it set the course for the national judicial system that has prevailed to this day; but the Congress could have chosen otherwise. If the Congress had chosen not to establish inferior courts, it would have set a very different course for the judicial department, but it would have been different in ways that it is difficult even to speculate about.

In 1789 two other national court structures were debated and defeated. They were defeated on the merits, not because either one would have failed to conform to the Constitution. Senator Richard Henry Lee of Virginia presented a proposal from the Virginia ratifying convention that would have limited inferior national courts to "cases of admiralty and maritime jurisdiction," leaving the state courts to serve as the lower national courts.[5] And Senator William Samuel Johnson of Connecticut, seconded strongly by Senator Pierce Butler of South Carolina, proposed that there should be "courts of *nisi prius*."[6] This would presumably have organized the national courts along the line of the then-existing English system, probably with the one national court sitting much like the King's Bench at Westminster and sending out its judges to try cases in the hinterlands. (The Massachusetts and New York courts were also organized this way in 1789.) Under this scheme of organization, issues of fact would be decided at trial, but questions of law could be reserved for a conference of the entire bench back at the capital. If either of these proposals had been adopted, the structure of the judicial system would have been greatly altered.

In short, the senators understood the Constitution to give them a large discretion, and the text supports them in this claim to authority. Moreover, we should remember that one-half of the membership of the Senate had been members of the Constitutional Convention.[7] When they act as though the Constitution vested them with great latitude in constructing the judiciary, their interpretation of their authority is entitled to considerable respect. Let us now turn to what they did.

15

ACTIVITIES IN THE SENATE

We do not have much direct evidence on the procedures that the Judiciary Committee itself followed in the course of its deliberations. However, the evidence that we do have, letters to constituents and friends, suggests that the committee followed the practice of the Continental Congress and the Constitutional Convention, that is, they proceeded by debating, and either adopting or rejecting, a series of general resolutions; the committee did not begin drafting an actual text until after certain basic resolutions were adopted. (The modern practice of beginning the legislative process by submitting a draft bill was not then used. As an aside, one might speculate that the notorious inefficiency of the modern legislature might be connected to the desuetude of the resolution procedure.) Letters indicate that by the end of April—three weeks into their deliberations—there was tentative agreement upon the broad outline of what was to become the First Judiciary Act.[8]

By May 11 the committee had reached sufficient agreement to be able to appoint a subcommittee to draft a bill.[9] The evidence suggests that this subcommittee comprised Senators Oliver Ellsworth of Connecticut, William Paterson of New Jersey, and Caleb Strong of Massachusetts, three Federalists who supported a strong central government and a strong highly articulated national judiciary.[10] A month later, on Friday, June 12, the Judiciary Committee met to consider the subcommittee draft and found it agreeable, although Senator William Maclay of Pennsylvania wrote in his diary that it was "long and somewhat confused."[11] Later that same day, Senator Lee reported the bill to the Senate for its first reading; the Senate responded by ordering printed copies to be prepared,[12] for use in debate and for distribution to constituents, and Monday, June 22, was assigned as the day for the second reading.[13]

The surviving manuscript of the subcommittee's efforts shows that, while it had been straightened out sufficiently to be reported, it was not in such good shape that a printer would not have had trouble with it. It contained strikeovers, marginal notations, amendments affixed by sealing wax, mixed-up pages, and even possibly duplications of clauses. Professor Goebel thinks that the printers must have had before them a manuscript "of a later rescension" than the one that has survived and is now in the National Archives.[14] However, there is one aspect of the manuscript bill that makes it almost certain that this is the copy that went to the printer. There are printer's marks on the manuscript exactly marking the four page-forms used in printing the bill.[15]

Two hundred fifty copies were printed, and senators and House members began sending out copies for comment on June 15.[16] Senator George Read of Delaware was unable to send out as many copies as he would have liked to, because "We are so restricted in our number of copies."[17] Probably to meet this need 120 additional copies were run off on or about June 21.[18] In all, records remain identifying at least twenty recipients of these copies, all of whom were asked for their comments.[19]

A second reading of the bill occurred from June 22 to July 6. A third reading "with a kind of saving privilege to make amendments"[20] occurred from July 7 through July 13. Then the bill was recommitted, probably to put it into final form for engrossing, and probably to the same subcommittee as before. Senator Paine Wingate of New Hampshire reported to his brother-in-law Timothy Pickering on July 11 that "The Judicial bill has had three readings in the Senate and is now to be committed in order to make some little alterations and amendments and then it will be ready to go to the other house."[21] On the morning of July 17 the Judiciary Committee "corrected"[22] the subcommittee's work; later that day, working from 11:00 A.M. to 4:00 P.M., the full Senate debated and passed the bill by recorded vote of fourteen to six.[23]

Amendments are reported in the *Senate Journal* commencing July 9 and up to recommittal on July 13,[24] but other amendments unreported therein are known to have been made before July 9,[25] and so we do not know whether amendments we cannot date were made during the second or third readings, during the period of the bill's recommittal, by the full committee when it briefly considered the results of the recommittal, or when the Senate briefly resumed debate. It is probable that no substantial changes were made after the report of the subcommittee on the morning of July 17, because the bill was probably in engrossed form at that time. The *Senate Journal* reports that the vote at 4:00 on July 17 was upon the "*engrossed* 'Bill to establish Judidial [sic] Courts of the United States.'"[26]

ACTIVITIES IN THE HOUSE: PASSAGE

The engrossed Judicial Bill was carried to the House on July 20.[27] The House ordered "100 copies be printed for the accomodation of the House."[28] The bill, printed by Thomas Greenleaf, was delivered on July 23.[29] The House procrastinated on the bill, finally debating it in late August and early September. On September 17 the bill passed on voice vote, with more than fifty amendments.[30] The amendments were viewed as but "small alterations,"[31] and "none of them materially alter the plan."[32]

An ad hoc committee of the Senate reported on September 19 that it agreed with most of the House amendments, but disagreed with four and amended one more. The Senate concurred.[33] On September 21, the House without debate receded from its four amendments to which the Senate had disagreed, concurred in the Senate's amendment to its amendment, and passed the bill.[34] The bill was signed by the president on September 24, thereby becoming a law of the United States and establishing the judicial department of the national government.[35]

RELATION TO OTHER LEGISLATION

There was of course other business being considered. The Departments of War and State were established, the latter of which had duties domestic as well as foreign. Financial affairs were ordered by the passage of a revenue act and tariff acts, and by the establishment of a Treasury Department. None of these acts appears to have greatly influenced the consideration of the Judicial Bill, although the practical need to have some way to enforce the revenue act and the tariff acts made the establishment of a judiciary a matter of some importance.

The principal legislation that the Senate prepared and that had importance to the shape of the Judicial Bill was the Crimes Bill. Both matters were apparently considered by the Senate as important subjects requiring early action. On May 13, two days after Ellsworth's subcommittee was assigned to draft a Judicial Bill from the committee's resolutions, the Senate appointed a separate committee to report a bill "defining the crimes and offenses that shall be cognizable under the authority of the United States, and their punishments."[36] All of those senators not on the Judiciary Committee were assigned to the committee on the Crimes Bill.[37] The work of the two committees probably moved apace, with each keeping the other informed of its progress, and with a steady interchange of ideas. The two Connecticut senators took leading roles on their respective committees.

The most striking piece of evidence that the Judicial Bill and the Crimes Bill were connected is presented by a floor amendment to the Judicial Bill. At an unknown point of time during the floor debate on the Judicial Bill, language was deleted that extended federal jurisdiction to all crimes "defined by the laws of the same."[38] Thereafter, on July 28, Senator William Samuel Johnson of Connecticut, on behalf of the Crimes Bill Committee, "reported a bill entitled, 'An act for the punishment of certain crimes against the United States.'"[39] Thus, although this committee had been appointed to bring in a bill *defining and punishing* crimes and offenses against the United States, its bill only provided for the *punishment* of certain crimes. The Senate's deletion from the Judicial Bill of the language referring to crimes "defined" by national law probably reflects its knowledge of the Crimes Bill Committee's decision not to define national crimes but, presumably, to leave their definition to the common law.

The Crimes Bill was considered by the Senate during much of August; it passed on August 31 and was sent to the House.[40] The Judicial Bill had been under consideration in the House since July 20, and it passed (as we have seen) on September 17. On the next day the House postponed consideration of the Crimes Bill until "the next session of Congress" and asked the Senate to concur in a resolution instructing the secretary of state to "procure from time to time, such of the statutes of the several states as may not be in his office." The Senate did so concur.[41] In other words, it seems inescapable that the House postponed acting on a national Crimes Bill until it could make a comprehensive study of the statutory criminal law that had been enacted in the several states.

Nevertheless, on September 21 the Senate resolved to recommend to the states that they should require their keepers of jails to receive prisoners of the United States "as shall be committed for offenses," and it was proposed that the United States would pay the local jailers for these services. The House concurred in this resolution the same day.[42] In other words, throughout its first session the First Congress had given every intention of extending to the national courts jurisdiction over crimes against the national government, even though no comprehensive bill relating to crimes was passed. The first comprehensive national law on crimes was not enacted until April 30, 1790,[43] being the same bill, amended slightly, as the Senate had drafted and adopted on August 31, 1789.[44] However, it is unthinkable that the First Congress would have left the new government defenseless against persons seeking its overthrow or engaged in other forms of criminal activity. The joint resolution of September 21 is evidence that members of Congress assumed that the national judiciary would exercise at least a temporary criminal jurisdiction over a common law of crimes not specified by national statute, until those statutes could be properly drafted.[45]

In the House of Representatives, the major legislative proposals that affected the Judicial Bill were those responding to demands for a Bill of Rights. As we have seen, the constitutional provisions for the judiciary, in

Article III and elsewhere, drew much opposition in state ratifying conventions and in the press. This opposition had chiefly to do with the sanctity of jury trials, with burdensome appeals, and with the breadth and vagueness of the powers the Constitution extended to the national judiciary. Opponents were concerned that the rights of middling and poor people as ascertained by local juries would be nullified through expensive appeals to a Supreme Court, sitting without a jury in a distant place.[46] Proponents of the Constitution told its opponents that their fears of vexatious litigation and rapacious national jurisdiction were groundless; opponents were assured that they were misreading the instrument, or that Congress would eliminate the perceived fears in its organization of the government.[47] These comments and promises, and the dangers to be guarded against, must have been constantly in the minds of the members of the First Congress.

In the state ratifying conventions there was support for more than two hundred amendments to the Constitution, embodying some eighty separate substantive changes.[48] Important alterations were proposed for the national judiciary. Some amendments would have guaranteed jury trials in civil cases in the national courts; others would have limited national-court jurisdiction over issues of federal law ("federal-question jurisdiction"). Virginia, North Carolina, New York, and the minority in Pennsylvania would have eliminated national-court jurisdiction in instances involving suits between citizens of different states ("diversity jurisdiction"). New Hampshire and Massachusetts, among others, would have provided that the amount in controversy in a diversity case be enormous ($1,500 in Massachusetts, $3,000 in New Hampshire) before such a case might be brought in a national court, or before it might be appealed to the Supreme Court ("amount-in-controversy requirement"). New York and Virginia proposed limiting lower national courts to admiralty jurisdiction; New York and Maryland proposed, in the words of the former, that national-court jurisdiction "is not in any case to be encreased enlarged or extended by any Fiction Collusion or mere suggestion"; and Virginia proposed that national jurisdiction should "extend to no case where the cause of action shall have originated before the ratification of this Constitution." New York wanted an express limitation on the power of national courts to decide land questions.[49] In sum, many people desired significant restrictions upon, or elimination of portions of, national-court jurisdiction, and the dilemma that members of the First Congress faced was to cater to these demands without seriously crippling the national judiciary.

On June 8 James Madison brought before the House of Representatives his proposal for nine amendments to the Constitution.[50] Two would have strengthened jury trials, while one would have placed an amount-in-controversy limitation on appeals to the Supreme Court.[51] Madison said: "I think it will be proper, with respect to the judiciary powers, to satisfy the public mind on those points which I have mentioned. [The amount-in-controversy limitation], with the regulations respecting jury trials in criminal cases, and suits at common law, it is to be hoped, will quiet and reconcile the minds of the people to that part of the constitution."[52] The proposed amendments were then considered by the House over the rest of the summer.

The Judicial Bill passed by the Senate on July 17 contained provisions that carried out all, or very nearly all, of the revisions contemplated by Madison's amendments. The bill placed an amount-in-controversy limitation on appeals to the Supreme Court,[53] and it restricted that Court's review to questions of law, thereby denying it the reexamination of facts. The bill provided for trial by jury in suits at common law. And it contained quite elaborate provisions governing criminal proceedings in the district circuit courts, which went a long way toward writing into the statute the revisions Madison had called for.

The House held the Judicial Bill while it debated the proposed amendments. Since the Judicial Bill met the most important objections to Article III that had been raised at the state ratifying conventions, all efforts to propose amendments to Article III were eventually defeated.[54] The House placed language in the Sixth Amendment expressly protecting the right of jurors to be drawn from the locality of a crime, after an ingenious Senate amendment to the Judicial Bill engineered by Richard Henry Lee to achieve a similar result was deemed insufficient.[55] Then the two provisions, the Judicial Bill and the resolution sending the proposed amendments to the states, were brought to final adoption almost simultaneously.[56]

The movement to amend Article III of the Constitution really had already been obviated by the provisions astutely placed in the Judicial Bill in the Senate, before the subject of amendments was given full consideration in the House. Only the Seventh Amendment's guarantee of civil jury trial was both responsive to the proposals to amend the Constitution and redundant of provisions in the Judiciary Act of 1789. The Judiciary Act thus succeeded in quieting the fears of those who had opposed Article III as originally drafted, without actually diminishing the powers granted to the national government in Article III.

A GENERAL DESCRIPTION OF THE FIRST JUDICIARY ACT

Exactly who should get credit for the ingenuity displayed in the First Judiciary Act is a controversy that cannot, and need not, be settled here. Ellsworth was given the lion's share of the credit for the act by most contemporaries, and Ellsworth is the one member of the Judiciary Committee reported by contemporaries to have assiduously politicked for the bill, but it was never claimed that the scheme was entirely his. The draft bill, as it was produced by the subcommittee, can be divided into three portions. The first, dealing with the organization of the judiciary, is in the handwriting of William Paterson. The second, dealing with the jurisdiction of the national courts, is in Ellsworth's hand. One section of the third portion of the bill, which deals with process, is in Caleb Strong's hand, while the remaining sections are in the hand of a clerk.

Though many modern commentators make an easy identification of handwriting and ideas, these facts as to handwriting may represent the manner in which the subcommittee divided up its task, rather than indicate the source of the ideas and compromises embodied therein. No important correspondence of Paterson, and very little of Ellsworth, survives in accessible repositories, and so we do not have direct evidence that would illuminate their ideas. Correspondence to Strong from his friends in Massachusetts passed along ideas that became a part of the scheme, but we have no way of knowing whether there was a direct cause-and-effect relationship, and Strong was not reputed among his contemporaries as having much credit for the result. All told, it is more probable than not that most of the vision and plan embodied in the bill was Ellsworth's, and henceforth in this book, Ellsworth will be given credit for the scheme of the judiciary, by way of shorthand. However, the scheme as a whole is more important than the attribution of authorship.

In the context of its day, the scheme embodied in the First Judiciary Act was as astute politically as it was legally. It was an ingenious collection of compromises, using both tight, detailed wording and broad, open-ended wording in different places; it established foundations upon which successors could build. Some proponents of the aggrandizement and centralization of national power, such as Alexander Hamilton, wished to establish an army of national judges who would carry national authority into every county. On the other hand, those who wished to restrict national power, such as Richard Henry Lee, desired a minimal national judiciary with only admiralty courts and a single Supreme Court, possessed of much less jurisdiction than that set out in Article III.

The act's compromise combined features of both schemes. At the lowest level would be district courts in each state, each with a locally resident judge. Their jurisdiction was to be limited to admiralty, petty crimes, and revenue collection. These district courts were not the powerful courts of the sort we know today, but they were to exercise a jurisdiction that would not have been denied to any national court by almost any contemporaneous observer.

The major national trial courts in the plan were to be the circuit courts. The states were grouped into three circuits; these courts did not have their own judges, but instead, they were to be staffed by two (of the six) Supreme Court justices "riding circuit" twice a year. The district judge resident in each state would become the third circuit judge, each in his own district. With the highest national judges regularly sitting in them, the prestige of their authority would be enhanced, and thus the prospect of appeals costly to the poor would be diminished, while the most serious questions likely to be brought into the new national courts would receive immediate attention by the nation's highest judges.

The circuit courts were to be vested with jurisdiction over important crimes, over cases involving out-of-state or foreign citizens, and over appeals from the district courts in admiralty cases. If cases involving out-of-state citizens or foreign citizens were begun in state courts, such cases could be "removed," or transferred, to the circuit courts from the state courts. Nothing was said in the act about whether the circuit courts had trial jurisdiction of cases "arising under" federal law or the Constitution. However, the Supreme Court was given appellate authority, via the writ-of-error procedure, over important questions of federal or constitutional law that were decided in state courts.

The Supreme Court also had a trial jurisdiction, primarily over interstate and international controversies. Its other business would be by way of writ of error from the circuit courts and the state courts. As stated above, the adoption of the writ-of-error procedure did much to dissipate disquiet over potential abuse of litigants and potential disregard of local juries. The sections on process also obviated or lessened many of the complaints about how the national courts would function, especially with regard to jury selection and jury trial.

SUMMARY

In the introduction and chronology, we have set forth several general theses about the content and significance of the First Judiciary Act, together with general history of its passage through the legislative process. The reader who is not familiar with the existing scholarship on the act may not have appreciated that almost all of our presentation has been controversial. The existing scholarship describes a very different act, and even when these different accounts share common details, the entire spirit of the description is different.

Differences in interpreting the First Judiciary Act spring largely from a scholarly preoccupation with the controversies that are current with us today. We are all naturally aware of the disputes over the proper role of the national judiciary that are live issues in current politics. And interestingly enough, there were analogous controversies in the late eighteenth century. However, there is a natural error that is easily made; one can read back modern preoccupations and assumptions into the controversies of times past. It is an error to presume that merely because the controversy—the role of the judiciary—is a constant, that political actors then understood the issues in the same terms that modern disputants would employ.

We are today preoccupied, for example, with problems of federalism and choice of law, and these concerns are part of our understanding of the problems that are raised by the jurisdictional powers of the national courts. When a national court has jurisdiction over a controversy, its first duty is to apply the federal law, which is acknowledged by all to be supreme in those matters to which it is applicable. However, there are numerous issues for which federal law gives no answers, and these issues regularly arise in cases that are within the jurisdiction of the national courts.

In this context of jurisdiction over a case that is not wholly governed by clearly applicable federal law, we moderns tend to make several assumptions about general problems of federalism. It is commonly assumed that there is a sharp distinction between federal and state law; that judges are empowered both to make final decisions about what the law is and to choose between federal law and state law; and that it is important to apply state law in appropriate instances in order to acknowledge the constitutionally founded sovereignty that remains to the states in our federal system. If federal law does not apply (or even does not *clearly* apply), then it is presumed that state law should apply. It is also presumed that such issues must have been seen as crucial in 1789, when the question of the relative power balance between the states and the new national government was uppermost in the thoughts of most people. Those who are preoccupied with such assumptions will search for an answer to these questions in the First Judiciary Act.

Section 34—added to the First Judiciary Act almost at the last moment—seems to provide an answer. It reads:

That the laws of the several states, except where the constitution, treaties or statutes of the United States shall otherwise require or provide, shall be regarded as rules of decision in trials at common law in the courts of the United States in cases where they apply.

If one reads back modern preoccupations into the debate over the First Judiciary Act, then one tends to give Section 34 of the act a far greater prominence than it should have, and thus one misinterprets it. Such a reader would see this section as giving a general instruction to the national judges on techniques for reconciling and harmonizing state and federal law; that reader would interpret Section 34 as instructing national judges to apply the state law of the state in which the national judge is sitting to all problems for which federal law does not clearly dictate an answer.

Professor Charles Warren had these modern assumptions in mind when he investigated the provenance of the Judiciary Act of 1789, attempting, in his own words, to throw "new light" on the subject.[57] He thereby misread Section 34 and the act. Moreover, he supplied an apparently authentic historical account of the act that supported this misreading, and thus he gave an unconscious anachronism new life and power by rationalizing it. The error here is twofold. Not only is Section 34 misinterpreted as to its content, in that it is now said to speak to a matter to which it did not speak, but the section is assumed to speak to a fundamental question of federalism. If Section 34 speaks to such a fundamental question, then it seems central to the act, instead of being a minor and peripheral provision. Other twentieth-century scholars and jurists, such as Justice Louis Brandeis and Professor Julius Goebel, Jr., have shared with Warren these same preconceptions and errors.

Reading the act through the lens of Section 34 is not a minor error; it has major consequences. If we assume that Section 34 is both central and crucial, and if we then misinterpret that section, and if we read the act as a whole with this assumption in place, then we see a very different act from the one that was written in 1789. We see a different kind of federalism from what they saw; we see a different sort of judiciary from the one that they imagined; and ultimately, we see law itself differently.

Let us now turn to the circumstances of history that will help us overcome the vice of being present-minded, and thus help illuminate the meaning of Section 34 and the whole 1789 act, and that will let us see the act as those who wrote it must have seen it. We shall start with the most general sort of facts; we shall start with the nature of the judiciary, and the meaning of law, as these were understood at the end of the eighteenth century.

CHAPTER III

The "Judicial Systems" of the Several States in 1789

INTRODUCTION

IN 1787–89 no state had a judicial system similar to a modern American judicial system. No state had a highest court known by the name of "supreme court" and no state had a highest court whose only, or even principal, function was the exercise of an appellate-review function over inferior courts.

While the trial function was exercised by judges, or members of the judiciary, this was not true of the appellate-review function, to the extent that it then existed. In speaking of judges, reference is being made to a governmental official performing the function of a judge, as generally understood today, either at the trial or appellate level, and without making any distinction as to whether the judge is a member of the legal profession or a layman.

But even to compare a late eighteenth-century judicial system with one of the modern day in meaningful manner it is necessary to take note of several changes that have taken place in the way the governmental structure, the judiciary, and the law were viewed in the late eighteenth century and at the present time. These changes can only be briefly summarized here, and the discussion is no attempt at a comprehensive coverage of the subject. A comparison of an eighteenth-century judicial system with one of the present day provides supporting evidence that these changes have taken place.

It cannot be emphasized too strongly that there is one important point that must constantly be kept in mind if one is to avoid misreading the Constitution and avoid misunderstanding the development of the Judiciary Act in the First Congress. This point is that in the eighteenth-century successive trials, even successive jury trials were common. The final result of these successive trials would be to reach the one and only "correct" result since each party had had the benefit of earlier "trial runs." It was the multiplicity of judges, and lawyers, and juries that would finally ensure the correct result. This approach to reaching the correct result is replaced in the modern system by the pronouncements of the highest appellate-review court, buttressed with doctrines of *stare decisis, res judicata,* and increasingly of collateral estoppel; each of these doctrines is highly technical and cannot be easily summarized in a book like this one; it is enough to say that doctrines are used to create finality, so that whatever has been decided shall not be redecided.

FOUND VERSUS MADE LAW

The eighteenth-century judge "found" the law; the twentieth-century judge "makes" the law. In the eighteenth century it was the *number* of judges seeking "to find" the law that was considered important; in the twentieth century it is the *hierarchical arrangement* into tiers of appellate and trial judges "making and applying" law that is considered important.

This is true as a generalization, but full explication requires some modification. At the present time, judicial lawmaking is closely related to judicial opinion writing, and even more importantly, to the publication of the opinions that are written. It is the opinion-writing and publishing judge engaged in appellate review who is typically viewed as the lawmaking judge. So he or she is. But any judge who writes an opinion and gets it published is treated by both the courts and the profession as a "lawmaking judge." The published opinions of at least some trial judges are respected in the legal world to the same extent as those coming from the judges sitting on the Supreme Court. Learned Hand's opinions as a federal district court trial judge are accorded the same respect and precedential value as Judge Hand's opinions written while he was on the United States Court of Appeals for the Second Circuit.

In the eighteenth century most judges did not write opinions and have them published. Thus in the modern sense, none of the eighteenth-century judges "made" law. Instead, all judges, and they were all trial judges, were engaged in the search to "find" the law.

In any search, of any nature, the prospects of success are enhanced by an increase in the number and competency of the searchers. This was as true in the search for "the law" as it is in searching for a lost child. And so the judicial systems of the eighteenth century were marked by having a multiplicity of judges sitting at the trial. This was true of inferior as well as of superior courts. All the justices of the peace were entitled to sit on the most insignificant of cases. The number who did sit was largely determined by availability, in light of problems of communication and transportation, and of inclination. There was some legislative regulation of the subject, particularly in requiring that one or more judges of the "quorum" be present, the "quorum" being understood as having something of a reverse meaning from what it carries today. These quorum judges (although this was not their official name) were those of the group, of whom one or more had to be present. The "chief judge or justice of the peace" was typically named as a member of the quorum.

Counsel too was engaged in a "search" for the true rule of law. A surprisingly large number of lawyers were retained by each side, each apparently being given the opportunity to argue the case as fully and as long as he had anything to say, whether repetitious or not of what had already been said. The bench sometimes called upon bystanding members of the bar for their opinions on the points in issue.

Lawyers were officers of the court, having a somewhat different function from judges, but nevertheless viewed as fellow searchers in seeking to find the one and only true rule of law. Consequently, their thoughts, or their arguments, were of equal importance with the thoughts of the judges. The only difference was that counsel argued, developing fully the arguments on each side, while the judges were neutral arbiters. But all had a common objective—finding the true rule of law.

All the eighteenth-century law reports show this to be the situation. The arguments of counsel are extensively reported, even though the decision of the court might be put into a single sentence. For the most part, all that is reported of the judges' viewpoints is the give-and-take of their argument with counsel, with a judge, sometimes, summarizing his decision in the way of conclusion. The reports of what the judges said or thought are not verbatim opinions written by the judges or by an official reporter, but rather are what someone—whether judge, lawyer, or law student—had in his notes or took down of what he heard during the argument.

The arguments of counsel have been largely dropped from modern law reports, at least as a separate section of the report of the case. The arguments, or some of them, may be summarized in the court's opinion, but arguments not considered significant or relevant by the court are simply ignored, or rejected in a laundry list of points raised and found to be "without merit."

The structure and content of the twentieth-century law report, when compared with that of the eighteenth century, reflects the significant differences between the views of the two centuries of the very nature of the judicial process and what "the law" is.

Even the jury, in the eighteenth century, was viewed as collegially involved in the judicial search for "the law." Juries not only found the facts, but they also had the final word as to what the law was. There was no need to "report" these jury determinations on the law since they would not be binding in any other court, nor for the matter in the same court in a different controversy.

In the absence of reports of how this process actually worked, little is known about these early judicial proceedings. There is evidence that each judge gave the jury his own views as to what the law was, and these views might very well differ from the views of his fellow judges. But that was all right because judges were only giving the jurors the benefit of their views, and it was up to the jury to choose among the views so expressed or to ignore all of them and lay down its own view of the "true rule of law."

In a judicial system having multijudge trial courts, each judge was allowed to have and express his own view of what the law was, and with the final determination of "the law" left to the jury, there was no place for the modern appellate-review court. Consequently, the rise of the modern appellate-review court is directly related to the decline of the law-finding (or lawmaking) function of the juries. The Horwitz[1] and Nelson[2] thesis that the late eighteenth- and early nineteenth-century judges engaged in the process of wresting control of defining "the law" from juries is correct, but in at least one respect is too simplistic. The development of appellate-review courts, with judges very much concerned in wresting control of "the law" from the juries, was the mechanism by which the process took place.[3]

In summary, all eighteenth-century courts were trial courts having a number of judges and juries all mutually engaged in "finding" the true rule of law. In the twentieth century the judicial structure has been stratified, divided into many single-judge courts and a few multijudge appellate-review courts. The jury has been excluded from the "lawmaking or law-finding process." In the twentieth century a few appellate-review judges "make" the law, and everyone—the citizen, the legislator and executive, and the judge of the lower court—is expected to comply and follow the law thus made by these higher-ranking judges.

A UNIFIED SOVEREIGN VERSUS THE SEPARATION OF POWERS

The background to the development of American governments was the existence of a single unified sovereign. This is not to overlook a long historical development in England, but only to state that the concept of sovereignty in England is concentrated in the Crown. Under the influence of Enlightenment philosophers such as Montesquieu, the Americans, when they became independent, were convinced of the desirability of having a divided sovereign—that is, a separation of government powers among the legislative, the executive, and the judicial.

The influence of this doctrine did not work a sudden change in American governmental structure. Indeed the separation of governmental functions has taken place over the entire history of the American government and still is not complete, and never will be. A legislative body—the Senate—sits for the "trial of impeachments." The trial of impeachments can hardly be considered a true legislative function under a rational separation of powers. Members of the Senate are "administrative judges" to carry out executive functions.

The pace at which the separation of powers (to the extent that it was adopted) took place differed in the American states.

The Massachusetts Frame of Government was introduced with a stirring statement of the separation of powers:

> In the government of this Commonwealth the legislative department shall never exercise the executive and judicial powers, or either of them: The executive shall never exercise the legislative and judicial powers, or either of them: The judicial shall never exercise the legislative and executive powers, or either of them: to the end it may be a government of laws and not of men.[4]

Neighboring Connecticut did not adopt a state constitution upon achieving independence. Instead it retained the same basic structure it had had since its settlement through both the colonial and early statehood periods. It was not until 1818 that Connecticut adopted a constitution; following the lead of Massachusetts it also proclaimed a distribution of powers, setting it forth as Article Second of the constitution.[5]

The structures of the judicial systems of these two states paralleled the growth of the idea of separation of powers. In Massachusetts the entire judicial function was vested in the judicial department of government. But in Connecticut the state's highest appellate-review function remained in the legislature until the constitution of 1818, when for the first time Connecticut had a true appellate-review judicial court.

The federal Constitution embodies the principle of separation of powers, but does so solely through the organization of the document, devoting separate articles to the three departments, but without ever proclaiming, as Massachusetts did, that one department should never exercise the powers committed to the other two. And when one examines the text carefully, important powers are shared by the several departments.

THE ENGLISH BACKGROUND

Inasmuch as in virtually all legal things Americans have, or are thought to have, an English background, it is necessary to review the judicial structure as it existed in England in 1787–89, as a background to examining the American judicial structures of that date.

In doing so, though, it should be kept in mind that it is simply impossible to determine with precision what was *generally* known in America about English law and English courts. There is a tendency to assume that everything known in England, by some process of transatlantic osmosis, was also known in the United States. Very little has been done about exploring the extent to which and the means by which English information sources were made available in the United States.[6] Too often there is simply reliance on all the modern sources of information, and then an assumption is made that these sources were equally available in the United States in the eighteenth century. Broad conclusions are then drawn, but without there being any nexus between existence of an eighteenth-century information source in England and *accessibility* to the same information in the United States.[7]

The single English work that was most familiar to Americans in 1787–89 must have been Blackstone's *Commentaries*.[8] This is shown by the list of subscribers published in the American edition as well as the frequency with which it was cited.

William Blackstone sensed that the proper arrangement of a judicial system was hierarchical with one supreme court at the apex. In his *Commentaries* he made a manful effort to describe the then-existing English courts in these terms, but the structure was too complex to be satisfactorily described in this way. By using procrustean techniques he was able to fit the "Public Courts of Common Law and Equity"[9] into an idealized hierarchical structure.

In the area where Blackstone discerned such an arrangement, that is, in common law and equity, Blackstone described an English system organized very much as a modern judicial system, with inferior courts—the *piedpoudre,* court-baron, hundred court, and county courts—at the bottom,[10] and the House of Lords at the top.[11] The principal trial courts, called superior courts, were the Court of Common Pleas, the Court of

King's Bench, the Court of Exchequer, and the Court of Chancery.[12] But even among these there was, as Blackstone saw it, some hierarchical arrangement, with the Court of King's Bench being the "supreme court of common law"[13] and the High Court of Chancery being a coequal "supreme court of equity."[14]

Above these four trial courts, two of which were also "supreme courts", stood the Court of Exchequer Chamber, which Blackstone described as a court "that hath no original jurisdiction, but is only a court of appeal, to correct the errors of other jurisdictions."[15]

Blackstone described this Court of Exchequer Chamber as though it were the one supreme judicial court of England: "Into the court also of exchequer chamber (which then consists of all the judges of the three superior courts, and now and then the lord chancellor also) are sometimes adjourned from the other courts such causes, as the judges upon argument find to be of great weight and difficulty, before any judgment is given upon them in the court below."[16] It is to be noted, though, that Exchequer Chamber was not an appellate-review court to which the parties appealed from decisions of inferior courts, but simply a conference of the judges of the trial courts.

But even so, Blackstone wrote, "From all the branches of this court the exchequer chamber, a writ or error lies to . . . The house of peers, which is the supreme court of judicature in the kingdom, having at present no original jurisdiction over causes, but only upon appeals and writs of error; to rectify any injustice or mistake of the law, committed by the courts below."[17]

Thus Blackstone describes the Court of Exchequer Chamber as a supreme court of appellate review, and then he also describes the House of Lords as an even more supreme court of "judicial" appellate review.

However, all the English courts did not fit into this structure. England also had courts ecclesiastical, military, and maritime,[18] and a large number of miscellany, which Blackstone called "courts of a special jurisdiction."[19] "The great court of appeal in all ecclesiastical causes" was the court of delegates.[20] Appeals from the courts military lay to the "king in person" and from the maritime courts to the "king in council."[21] Blackstone says nothing about an ultimate appeal to the House of Lords in these types of causes.

It is not necessary to question the accuracy of Blackstone's description to show that England did not at the time of his writing have a hierarchical judicial system comparable to that existing today. Robert Stevens has written[22] that until the end of the eighteenth century there was a "subservience of the formal legal system to the political sovereign" and that this was "nowhere better illustrated than in the final appeal to the Lords."[23]

Stevens says, although parenthetically only, that in England by the Tudor period there had been established "a hierarchy of judicial appeals," yet he does not describe that hierarchy.[24] Instead his description of nineteenth-century developments raises doubts as to whether England earlier had a judicial hierarchy of appeals in any meaningful sense.

Stevens describes how in the early 1830s the modern hierarchical arrangement of appellate-review courts was established in England. In 1830 Lord Broughman "established a new court of Exchequer Chamber to replace the strange system of appeal courts of that name that had lumbered on from Elizabeth's days. The court of King's Bench lost its eclectic appellate jurisdiction; writs of error lying directly from the House of Lords to the courts of original jurisdiction were abolished; and the Exchequer Chamber was made a mandatory intermediate appeal court from the three common law courts: King's Bench, Common Pleas, and Exchequer."[25] In 1832 the Court of Delegates, which since the sixteenth century had been the final court of appeal in ecclesiastical and admiralty courts, was abolished and its jurisdiction transferred to the Privy Council, described as "the basic organ of the executive, which had also retained extensive judicial functions."[26]

By 1833 "both the House of Lords and the Privy Council had taken on the more obvious guise of courts and were becoming increasingly independent of the legislative and executive organs whose names they bore."[27]

During the American colonial period, it was possible to take an "appeal" to the Privy Council, or perhaps more accurately to the Council Committee for Trade and Plantations.[28] There has been a tendency to treat the Privy Council as an appellate-review judicial court in the modern sense. Instead it was an executive body that not only considered judicial appeals but also reviewed the legislation of the colonial legislatures, disallowing legislation of which it did not approve.

Joseph Henry Smith, in his study of appeals from America to England, says that there was "normal conciliar policy of permitting appeals to the King in Council from only the superior courts in the respective plantations."[29] But this, even as stated by Smith, was only a matter of *policy* or practice, and as Smith himself shows in discussing the subject, the policy was sometimes departed from. This is not surprising, though, since the judicial organization of the colonies was not such that one could find one superior or supreme court in each colony that stood at the apex of a colony's judicial system, from which, under a hierarchical arrangement, an appeal to England would lie. The fact seems to be that there was no pre-requisite of exhausting colonial appeals before appealing to the Privy Council. It was of course more economic to exhaust remedies on this side of the Atlantic before seeking remedy in England, but this is something different from requiring exhaustion of colonial remedies or allowing an appeal to the Privy Council only from the "highest" colonial court.

CHARACTERISTICS OF AN APPELLATE-REVIEW COURT

Obviously, the delegates to the Constitutional Convention of 1787 and the members of the First Congress were familiar with the structure of their own state judiciary systems. The national system was developed in light of that knowledge. But contrary to what may be generally thought, the national judiciary was not modeled on the then-existing judicial systems of the states, or of England, but represents a new departure from established systems. This departure in the national system is not so much a radical or sharp break with the past, but rather the assumption of a leadership role. At the time the process of organizing the state judicial systems was in a state of flux. In organizing the national system, the men of the period used what must have been considered the "best ideas" of the period. Inasmuch as these ideas were good ones, especially for a rapidly growing and expanding nation, the national system became the model upon which the state judiciaries were based. The consequences of some of the novel provisions used for the national system could only then be dimly perceived, if perceived at all.

The principal characteristic of the modern judicial system is its hierarchical structure. It is vertically structured, with a number of coequal courts at each vertical level, the number of such courts at each level decreasing sharply as the vertical structure is ascended. At the apex is one supreme, appellate-review court.

Today this hierarchical structure is so taken for granted that it seems almost impossible to have any other structure. And this leads to an assumption that judicial systems in 1787–89 were similarly structured, and their every act is interpreted as though they were so structured.

But the fact is that the basic court system structure in 1787–89, both in the American states and in England, was horizontal. There were different levels of courts, which by definition means that some were "superior" and others were "inferior." *All were trial courts.* The primary function of the superior courts was the exercise of a trial jurisdiction.

There was an embryonic appellate-review function in the judiciary and

35

again, by definition, to the extent it existed, this function called for "superior" courts to review the "inferior" courts. But there were many courts with specialized jurisdiction, that is, jurisdiction outside the categories encompassed by "law and equity." These included the courts of admiralty, of probate, of the church, and of the law merchant. These specialized courts are not easily classified as either superior or inferior courts. The subject matter of their jurisdiction was in some instances drawn within that of the law and equity courts. The best known example is Lord Mansfield's incorporation of the law merchant into the common law that was being administered by the King's Bench. The thrust, at least from the time of Coke, seems to have been conversion of this horizontal court structure into a vertical hierarchy of courts.

The present-day national judicial system illustrates the vertical hierarchical judicial structure to which judicial organization has tended. One supreme court at the top; thirteen courts of appeal at the next lower level; district courts at a still lower level, these being the principal trial courts; and below them a large number of magistrates, representing the lowest trial level. Being a federal system, the Supreme Court of the United States also sits as the one supreme court reviewing the fifty state judicial systems, each of which is again organized in a hierarchical structure.

In 1787–89 the highest judicial court in eleven of the thirteen states had all four of the following characteristics:

1. The highest judicial court was first and most importantly a trial court. While it might have some functions in the nature of appellate review, they were of secondary significance.

2. The appellate-review function was performed by some part of the legislature, or the executive, or by some combination of legislative, executive, and judicial officials. The ultimate reviewing authority of judicial proceedings was not vested exclusively in the judiciary in any state.

3. Every judge was a trial judge, and he participated along with others in reviewing his own actions as a trial judge, and might or might not have a vote in this review.

4. Judges did not write opinions and so there were no opinions to publish.

The other two states are Maryland and Virginia. As early as 1776 Maryland had provided on paper for a "modern" appellate-review court, but did not have such a court; it was not until three-quarters of a century later that Maryland actually established a true appellate-review court. As a result of legislation adopted in 1788, Virginia was in the process of establishing a true appellate-review court.

The modern appellate-review court has four characteristics distinguishing it from all the American courts of the late eighteenth century. These characteristics relate to the structure of the court and its place in the whole judicial system. As a part of the modern court's function, certain distinctive law-reporting characteristics have developed. These four characteristics are as follows:

1. The principal function of the court is to review lower-court proceedings, and only incidentally, if at all, to function as a trial court;

2. The court is completely separated from the executive and legislative branches, and its members are all judicial officers;

3. The court and all of its permanent members are separate and distinct from the trial courts and lower appellate courts, which lower courts have their own permanent members;

4. The judges write opinions for publication. These opinions are published:

   a. verbatim;

   b. on a regular basis, continually and timely; and

   c. with some "official" sanction.

The accompanying tables cover courts in the states in the Union at the end of the eighteenth century, and courts of the United States, and the tables state two dates: (1) the dates on which each jurisdiction took the "last step" necessary to establish within its judicial system a true appellate-review court, that is, a court having the three structural characteristics prerequisite to such a court; and (2) the date on which each jurisdiction established a modern system of law reporting. These dates are offered as a reasonable interpretation of the evidence and are not graven in stone. There is a tendency for formal recognition of legal developments to follow upon and not to precede the development so formalized. Moreover, one's interpretation of evidence very well may be colored by what one is seeking. Most discussions of the development of state judicial systems and of their supreme courts seem to assume that earlier judicial structures were the same as at the time of the writing, and so the evidence is interpreted in that light. The present writer may have erred in the opposite direction. But the evidence seems clear that the modern appellate-review court did not come into existence until the nineteenth century.

Following Independence, there was a great deal of diversity in the judicial systems established by the individual states. Legislatures made frequent changes, adding new features, dropping old ones, and changing those retained. Sometimes legislation reorganizing a judicial system was never put into effect, but instead new legislation was passed establishing still a different kind of judicial system. Consequently, it is difficult to trace the development of the state judiciaries from colonial times to the modern system. However, more or less standardized judicial systems did evolve, the principal feature of which is the modern appellate-review tribunal.

All four of the characteristics that have been listed evolved together, each feeding upon the other, so to speak. The evolution was concurrent, not consecutive. For example, judges did not write opinions until opinions were published. But at the same time opinions were not published until judges wrote them. It is not possible, or at least not practicable, to have the one without the other. To ask which came first is very similar to asking, "Which came first, the hen or the egg?"

The date 1789 is as satisfactory as any for dating the beginning of the development of the American appellate-review court. It is the year in which the first "true" American law report was published and the year the national judicial system was established. Both of these events had large significance in the development of the modern American appellate-review court.

AN APPELLATE-REVIEW COURT IS NOT A TRIAL COURT

The words "appeal" and "appellate" have always had several meanings but there has been a shift in the legal context in the primary meaning given to the words in the years since 1787–89. The shift has been subtle and largely unnoticed. In 1787–89 an appeal was a part of the *trial* process. Just as the highest state courts were trial courts, so too an appeal to the highest state court was a procedure for obtaining either a trial in the first instance or a second or third trial in the state's highest court. Today the usual meaning of an appeal is a seeking of appellate review of a proceeding or trial in an inferior court. This accords with the modern function of the highest courts of the states as appellate-review courts.

A comparison of the definition of today's "appeal" in *Black's Law Dictionary* with the definition given in *Conductor Generalis,* published in the eighteenth century, shows how the principal meaning of the word in the legal context has changed:

Black's Law Dictionary says an "appeal" is a:

Resort to a superior (i.e. appellate) court to review the decision of an inferior (i.e. trial) court or administrative agency.[30]

Conductor Generalis says of the word "appeal":

This word hath two significations in law; the one is removing a cause from an inferior court or judge, to a superior; as from one or more justices, to the quarter sessions.

The other kind of appeal (which is the subject of this title) is a prosecution against a supposed offender, by the party's own private action; prosecuting also for the crown, in respect for the offense against the publick.[31]

While the word "removing" in the first paragraph of this definition may include removal for purposes of appellate review, the more usual meaning was removal for purposes of *trial*. This is made evident by referring to the definition of the same word in Johnson's *Dictionary of the English Language*, published in 1755. Johnson says:

An *appeal* is a provocation from an inferior to a superior judge, whereby the jurisdiction of the inferior judge is for a while suspended, in respect of the cause; the cognizance being devolved to the superior judge.[32]

An earlier usage of the word "appeal" was that of an accusation, as in the private citizen's appeal of a felony.[33] But the procedure described by this meaning had fallen into disuse by the time Blackstone wrote.[34]

Although the use of an appeal to secure a new trial has frequently been noted by scholars and commentators, they tend to fit such procedure into a modern hierarchical or pyramidal arrangement of courts.[35]

The eighteenth-century meaning of appeal still prevails in some jurisdictions today. An appeal that involves a "removal" for trial in the first instance is ordinarily described by that term, "removal," but "appeal" is still the term used to describe the losing party's seeking an entirely new trial in a higher court.[36]

Another technique for removing a case from an inferior court to a superior court for trial was by writ of *certiorari*. This was the procedure followed in Pennsylvania,[37] and was also available in Virginia.[38]

The extent of the use of "appeals" to obtain new trials in a different court, not once, but twice, is evident in an exchange of correspondence in 1789 between Justice David Sewall of the Supreme Judicial Court of Massachusetts and Senator Caleb Strong of the same state regarding the proposed federal Judicial Bill. Justice Sewall[39] wrote Caleb Strong on May 2, giving him the benefit of his comments on the sketch of a national judicial system, which Strong had sent to him on April 22. "I have communicated your last to the Chief Justice & Judge Sumner the only Judges that have attended here. The chief Justice has copied out the Sixth, and I

39

have requested him to consider it particularly, & write you on the Subject but Whether he will or not he has made me no particular promise."[40] Justice Sewall set forth both the then-current practice in Massachusetts and the lessons to be learned from it in establishing a national judicial system:

> The power of granting new Trials should be placed in every Court. This is perhaps a part of the Judicial Power, and in their Original formation it may be best to expressly make it such under certain modifications and restrictions, and this method may answer all the purposes of Reviews, or Appeals with power to determine the Fact, in the Court appealed unto. We in Massachusetts have been used to various Trials of the same Facts by different Jurys of Course. But the time will come when the Ill consequences of this mode will appear—and if no Reviews were now had, but such as upon the particular Cause in question Justice and Equity required it would be pro bono in the opinion of some. Appeals therefore in the nature of a Writ of Error in some matters in the federal Courts may be more expedient. The Provision for a Writ of Error *from the "ultimate determination of a Cause in the highest Court of Law in Equity* of a State," as mentioned in the Scetch to th [*sic*] S. Fed. Judicial is a necessary, and usefull [*sic*] Provision.[41]

It was these *successive trials* in the same case that formed the basis for much of the criticism of Article III in the proposed Constitution, and led to proposed amendments to restrict the jurisdiction of the national judiciary.

Madison recognized that in this area of "appeals" the judiciary article was subject to legitimate criticism. He assured the people of his district that he wanted "to put the judiciary department into such a form as will render vexatious appeals impossible."[42] In 1748 the General Assembly of Virginia had passed legislation to prevent "trifling and vexatious appeals from the county courts" to the general court by prohibiting attorneys practicing before the general court from also practicing in the county court. Obviously, an attorney practicing in the county court would think twice before appealing for trial or obtaining a second trial in the general court if by doing so he lost his client to another attorney. This very well may have been the most effective way to prevent "trifling and vexatious appeals." It seems almost self-evident that the statute was not directed at appeals in the modern sense of appellate review.[43]

The First Congress in the provisions of the Judiciary Act of 1789 met both the demands for amendment of Article III of the Constitution, and the problems raised by Justice Sewall. This was done by limiting appeals to the use of writs of error;[44] the only appeals permitted to the Supreme Court from either the circuit courts or the state judiciaries are by writ of error. By this relatively simple technique the appellate jurisdiction of the national courts, both the circuit courts and the Supreme Court, was limited to an *appellate-review* function. They were denied authority to hold new trials upon appeals. In the exercise of the diversity jurisdiction, in appropriate cases, a removal for trial in the first instance was permitted, but the procedure is called "removal" and not "appeal."[45]

THE VARIETIES OF AMERICAN JUDICIAL SYSTEMS

The federal Constitution establishes "one supreme Court." Neither England nor any American state provided a model for this court. The Constitution guards against having a legislative body at the judicial apex, by adopting the doctrine of separation of powers. It guarded against having more than one coequal supreme court, as one for equity and another for common law, by specifically providing that there should be only one supreme court.

The English judicial system, with its plethora of courts, obscure jurisdictions, and unclear hierarchical arrangements, was patently unsatisfactory, and was a model rather to be avoided than emulated. There is some indication that in 1787 American state judicatories were tending toward developing a hierarchical arrangement. But as of 1787 no American state had "one supreme Court" either in name or in fact. (One might say that Maryland had the equivalent on paper in a Court of Appeals, but it was on paper only.)

Professor Goebel describes the colonial judiciaries in the following way: "The principle employed in the establishment of courts was the distinction between inferior and superior jurisdiction. . . . The inferior-superior dichotomy was in the main determined by monetary limitations of the amount in controversy in civil actions, the seriousness of the crime in criminal proceedings."[46] Literally, the description is accurate, but when it is read as referring to appellate review it is very misleading.[47]

As has been pointed out, at the end of the eighteenth century England did not have a hierarchical judicial structure, nor were appeals from the American colonies routed along any such well-defined structure.

Both colonial and English legislative bodies by the use of private bills could settle controversies that are today considered judicial in nature and can be resolved only through the judicial courts. In the eighteenth century such controversies could be settled by the legislature by public acts, the same as today, but also by private acts. A judicial proceeding had not yet become as clearly defined as it is today.

At the end of the eighteenth century "an appeal" meant an appeal to any higher authority—judicial, executive, or legislative—with the ultimate appeal to the Crown, or indeed to the Almighty. At the same time the word was used as a term of art in matters legal, but used in ways so various as to defy easy summary. Today the word can still be used in the sense of an appeal to higher authority, but it has come to have customary meaning in a legal context of an appeal to higher judicial authority, in the sense of seeking review, that is, appellate review.

In 1787–89 there were almost as many different types of judicial systems in the American states as there were states.[48] At one extreme was Georgia, which did not even establish a state supreme court until 1846, and Delaware, which did not establish a true appellate-review court until 1951. At the other extreme was Maryland, which as early as 1776 provided *on paper* for a Court of Appeals with the principal characteristics of an appellate-review court.

There was some variation along regional lines in the organization of the state judicial systems in 1787–89. In three of the New England states— Massachusetts, New Hampshire, and Rhode Island—there was an opportunity for multiple trials. The decision, either real or sham, resulting from a trial in an inferior tribunal could be appealed to a superior tribunal, where a second and entirely new trial could be had. And this in turn could be appealed in Massachusetts and a new third trial could be had. However, New England, except for Connecticut, took the lead in committing judicial proceedings exclusively to judges, thus effecting a separation of the powers of the judiciary from the other two branches of government.

Connecticut and the middle-Atlantic states—New York and New Jersey—provided for an appellate-review function, but did not vest it in an exclusively judicial agency, but rather in some combination of officials from all three branches of government, with a tendency for the legislative branch to predominate. In these states the judiciary was separated from the other branches insofar as the "trial" function was concerned, but the appeal or appellate review tended to follow the English model of being exercised primarily by the legislative body. Pennsylvania required appointment of a number of citizens, instead of members of either the legislature or executive branches, to the appellate-review tribunal, although there was no express disqualification of executive or legislative officials from serving.

The southern states of North Carolina, South Carolina, and Georgia delayed establishment of a separate court to exercise appellate-review functions. Instead in North and South Carolina the judges of the trial courts gradually came to have meetings, informal at first and by legislative direction later, to consider questions appropriate for decision by an appellate-review tribunal. These meetings were called Courts of Conference in North Carolina and Adjustment Courts in South Carolina; they considered a limited number of questions such as motions to grant new trials. Their operation is reminiscent of the *nisi prius* system in England, but the procedure was much less formalized.

Georgia long delayed establishing even this rudimentary form of appellate review, but then, near the middle of the nineteenth century, with a single stroke Georgia established a modern appellate-review court.

Maryland was the only state to establish a modern style supreme court when it became independent in 1776. Prior to Independence, the highest judicial body in Maryland was the governor and his council.[49] In its constitution of 1776, Maryland provided that the legislative, executive, and judicial powers of government ought not to be exercised by the same man or body of men.[50] Accordingly, a separate judicial system was established, to include a General Court, a Court of Chancery, and a Court of Admiralty. The constitution also provided for a separate Court of Appeals to sit on appeals from these other three courts.[51]

But it was not until the end of 1778 that the Maryland General Assembly provided for the organization of this court, when a Court of Appeals of five members was established and elected.[52] Even after the Court of Appeals had been established on paper, it was not until 1783 that the court was formally organized and began functioning.[53] When it did so the only cases on the docket were those that had been pending before its predecessor, the governor and his council, when it last met in May 1776.

The number of appeals was small, so that service as a judge of the court was only a part-time activity, much less demanding than being a judge of a trial court. As a consequence the salary was less than for trial judges, and so it was hardly a very attractive post. As a result, the constitution was amended in 1805 so as to reorganize the judicial system. Under the reorganization, Maryland was divided into six districts for trial purposes, with a chief judge and two associate judges presiding in each district. The chief judges of the six districts constituted the Court of Appeals.[54] And so

43

Maryland, having found a Court of Appeals manned by separate judges to be unsatisfactory, returned to a judicial structure that used the same judges to exercise both the trial and appellate-review functions.

The Virginia Court of Appeals established in 1788 had all of the structural characteristics of a modern appellate court. It was separate from the trial courts and it was composed only of judges, also different from the trial judges. It can appropriately be called the earliest American appellate-review court that has continuously functioned. The Court of Appeals of Kentucky grew out of the special recognition given to the Kentucky District in the organization of the Virginia judicial system, taking on the characteristics of the parent, and so it became one of the earliest American appellate-review courts.

In 1789 the principal characteristic of state judicatories was their *horizontal* arrangement. "Superior" courts as well as "inferior" court were trial courts. The important function of the superior courts was the trial function, not the appellate-review function.

The principal example of a "national" court established before 1789 is the Court of Appeals in Cases of Captures, established by the Continental Congress. On January 15, 1780, the Continental Congress considered a report—in the handwriting of Oliver Ellsworth—outlining a plan for establishing a Court of Appeals in Cases of Capture. The report recommended "[t]hat a court be established for the trial of all appeals from the courts of admiralty in these United States." It was further recommended "[t]hat the trials therein be according to the usage of nations and not by jury."[55] A motion by New Hampshire to delete this last provision was defeated by a vote of ten states to two.[56] The resolution was apparently agreed to at this time.[57]

On June 27, 1786, the Continental Congress directed the judges of this court "in every cause which has been or may be brought before them to sustain appeals and grant rehearings or new trials of the same, wherever Justice and right may in their opinion require it."[58] If there had been any doubt about it, this resolution directs the Court of Appeals to review the whole case, and if necessary in the interest of justice, to do so more than once.

DATES THAT MODERN APPELLATE-REVIEW COURTS WERE ESTABLISHED

The year in which each of the original thirteen states, and the United States, established its modern appellate-review court is set forth in table 3.1.

TABLE 3.1
Establishment of Appellate-Review Courts

State	Date	Citation
New Hampshire	1901	1901 N.H. Laws, Ch. 78
(Reorganizes supreme court giving the supreme court appellate-review function and a superior court the trial function)		
Massachusetts	1859	1859 Mass. Acts, ch. 196
(Separates superior court with trial function from supreme judicial court)		
Rhode Island	1905	1905 R.I. Pub. Laws, tit. I, ch. 1
(Establishes superior court with trial function)		
Connecticut	1889	1889 Conn. Pub. Acts, ch. 194
(Allows supreme court of errors discretion in performing circuit-trial function)		
New York	1847	1846 Const. Art. VI, § 2; 1847 N.Y. Laws, ch. 280, Art. II
(Establishes court of appeals of judges only, eliminating senators from membership)		
New Jersey	1844	1844 Const. Art. VI, § 1
(Establishes court of errors and appeals with membership consisting only of judges)		
Pennsylvania	1874	1874 Const., Art. V, § 3
(Confirms supreme court's appellate-review function "as is now or may hereafter be provided by law.")		
Delaware	1951	1951 Del. Laws, ch. 109, amending 1897 Const. Art. IV
(Establishes supreme court with separate judges)		
Maryland	(1776)	1776 Md. Const. Art. 56 (never fully effectuated)
	1851	1851 Const. Art. IV, § 2
(Although 1776 constitution establishes a court of appeals, it was not until 1851 that the constitution establishes a court of appeals to have "appellate jurisdiction only")		
Virginia	1788	1788 Laws, ch. LXVIII
(Establishes court of appeals with judges different from trial judges)		
North Carolina	1818	1818 Laws, ch. 1
(Establishes supreme court of three justices)		
South Carolina	1868	1868 S.C. Acts, No. 28
(Establishes supreme court consisting of judges separate from trial judges)		
Georgia	1845	Laws 1845, Act of Dec. 10 carried into effect constitutional amendment of Art. III, § 1, made in 1835

TABLE 3.1, continued

State	Date	Citation
("The said court shall have no original jurisdiction, but shall be a court alone for the trial and correction of errors in law and equity from the superior courts of the several circuits.")		
United States	1789	U.S. Stat. at Large, Vol. 1, Ch. 20, §§ 22, 25
(Provides for appellate review by writ of error)		

This table shows the date on which the state's modern appellate-review court was established, and gives a citation to the authority relied upon for using this date, as well as a description of this "last step" in the development of the court. It would be surprising if some knowledgeable authorities on the subject would not disagree with the date selected. The development of state appellate-review courts is not marked with signposts and even what signs there are are not always easy of interpretation. There is always a strong tendency to interpret the past in light of the present. The result is that the modern appellate-review court is assumed to have existed long before it can truly be said to have come into existence.

DATES THAT MODERN LAW-REPORTING SYSTEMS
WERE ESTABLISHED

In some states a modern system of law reporting was established at the same, or about the same time as an appellate-review court was established. In other states law reporting of the state's highest *trial* court preceded the establishment of an appellate-review court by a half century or more.

The dates on which a modern system of law reporting was established in each of the original thirteen states, and the United States, are set forth in table 3.2. A modern system of law reporting is defined as one in which the decisions of a court, and the reasons for the decisions, are published on a regular and timely basis, so as to be generally available to all courts, the legal profession, and the public. No distinction is made between law reports privately published and those published by state authority, as by a state reporter. Nor is any distinction made between reports that publish verbatim the opinions of the court and reports publishing a reporter's statement of the decision. (In early reports it is often impossible to determine whether the report is an opinion or a statement based on the reporter's notes and other materials.)

TABLE 3.2
Origins of "Modern" Law-Reporting Systems in the Thirteen Original States
and the United States: Dates, Reporters, and Style of Reports

State	Date of Publication	Reporter
New Hampshire	1819	Nathaniel Adams

(Reports of Cases Argued and Determined in the Superior
Court of Judicature for the State of New-Hampshire, from
September 1816, To February 1819)

Massachusetts	1805	Ephraim Williams

(Reports of Cases Argued and Determined in the Supreme
Judicial Court of the State of Massachusetts, from
September 1804 to June 1805—Both Inclusive)

Rhode Island	1847	Thomas Durfee

(Rhode Island Reports [Bound volume, 1851, incorporates
pamphlet reports begun by Durfee in 1847])

Connecticut	1815	Thomas Day

(Connecticut Reports [Bound volume, 1817, incorporates
pamphlet published in 1815])

New York	1804	George Caines

(New York Term Reports of Cases Argued and
Determined in the Supreme Court of that State)

New Jersey Law	1808	William Sanford Pennington

(Reports of Cases Adjudged in the Supreme Court of
Judicature of the State of New Jersey)

New Jersey Equity	183?	N. Saxton

(Reports of Cases Decided in the Court of Chancery of the
State of New Jersey)

Pennsylvania	1809	Horace Binney

(Reports of Cases Adjudged in the Supreme Court of
Pennsylvania)

Delaware	1837	Samuel M. Harrington

(Reports of Cases Argued and Adjudged in the Superior
Court and Court of Errors and Appeals of the State of
Delaware)

Maryland	1852	

(Maryland Reports)

Virginia	1807	William Waller Hening and William Munford

(Reports of Cases Argued and Determined in the Supreme
Court of Appeals of Virginia)

North Carolina	1818	John Louis Taylor

(North Carolina Term Reports)

South Carolina	1819	John Mill

(Reports of Judicial Decisions in the Constitution Court of
South Carolina)

Georgia	1847	

(Georgia Reports)

United States	1804	William Cranch

(United States Reports)

THE RELATIONSHIP BETWEEN THE DEVELOPMENT OF
APPELLATE-REVIEW COURTS AND MODERN LAW REPORTING

The modern system of law reporting could not develop until judges wrote opinions and made them available for publication on a timely and regular basis. At the same time, there was no incentive for judges to craft judicial opinions until a system developed whereby the opinions would be published.

The two developments are interdependent. We could not have the one without the other. The mainstay of early law reporting was the reporting of trial decisions, with some reporting of appeals when such took place. But with the development of the appellate-review court, law reporting became increasingly identified with the reporting of the opinions of these courts. There is still some reporting of trial court decisions, particularly of the United States district courts, but both the heart and the bulk of law reporting today is the reporting of the "law" being made by the appellate-review tribunals.

The relationship between law reporting and appellate review is illuminated in table 3.3, which for comparative purposes shows the dates on

TABLE 3.3
Establishment of Modern Appellate Review Courts
and Law-Reporting Systems

State	Appellate-Review Court	Law Reporting (Date of Publication)
New Hampshire	1901	1819
Massachusetts	1859	1805
Rhode Island	1905	1847
Connecticut	1889	1815
New York	1847	1804
New Jersey	1844	1808 Law 183? Equity
Pennsylvania	1874	1809
Delaware	1951	1837
Maryland	1851 (1776)	1852
Virginia	1788	1807
North Carolina	1818	1818
South Carolina	1868	1819
Georgia	1845	1847
United States	1789	1804

which each state and the United States established a modern appellate-review court and a modern system of law reporting.

WERE STATE STATUTES AVAILABLE?

Moderns find it easy to assume that state cases and state statutes were readily available in 1789, since law today is superbly indexed, and since today's law libraries are inundated with case-law and statute books. But we have just seen that judicial decisions, much less reports of them, were almost unknown and certainly not ordinary in 1789. Similarly, for some of the same reasons, a complete compilation of the existing statute law of the states, or of any state, would have been difficult to discover in 1789.

It is instructive to contrast the exhaustive recent work of Professor Goebel in this regard. Goebel's discussion of the origin and meaning of the Judiciary Act of 1789 finds it "rooted in the law and custom of divers American jurisdictions." He thinks that this evidenced "a subtle species of continuity," the new national system having been "planted in the soil of American tradition" and being directed by Section 34 of the act to "regard[ ] state laws as rules of decision."[59]

Goebel's major historical premise is that "no belief was more ingrained in this country [in 1789] than that courts were properly to be ordered in terms of inferior and superior jurisdiction." So sure is Goebel that "the hierarchical arrangement of courts" existed then in the states much as it does now, that "no preliminary canvas of state laws" was undertaken to ensure that the premise was true.[60] We have seen that his premise, however, is incorrect.

Similarly, Goebel assumes that the statute law of the states was collected and available for the use of the committee. And similarly, Goebel is again in error. There was no satisfactory collection of state statutes available to the members of the First Congress, or available anywhere in the United States.

According to Goebel, the First Congress must have had access to books relating to state jurisprudence in which the incidents of procedure and practice could be found. "The provisions which are renditions of state statutes could, we believe, hardly have been drafted from memory alone. This raises the problem of the availability of the sources."[61] Goebel thinks that it was doubtful whether the statutes of sister states would have been found in the private law libraries in New York,[62] a conclusion that all the evidence shows was valid.[63]

Actually, the members of the First Congress were given access to the library of the New York Society, which was housed in the same building as that in which the Congress met.[64] The New York Society published in 1789 *A Catalogue of the Books belonging to the said Library*.[65] This catalogue shows that the library contained *no* American statutes, although it did contain a copy of Kirby's *Reports*.[66]

Goebel categorically states, "It is, however, certain that the new Congress itself had inherited a collection of such statutes," pointing out that on July 27, 1785, the Continental Congress had passed a resolve requesting each state to send thirteen copies of all laws enacted since 1774, with the view to retaining one copy for Congress and sending twelve copies to the states other than the one whose laws were involved. Follow-up requests were made on August 29, October 7, and November 9. Goebel reports there was "such compliance as was possible," but does not indicate how extensive that was. He cites a letter from Charles Thomson, the secretary of the Continental Congress, to Washington, dated July 23, 1789, saying that the books, letters, and papers of the Continental Congress had been deposited "in rooms in the house where the Legislature of the United States now assemble." Goebel concludes, "The statutes were presumably available for the use of the Senate Committee," but he himself did not trace to this collection of state law the state statutes that he says are the source of the provisions of the Judiciary Act, and in fact he used collections of state statutes not published until after 1789.[67] The records of the Continental Congress show that Thomson never did have much success in collecting the then-current statutes of all the thirteen states.[68] There is no evidence that any state sent along its session laws each year, in an attempt to keep Congress current.

Apparently no state had achieved a complete codification of its statutes by 1789, or by 1800, much less were there any attempts continually to integrate recently passed laws into a codification.[69] It is likely, therefore, given the prevailing opinion that law was found and not made, that statutes too were at bottom merely attempts to approximate the true law, that not many people were interested in the kind of complete codification of statute laws moderns find indispensable and basic. Moreover, it was difficult and expensive to come across such collections of the laws of a state that did exist. In the Northwest Ordinance, Congress required "the governor and judges . . . [to] adopt . . . such laws of the original States . . . as may be necessary, and best suited to the circumstances of the district."[70] Governor Arthur St. Clair, reporting to President Washington in August, 1789, noted the difficulties this entailed: "[I]t was found that the Judges were not possessed of the Codes of the different States—that few of the

Laws in the Collections they were in possession of would apply."[71] There should be not much wonder that Secretary Thomson had a difficult time acquiring a collection of state statutes pursuant to the 1785 legislation, and it is clear that Congress had no complete set of codifications of state laws available to it in the summer of 1789.

SUMMARY

No state in 1789 had either judges who wrote opinions or reporters who published opinions, or courts that could instruct other courts about what state law was. The highest courts of many states were composed of neither judges nor lawyers. Judges did not make law; with the collegial assistance of counsel, of jurors, and sometimes of members of the executive and legislative parts of the government, they engaged in a continual struggle to discover the law. They approximated rather than made law. A "superior" court was distinguished from an "inferior" one by the fact that it contained more searchers; it was not a court that dealt solely with appealed legal issues, nor a group of legally trained judges distinct from those inhabiting "inferior" benches, nor a top rung in a hierarchical ladder of power and authority. The judgments of "superior" courts did not need to be published because they were ephemeral and transitory "opinions" *about* the law, not permanent and authoritative statements *of* the law. Codes of state statutes were incomplete or nonexistent, and those that existed were at least in large part essentially inaccessible.

In short, no state court in 1789 could have declared what the law of that state was. There was in fact no such authoritative source for the law of a state. Consequently, Congress could not have required the national courts to look to the opinions of state courts to ascertain what state law was; this would have been unthinkable.

In order to have authoritative declarations of law one must have a hierarchical court system, in which there exist "higher" courts that can rule authoritatively upon questions of law which have been passed up from the "lower" courts. In other words, one must have the sort of court structure that was the innovation of the First Judiciary Act. However, Congress did not create a hierarchical structure so as to generate authoritative declarations of law. Instead, this structure was invented to solve a political problem. Opponents of the new Constitution had objected that Article III's provision that "the supreme Court shall have appellate Jurisdiction, both as to Law and Fact" was potentially dangerous and oppressive; the danger was that local juries could be ignored, and the oppression could stem from a wealthy litigant dragging a poorer litigant to the capital to retry questions of fact. The hierarchical structure of the First Judiciary Act addressed the question by limiting the highest court to questions of law. As a by-product of this innovation, when added to the notion of judicial review that was concurrently being invented to solve other political problems,[72] the highest court created by the act developed the power to declare the law. The historical irony is that we moderns regard the unintended by-product—declaring the law—to be the very essence of the matter.

CHAPTER IV

Organization of National Courts Under the Judiciary Act of 1789

INTRODUCTION

THE PROBLEMS OF ESTABLISHING a national judiciary in 1789 were immense. Puzzles abound in the 1789 act as a result, since these problems demanded both novel solutions and open-ended phraseology, the latter not only because of hesitation and uncertainty, not only to allow flexibility and leeway, but also because of the political compromises necessary to achieve a working court system acceptable to most people. Modern present-mindedness places blinders on readers of the 1789 act. Moderns fail to notice some of the puzzles, and they find answers to others that are consonant with their own knowledge and beliefs about courts. Moderns (usually unreflectively) impose closure to ratify the present.

We shall proceed to examine several of these puzzles, both to demonstrate the open-endedness and uncertainty inherent in some provisions of the act, and to show how other provisions aid in understanding Section 34.

DOES THE CONSTITUTION ITSELF VEST JURISDICTION IN THE JUDICIAL DEPARTMENT?[1]

Article III, Section 2, of the Constitution says, "The judicial power shall extend" and then lists a series of affirmative grants, leaving the residuary subjects to the states. This form of expression has led to the view that the national courts are courts of "limited" jurisdiction. Yet the Constitution does not say this.

To test where the balance lies between the national courts and the state courts, the provisions of Article III, Section 2, can be phrased negatively, that is, in terms of what is not within the national jurisdiction rather than what is within it. The result is something like this: "The judicial power of the United States shall extend to all controversies, except those between citizens of the same state or between aliens, and even these controversies are within the judicial power of the United States when involving subjects within the legislative power of Congress under Article I, Section 8." When so phrased, it is obvious that the "important" national judicial power is vastly more extensive than that left to the states. The United States Supreme Court is the only American court with *complete* judicial jurisdiction, whether it is called general, limited, or whatever, for it is the only American court that determines its own jurisdiction, and from which determination there is no appeal to any higher judicial court.[2]

When the First Congress read the Constitution, it could see the potential in Article III for overwhelming the state judicatories. But there remained the question of the constitutional ability of Congress to define or to limit the jurisdiction granted by Article III. The powers of the Congress, and many of the powers of the president, are directly vested in those agencies by the Constitution itself. No enabling legislation was necessary, and no legislative limitations would be valid. The Constitution uses the words "shall be vested" when speaking of the power of each of the three major divisions of the national government, including (see above) the judiciary. Should the judiciary be nevertheless considered different, in that the "judicial power" stated in Article III, Section 2, must be conveyed to the judges by some explicit legislation? Could, more importantly, this conveyance be only of a part of the jurisdiction delineated in the Constitution?

To a very considerable degree the Judiciary Act of 1789 temporizes. It is so worded that it neither adopts nor rejects an interpretation of the Constitution under which the Constitution itself vests its large judicial power in the federal judicial department, or whether this vesting is subject to the control of Congress.

The question of the power of Congress was broached when debate began in the Senate on the Judicial Bill on June 22, a debate that Charles Warren says "was the crucial contest in the enactment of the Judiciary Act."[3] The debate arose on a motion by Richard Henry Lee of Virginia. In his *Journal,* William Maclay set forth the motion and described the debate in the following passage:

> *June 22nd*—But now Mr. Lee brought forward a motion nearly in the words of the Virginia amendment, viz., "That the jurisdiction of the Federal courts should be confined to cases of admiralty and maritime jurisdiction." Lee and Grayson supported this position. Elsworth answered them, and the ball was kept up until past three o'clock. The question was going to be put. I rose and begged to make

a remark or two. The effect of the motion was to exclude the Federal jurisdiction from each of the States except in admiralty and maritime cases. But the Constitution expressly extended it to all cases, in law and equity, under the Constitution and laws of the United States; treaties made or to be made, etc. We already had existing treaties, and were about making many laws. These must be executed by the Federal judiciary. The arguments which had been used would apply well if amendments to the Constitution were under consideration, but certainly were inapplicable here.[4]

Lee's motion was not a motion to amend the Judicial Bill, either by addition or deletion. It was a general proposition, such as was used in the federal convention.[5] It dealt with diversity, its implication being to take that jurisdiction away from the national courts to be created in the bill. The question debated was whether to give the "Federal" courts a diversity jurisdiction.

Warren erroneously sees this debate as involving federal-question jurisdiction:

> The broad pro-Constitution men took the position that Congress had no power to withhold from the Federal Courts which it should establish any of the judicial power granted by the Constitution. On this point, they were forced to yield; for the Congress withheld from the Federal Courts much of the jurisdiction which it might have bestowed under the Constitution. On the other hand, the narrow pro-Constitution men were anxious to give to the Federal Courts as little jurisdiction as possible and to leave to the State Courts, in the first instance, jurisdiction over most of the Federal questions, subject to Federal revision through the appellate power of the United States Supreme Court. On this point, this faction also was forced to yield. The result was a compromise.[6]

While Warren's statement of the viewpoint of the broad pro-Constitution men seems to be a correct statement of the view that the Constitution itself vests the national judicial power in the judicial department, the narrow pro-Constitution men were not denying that point, but rather seeking to have the state courts established as a part of that judicial department—as the lower national courts.

It is possible to view jurisdiction left to the state courts as being left to the state courts as *state courts* or as *lower national courts*. Lee wanted it left to them as lower national courts, or at least this is a tenable interpretation of his position in this debate.[7] On this view, no one was suggesting that Congress had a power to restrict or limit the Article III grant.[8]

The debate took up part of two days. In the end, the Senate agreed with the majority of its committee and rejected Lee's motion. It is well to keep in mind, though, that the decision might have been different.

If the Senate had decided to give the inferior national courts only an admiralty jurisdiction, it would have had to decide what to do with the rest of the "judicial power of the United States." It could have decided that the state courts should act as lower national courts—as Lee and others desired—or it could have left the rest of the judicial power in the one Supreme Court. Both alternatives assume that the powers of Article III are automatically vested in the judicial department.

A third possibility—having the contrary assumption—is the way that the national judicial system eventually developed. It is now orthodoxy that the federal courts have only the jurisdiction expressly given to them by Congress, so that to the extent the judicial power is not actually vested by congressional action in the federal courts it remains with the states. Even today the full implications of this view are unclear, as witnessed by the recurring debates over whether Congress can limit the "appellate jurisdiction" of the Supreme Court. Even more telling is to ask what the situation would have been if the First Congress had not written Section 25 into the Judiciary Act. Section 25 gave statutory authorization to Supreme Court review of state judicial decisions on constitutional and federal-law issues.

One cannot say with any confidence whether the First Congress even considered its possible power to limit or restrict Article III jurisdiction. Article III, Section 2 gives Congress the power to regulate the "appellate jurisdiction" of the Supreme Court; nothing is said about regulating "original jurisdiction." The *whole* of the judicial power of the United States outlined in Article III was recognized in the Judiciary Act.[9]

The act contains no "true" amount-in-controversy limitations on the exercise of national jurisdiction. There are three provisions that may appear to contradict this statement, two concerning suits by the United States in the district and circuit courts and the other concerning the removal of cases from the state courts to the circuit courts for trial. All are explainable on other grounds.

Section 9 gives the district courts jurisdiction of suits at common law where the United States sues only when the matter in dispute is $100 or more. Section 11 limits circuit-court jurisdiction over suits by the United States of a civil nature at common law or equity, to those where the matter in dispute is more than $500. These are self-limiting restrictions. The United States can determine whether to sue, and so it should be able to impose on itself a limitation that it will not sue unless there is at least $100 or $500 in dispute.

Section 12 requires that the amount in dispute must exceed $500 in order for a diversity or alienage suit to be removed from a state court to the circuit court for trial. Even though there is no dollar limitation on the bringing of diversity or alienage suits under the original jurisdiction of the circuit courts, this limitation in removal cases can be rationalized since it simply involves the distribution of the judicial power among inferior courts. The constitutional grant, without any dollar limitation, is left intact for suits where the amount in dispute is under $500 and can still be brought under the original jurisdiction of the circuit courts.

Many assume that Section 11 required a $500 amount in controversy before federal jurisdiction could be established over a diversity or an alienage suit. The language and punctuation of the relevant passage, however, demonstrate that no such limitation was imposed. The passage is as follows:

> That the circuit courts shall have original cognizance, concurrent with the courts of the several states, of all suits of a civil nature at common law or in equity, where the matter in dispute exceeds, exclusive of costs, the sum or value of five hundred dollars, and the United States are plaintiffs or petitioners; or an alien is a party, or the suit is between a citizen of the State where the suit is brought, and a citizen of another State.

The semicolon clearly restricts the amount-in-controversy requirement to the instance that precedes it, namely, actions brought by the United States.[10]

The strongest reason for saying that the Judiciary Act of 1789 did not impose any dollar limitations on the diversity jurisdiction where the suits were brought originally in the circuit court, is to look at the provisions of the Judicial Bill in comparison with the proposed constitutional amendments that were developed at the same time.

Madison proposed a constitutional amendment providing that there should be a right to trial by jury in suits at common law, between man and man, regardless of the amount in controversy.[11] The House, in adopting the Resolve of August 24, continued the principle, proposing, "In suits at common law, the right of trial by Jury shall be preserved."[12] But on September 9, the Senate changed this provision so as to limit it to suits "where the value in controversy shall exceed twenty dollars."[13]

It would have been absurd for the First Congress to put a $500 limitation on original suits at common law in the circuit courts, while at the same time proposing a constitutional amendment cutting that amount down to $20. How could the Congress have justified making a different provision in the Judicial Bill than it was going to require by constitutional amendment? To avoid this inconsistency it must be assumed that there was no dollar limitation placed on original suits at common law in the circuit courts under the diversity jurisdiction. This is what Section 11 of the statute says, and it takes a perverse reading of it to obtain an interpretation that there was a $500 limitation.

Nevertheless, the First Congress wanted to impose restrictions on access to the national courts. Since its power to do so by imposing dollar restrictions was doubtful, it turned to other measures. Plaintiffs were discouraged from resorting to the circuit courts where only small amounts were in dispute by a denial of costs and possible imposition of costs[14] on a successful plaintiff who nevertheless recovers a small amount. Section 20 of the 1789 act provides:

> That where in a circuit court, a plaintiff in an action, originally brought there, or a petitioner in equity, other than the United States, recovers less than the sum or value of five hundred dollars, or a libellant, upon his own appeal, less than the sum or value of three hundred dollars, he shall not be allowed, but at the discretion of the court, may be adjudged to pay costs.

But the imposition of similar restrictions on the successful libellant is puzzling. There had to be $300 in dispute in order for an "appeal" to lie from the district to the circuit court.[15] So this provision apparently applies only when the amount in dispute exceeds $300 in the district court, but the appealing libellant recovers less than $300 in the circuit court. It is odd that such a picayune provision should have been included in this act. It seems rather more probable that there is some connection between this provision and the "appellate jurisdiction" given to the circuit courts in the last sentence of Section 11.[16]

Yet another example of the open-ended and ambiguous nature of important Judiciary Act provisions, reflecting congressional doubt about the wisdom of, or their power to fashion, limitations on Article III jurisdiction lies in the treatment afforded "federal questions." The Judiciary Act of 1789 does not expressly extend the national judicial power to "all cases, in law and equity, arising under this constitution, the laws of the United

States, and treaties made, or which shall be made, under this authority."[17] But it does not expressly deny that jurisdiction either.

The myth that this silence nevertheless constitutes a denial of the jurisdiction has come to be orthodoxy. The myth found reaffirmation and reinforcement in Charles Warren's reading of a letter published in the *State Gazette of North Carolina* on July 30, 1789, explaining what had been done so far in the First Congress about the judiciary.[18] Warren reads the statement in that letter that the circuit courts were to "take cognizance of all cases of Federal jurisdiction" as referring to a federal-question jurisdiction. In context, as is explained in Appendix 1, it appears that the writer of that *State Gazette* letter was referring to the diversity jurisdiction as being within the "Federal jurisdiction." As read correctly, the letter provides no evidence that the Judiciary Committee ever intended expressly to give the national courts a federal-question jurisdiction; and so, when the reported bill did not do so, the committee had not, as Warren erroneously thinks, "eliminated" the federal-question jurisdiction.[19]

Warren concludes, "Congress withheld from the Federal Courts much of the jurisdiction which it might have bestowed under the Constitution."[20] Some credence to this view is to be found in the Judiciary Act of 1801, which explicitly gave the circuit courts jurisdiction "of all cases in law or equity, arising under the constitution and laws of the United States, and treaties made, or which shall be made, under their authority."[21] This could have been a ratification of an already-existing jurisdiction. The 1801 act, however, was soon repealed.[22]

In fact Warren in another place understands the First Congress to have left the federal-question jurisdiction in limbo, placing it neither with the national courts nor with the state courts. He says that "the narrow constructionist party failed in their attempt to leave to the State Courts jurisdiction over Federal questions" but succeeded in the following years by statute in vesting such jurisdiction in the state courts until *Prigg v. Pennsylvania*[23] "put an end to any attempt to enforce the doctrine of Congressional power to vest Federal jurisdiction in State Courts or officers."[24]

In 1875 Congress again expressly provided that the circuit courts should have jurisdiction "of all suits of a civil nature at common law or in equity . . . arising under the Constitution or laws of the United States, or treaties made, or which shall be made under their authority"[25] but in doing so placed a dollar limitation of $500 on the jurisdiction. This statute reads equally well as giving the federal courts for the first time a federal-question jurisdiction, limiting it to situations in which the matter in dispute exceeds $500, or as placing the $500 limitation on the exercise of a federal-question jurisdiction on which there had previously been no such limitation.

Commentators have, unquestioningly it would seem, accepted the notion that the Judiciary Act of 1789 did not give the national courts a federal-question jurisdiction, although recognizing that it appears to go against the common sense of establishing a national judiciary in the first place. Wright's *Treatise* says: "Although this federal question jurisdiction was one of the principal reasons that the Constitution authorized Congress to create a system of inferior federal courts, with one short-lived exception it was not until 1875 that the Congress gave the federal courts general original jurisdiction over these cases."[26] But neither Warren nor later commentators have given any examples of national laws over which the national judiciary did not exercise jurisdiction. It is hardly conceivable that the government hobbled along for nearly a century not giving the national judiciary the jurisdiction it was expected to have.[27]

Congress simply did not say whether it was giving the federal courts *all* the jurisdiction authorized by the Constitution, or only a part of it. It sufficed for the purposes of Congress to make specific mentions of the subjects in which it was particularly interested.

A SUPREME COURT OF TRIALS AND ERRORS?

Another example of the open-endedness of both the Constitution and the Judiciary Act lies in the name and structure of the nation's new high court. Neither is very clear. The Constitution provides in Article III, Section 1, that there shall be "one supreme court." But the Constitution does not name that court. In the first printed copies of the Constitution the phrase is rendered as above, that is, all in lower case. The engrossed Constitution refers to it as "one supreme Court," the engrosser capitalizing "Court" as was his practice of capitalizing all nouns. Any effort to capitalize *Supreme Court* in the Constitution runs into difficulties in the rendition of the phrase "both of the supreme and inferior courts," which appears in Article III, Section 1.

Confirmation of the fact that the nation's highest court is not named in the Constitution is found in the style of the heading on the first page of the Minute Book of the Supreme Court, which reads: "At the Supreme Judicial Court of the United States begun and held at New York . . ." (February 1, 1790).[28] Warren, apparently operating on the assumption that the Court is named by the Constitution itself, called this a curious "error."[29]

In the first Minutes of the Court, adjourning to the next day for lack of a quorum, the Court is referred to as the "Supreme Court of the United States," and so it has been known ever since. But this is all that is known about how the Court got its name.

The First Congress in enacting the Judiciary Act of 1789 did not give the highest court a name, although the Congress recognized that there should be one supreme court.[30] This was not an oversight, for the First Congress did name the other national courts, and in doing so, used capital letters. Section 3 provides "[t]hat there be a court called a District Court" in each of the districts set up, and Section 4 provides that there should be courts held in each of the three circuits "which shall be called Circuit Courts."[31]

There is some indication that in the First Congress the Judiciary Committee considered establishing a national judicial system like that of Massachusetts and states with similar systems. These systems were, themselves, modeled closely on the one existing in England, the *nisi prius* system, where one or more supreme or superior courts exercises the principal trial jurisdiction over the entire country or state. England had several such countrywide superior trial courts—King's Bench, Common Pleas, Exchequer, Admiralty, and others. Massachusetts had one, the Superior Court of Judicature, whose name was changed in 1781—although without significant change of function—to the Supreme Judicial Court.

The trial jurisdiction of these courts was exercised by one or more of the justices going out into the counties, and holding trials, reserving questions of law for the full court back at the seat of government, Westminster or Boston.

In the letter published on July 30, 1789, in the *State Gazette of North Carolina,* referred to and discussed in appendix 1,[32] the writer said the Judiciary Committee had agreed upon a circuit court that should "act as a nisi prius Judge, in cases originating in the Supreme Court, and as a Court of Appeals from the Admiralty Court."

After Lee's motion to limit the inferior national judiciary to admiralty courts was defeated on June 23, the Senate turned to consideration of the actual provisions of the Judicial Bill. The only information available on this debate is found in Maclay's *Journal.* It is extremely murky and is set forth in full below so readers can draw their own conclusions as to what the debate was about:

> The first clause of the bill was now called for. Grayson made a long harangue. I mentioned that I thought this an improper time to decide absolutely on this part of the bill. If the bill stood in its present form

and the Circuit Courts were continued, six judges appeared to be too few. If the Circuit Courts were struck out, they were too many; that it would have pleased me better; but as we were in committee I would not consider myself as absolutely bound by anything that happened now, but would reserve myself until the second reading in the Senate. Mr. Elsworth rose and made a most elaborate harangue on the necessity of a numerous bench of judges. He enlarged on the importance of the causes that would come before them, of the dignity it was necessary to support, and the twelve judges of England in the Exchequer Chamber were held up to view during the whole harangue, and he seemed to draw conclusions that twelve were few enough. I readily admitted that the information respecting the English courts was fairly stated. But in England the whole mass of litigation in the kingdom came before these judges, the whole suits arising from eight or nine millions of people. Here it was totally different. The mass of causes would remain with the State judges. Those only arising from Federal laws would come before the Federal judges, and these would be comparatively few indeed. When they became numerous it would be time enough to increase the judges.

Mr. Grayson rose again and repeated his opinion that numbers were necessary to procure respectable decisions, I replied that, in my opinion, the way to secure respectable decisions was to choose eminent characters for judges; that numbers rather lessened responsibility, and, unless they were all eminent, tended to obscure the decisions. The clause, however, was passed. Adjourned at the usual hour.

June 24th.—Rode out early this morning, but returned before eight. Attended [Senate] at the usual time. The bill for the judiciary was taken up. The first debate that arose was whether there should be Circuit Courts or courts of *nisi prius*. This distinction was started by Mr. Johnson, from Connecticut. Was adopted, and spoke long to by Mr. Butler. This kept us most of the day. I did not give a vote either way—indeed, I do not like the bill. The vote was for district courts. We proceeded to a clause about Quakers taking an affirmation.[33]

This debate was begun around the seemingly innocuous first clause, providing for six Supreme Court justices. Those who wanted a large number of justices on the Supreme Court seemingly were envisioning a judicial system like that of England or Massachusetts in which these judges would go out and try cases. The only restriction imposed by the Constitution on this type of judicial organization was that there should be only *one* such supreme or superior court, thus avoiding the multiplicity of superior courts that existed in England.

Maclay writes as though a system using circuit courts and one using courts of *nisi prius* were two different and opposing systems, and says the vote was for district courts. This leaves his meaning in the air. The Judiciary Act of 1789 provides for both district courts and circuit courts. Does it provide for a *nisi prius* system or not? While Section 11 of the act provides that the circuit courts "shall have original cognizance" of suits of a civil nature at common law or in equity, the act makes no provision as to how and where these suits should be actually commenced. The Process Act, passed almost simultaneously with the Judiciary Act, requires the process to issue from the supreme or circuit courts to "bear test of the chief justice of the supreme court" while the process from the district court was to "bear test of the judge of such court."[34] This is some indication that the circuit courts were not viewed as a separate court, but as a part of the one supreme court: in other words, as something resembling a *nisi prius* system.

The most that can be said is that the language of the Judiciary Act of 1789 is sufficiently flexible so that the Supreme Court could have developed as a superior court with trial jurisdiction over the entire country, the jurisdiction being exercised by the justices going out on circuit and reserving questions of law for the full court.

GEOGRAPHICAL BOUNDARIES OF DISTRICT COURTS

Since there is nothing in the Constitution requiring the establishment of district courts, there is nothing requiring that the districts follow state lines. Alexander Hamilton in *The Federalist No. 81* suggested that a quite different arrangement might be useful. He wrote: "I am not sure but that it will be found highly expedient and useful to divide the United States into four or five, or half a dozen districts; and to institute a federal court in each district, in lieu of one in every state. The judges of these courts, with the aid of state judges, may hold circuits for the trial of causes in the several parts of the respective districts."

The draft Judicial Bill that the subcommittee reported to the Senate established eleven districts for the eleven states that had then ratified the Constitution, nine of which precisely followed state lines. However, New Hampshire District was "to consist of the state of New-Hampshire, and that part of the State of Massachusetts, which lies easterly of the state of New-Hampshire." This drew a protest from the president of New Hampshire, lawyer John Pickering, who wrote under date of July 1 to Paine Wingate that it "shocked your constituents here with abhorence." Pickering suggested that if the whole territory of Massachusetts could not be made one district, "Let the eastern territory of that Commonwealth be made a separate district."[35] It is interesting to note that Pickering's objections were founded on notions of prestige, not upon the difficulty of determining what law would apply in a district straddling state lines.

In the final bill as passed by the Senate, Pickering's suggestion was followed and a separate Maine District was established. Virginia also became two districts, as there was to be a separate Kentucky District. In order to fit these two new and remote districts into the circuit court system, a new Section 10 was added to the bill. Section 10 provided for writs of error from Maine District to be heard in the Circuit Court for Massachusetts District, while Section 21 similarly provided for appeals in admiralty.[36] But as regarded Kentucky District, Section 10 provided that "writs of error and appeals shall lie from decisions therein to the Supreme Court in the same causes, as from a circuit court to the Supreme Court." This section is out-of-joint with Section 22, which made no provision for "appeals" from the circuit court to the Supreme Court, providing (as we have seen) only for writs of error.

Since 1789 the district courts have always been organized so as not to cross over state boundaries, with the one major exception of the Judiciary Act of 1801, which provided for a District of Potomac,[37] covering parts of Maryland and Virginia and including the District of Columbia.[38] Similarly, circuit court lines have followed state boundaries. This coterminousness of national court lines and state boundaries has led to a view that there is something inevitable and peculiar about the arrangement. It has become easy to assume that this arrangement was made so that there would be a district federal judge familiar with the state law of his district, because moderns assume a requirement in diversity cases that he should be applying this unique state law. No such assumption motivated the drafters of the original 1789 Judicial Bill or the Judiciary Act of 1801, though if Section 34 had the meaning now imputed to it they *must* have shared such an assumption. No one in 1789 even noticed a problem, from the standpoint of choice of law.

DIVISION OF JURISDICTION BETWEEN DISTRICT AND CIRCUIT COURTS

The circuit court is the superior court and the district court is the inferior court. It is the circuit court that reviews the judgments of the district court. In light of this, what is the basis for the division of jurisdiction between the two courts?

Section 9, defining the jurisdiction of the district courts, was probably the one most frequently amended from the floor of the Senate.[39] In end result the jurisdiction given was of two types. One type follows the superior court/inferior court division while the other invests the district court with exclusive original jurisdiction over one of the important subjects of the judicial power of the United States.

The superior/inferior division is represented by the criminal jurisdiction conferred on the two courts. The district courts are given jurisdiction of offenses and crimes where the punishment cannot exceed thirty stripes of whipping, a fine of $100, or imprisonment of more than six months. The circuit courts have concurrent jurisdiction of these offenses and then have exclusive jurisdiction of all crimes carrying a greater punishment.[40]

The district courts were given exclusive original federal jurisdiction in only one important type of case: in "civil causes of admiralty and maritime jurisdiction." Even this was diluted by "saving to suitors, in all cases, the right of a common law remedy [in state courts], where the common law is competent to give it." The admiralty jurisdiction is stated to include "all seizures under laws of impost, navigation or trade of the United States" on the high seas and navigable waters,[41] and so in these proceedings there would be no right to trial by jury. The district courts also were given exclusive original jurisdiction over seizures on land and of suits for penalties and forfeitures incurred under the laws of the United States,[42] wherein there was a right to trial by jury. Section 9 concluded by specifying that "the trial of issues in fact, in the district courts, in all causes except civil causes of admiralty and maritime jurisdiction, shall be by jury," probably additional reassurance to those upset about the failure of the Constitution to guarantee jury trial in all traditional instances.

Most other original jurisdiction of the district court was concurrent with that of the circuit court, so that plaintiffs in these cases were free to bring their suits either in the district court or in the circuit court. This included suits by aliens for torts in violation of international law or treaty and suits by the United States where at least $100 was in controversy.[43]

On "appeals" of admiralty cases from district courts to the circuit courts, the whole case was open to reconsideration.[44] The review was the equivalent of a "trial *de novo*." And on this review Section 4 allowed the district judge no vote, being permitted only to assign the reasons for his decision. Only the Supreme Court justices, sitting as members of the circuit court, could vote.

Section 11 gave the circuit courts exclusive national jurisdiction both of diversity cases and of cases where the United States is plaintiff or petitioner,[45] but this jurisdiction is concurrent with that of the several states. Its judgments and decrees in these actions were subject to review by the Supreme Court on writ of error pursuant to Section 22, although with a $2,000 jurisdictional limitation.

Why is the "inferior" court given the admiralty jurisdiction and the "superior" court given the diversity jurisdiction? It would seem that the justices of the Supreme Court would be the more familiar with admiralty law—a branch of international law, with no local peculiarities or ties—and the judge of the district court, if (as was likely) he was a resident of the state, would be more familiar with state law. So the arrangement of diversity jurisdiction is topsy-turvy, if one assumes that state law was supposed by the Judiciary Act drafters to be automatically applied in such cases.

But if consideration is given to the nature of admiralty and to the purpose of the diversity jurisdiction without making such an assumption, a rational pattern appears. Admiralty law was considered to be the same in all jurisdictions, whether American or foreign. This would be easier of determination by a resident district judge, with access to his own private law library and the libraries of other practitioners, than by the peripatetic justices of the Supreme Court who would not have easy access to their own lawbooks. Besides, the district judge was subject to correction by an "appeal" to the circuit court, where the whole matter would be reviewed.[46]

Diversity jurisdiction presumed at least a suspicion of localistic bias on the part of local judges toward the out-of-state citizen, and thus required adjudication by wholly disinterested judges, or at least as disinterested as could be found. This called for justices of the Supreme Court to sit on the circuit court and hear such suits. No judgment in a circuit court could be entered without the concurrence of at least one of these justices of the Supreme Court.[47] The opinions of the disinterested Supreme Court justices were so important that the Judiciary Act did not disable a justice from voting in the Supreme Court's review of a case he had participated in on circuit. The Senate rejected efforts to amend the act so as to deny the Supreme Court justice who heard the case at trial a vote on review.[48]

APPELLATE REVIEW: APPEALS, WRITS OF ERROR, AND RETRIALS

As we have noted, the provisions for appellate review in Article III, Section 2 generated a great deal of political controversy. In considering this subject, one must keep in mind the eighteenth-century meaning of the word "appeal," for thinking of an "appeal" in the modern sense quickly leads to error.

66

The "appeal" was the method of superior court review in civil-law jurisdictions, jurisdictions that did not use the jury (such as admiralty). An appeal would, in such a system, open the way to a consideration of the whole case by the superior court. An appeal might have been taken either before or after an initial trial in the inferior court. When it was taken after the initial trial the result is that there was a second trial, *de novo,* in the superior court. On appeals both facts and law were open for consideration, either as an initial proposition or by reconsideration.

The "writ of error" was a method of obtaining review in common-law actions. Only questions of law were open to review in the superior court; questions of fact were not subject to review, because of the sanctity of the jury. Thus review by the superior court was limited. But this limitation might sometimes have been avoided through use of extraordinary writs such as those of *certiorari, mandamus,* prohibition, and *habeas corpus.* Review of facts, though, was accomplished only in "extraordinary" cases.

Even such a strong supporter of the Constitution as Madison recognized that the judicial article was defective as it related to appeals, but Madison was thinking of "appeals" in the sense of retrials, not in the modern sense of appellate review. At the time of the elections to Congress, it was bruited about in Madison's district that he was opposed to amendments to the Constitution. In an endeavor to combat these reports, Madison wrote letters to several persons setting forth his real opinions, in the hope and with the wish that they would give publicity to these views.[49] Madison said he favored amendments that would "serve the double purpose of satisfying the minds of well meaning opponents, and of providing additional guards in favour of liberty."[50] Among the amendments he favored, "There is room likewise in the Judiciary department for amendment. It ought to be so regulated, as to render vexatious, and superfluous appeals, impossible."[51]

In dealing with the review process in the Judiciary Act, the Senate carefully chose its words. As drafted by Ellsworth and as introduced into the Senate, the Judicial Bill permitted reexamination by the circuit court of civil actions in the district court "upon a *petition* in error" (emphasis added). And then the bill further gave the Supreme Court the power to reexamine circuit court decisions in both civil actions and suits in equity "upon a like process." What Ellsworth meant by "petition in error" is not clear. There was not in 1789, nor is there today, any well-established distinctive judicial procedure known as "petition in error."[52] Ellsworth may have been using the word "petition" in the same way he used blanks for dollar amounts and for numbers of days, that is, as a "neutral" word to be given greater precision later. Perhaps, like "removal" in Section 12, he was attempting to coin a new term, allowing the new courts to give it meaning. If Ellsworth had meant "writ of error" he would have used the term, for the procedure was well known in Connecticut, and in fact the legislation establishing the Connecticut Supreme Court of Errors in 1784 provided for review by writ of error.[53] By amendment from the floor, the Senate changed the word "petition" to "writ."[54]

This well may have been the most important policy decision embodied in the Judiciary Act. At one and the same time it eliminated the need for a constitutional amendment, such as envisioned by Madison to eliminate retrials on appeal, and it avoided adoption of the objectionable Massachusetts procedure, outlined by Justice Sewall of the Supreme Judicial Court of Massachusetts in a letter Sewall wrote to Senator Caleb Strong under date of May 2:

> The power of granting new Trials should be placed in every Court. This is perhaps a part of the Judicial Power, and in their Original formation it may be best to expressly make it such under certain modifications and restrictions, and this method may answer all the purposes of Reviews, or Appeals with power to determine the Fact, in the Court appealed unto. We in Massachusetts have been used to various Trials of the same Facts by different Jurys of Course. But the time will come when the Ill consequences of this mode will appear—and if no Reviews were now had, but such as upon the particular Cause in question Justice and Equity required it would be pro bono in the opinion of some. Appeals therefore in the nature of a Writ of Error in some matters in the federal Courts may be more expedient. The Provision for a Writ of Error *from the "ultimate determination of a Cause in the highest Court of Law in Equity* of a State," as mentioned in the Scetch to the S. Fed. Judicial is a necessary, and useful Provision.[55]

The act as passed carefully prevents the Supreme Court from being able to retry any cases. The most important device to this end is the "writ of error." Section 13 allots to the Supreme Court "appellate jurisdiction from the circuit courts and courts of the several states, in the cases herein after specially provided for." Section 22, with regard to cases in the circuit courts, and Section 25, with regard to cases in the state courts, permit Supreme Court review by writ of error only. Section 22 further provides that "there shall be no reversal . . . on such writ of error . . . for any error in fact," and Section 25 provides for proceedings upon the writ of error "in the same manner and under the same regulations . . . as if the judgment or decree complained of had been rendered or passed in a circuit court." Only errors of law are to be considered.

This result is strengthened by a second device: The Supreme Court may hear writs of error only after "final" judgments or decrees, according to Sections 22 and 25. The notion of "appeal" in the eighteenth century, it should be recalled, allowed transfer to the superior court *before or after* trial.

Appeals were allowed by the Judiciary Act from district to circuit courts in admiralty cases, meaning, as we have seen, a trial *de novo* in the circuit court. But Section 21 allowed such appeals only from "final decrees" (where the amount in dispute is over $300), eliminating the possibility of transfer *before trial* upon appeal. This "after trial" approach was further provided for by giving the district courts in Section 9 "exclusive original cognizance of all civil causes of admiralty and maritime jurisdiction"—exclusive of the circuit courts and Supreme Court as well as exclusive of the state courts.

However, the circuit courts were also given jurisdiction by the last sentence of Section 11, providing that the "circuit courts shall also have appellate jurisdiction from the district courts under the regulations and restrictions herein after provided," and by a phrase in Section 22 providing for jurisdiction over cases "removed there by appeal from a district court."[56] The act otherwise provides in Sections 21 and 22 for review by appeals or writ of error from "final" decrees, so the quoted seemingly coordinate language from Sections 11 and 22 seems to provide for appeals *before trial* of cases where the district court did not have "exclusive original" jurisdiction—such as suits by the United States, or suits by aliens for torts under international law or treaties.[57] Insofar as reported cases show, this appeal-before-trial jurisdiction of the circuit courts fell into desuetude without ever being used, but it does indicate how carefully the notion of "appeals" was dealt with in the act. Appeals of this sort—transfers before trial—were clearly not to be permitted to the Supreme Court.

The structure of the act is that the Supreme Court is given power to review civil actions at law and suits in equity in the circuit court where the original trial was in the circuit court. It is given no power to review a case in which the original trial was in the district court, and regarding which the circuit court exercised only a review function, such as admiralty cases. Moreover, the First Congress limited the "trial" jurisdiction of the Supreme Court to those cases that arose under its original jurisdiction. This was still a potentially extensive trial jurisdiction since it covered controversies in which a state or an ambassador was a party.[58]

One loophole was, however, put into the act. The door was left ajar to Supreme Court reexamination of facts by the provision in Section 13 giving the Supreme Court the power to issue writs of prohibition to the district courts in admiralty cases and the power to issue "writs of mandamus, in cases warranted by the principles and usages of law, to any courts appointed, or persons holding office, under the authority of the United States." Litigants and lawyers used the opening to seek Supreme Court review of the facts, as well as the law. Prohibition was used in *United States v. Peters*[59] to bring to the Court an admiralty case. Beginning in 1792 in *Hayburn's Case*[60] mandamus was pressed into use.[61]

It was only a small loophole, to be used in extraordinary instances, and (at least with regard to prohibition) carefully restricted. By implication, the Supreme Court was not permitted to issue the more comprehensive and intrusive writs of *certiorari* and injunction.[62] Basically the act was designed to stifle alarm over Supreme Court retrial of facts by denying it the power to do so.

The result, although it was not apparently an intended result, was (as we have noted) to commence the establishment of a hierarchical arrangement of the judiciary, by restricting the appellate process in the national courts to reviewing questions of law, at least in regard to civil actions at law and suits in equity. The next step, also apparently unintended as such, came by judicial interpretation of the act in 1796.

OLIVER ELLSWORTH AS CHIEF JUSTICE IN 1796 REWRITES THE JUDICIARY ACT HE HAD DRAFTED IN 1789

As we have seen in this chapter, the Judiciary Act of 1789 gave the Supreme Court sitting as a whole no power to review admiralty and maritime cases tried in the district courts, except such as may be exercised through use of a writ of prohibition or *mandamus*. The strictures placed on Supreme Court review of admiralty and maritime cases quickly proved unsatisfactory and were simply ignored. This very well may have been done by agreement between the parties, and with the acquiescence of the Court.[63]

The first reported instance of Supreme Court review of an admiralty case is *Glass v. The Sloop, Betsey.*[64] The procedure by which the case reached the Court is not clearly reported, although the parties are referred to in the language of an "appeal" as appellants and appellees. In a note the reporter, Alexander Dallas, points out that "the appeal had not been presented to any court or judge of the United States,"[65] but this defect seemingly was waived by agreement of the parties and with the consent of the Court. In *United States v. Peters* there was "a motion for a prohibition to the district court of Pennsylvania,"[66] using the loophole of Section 13 previously noted.

In most other early admiralty cases Supreme Court review was simply by writ of error directed to the circuit court,[67] although in one case it is reported that the procedure was by "a writ of error, in the nature of an appeal."[68]

Made chief justice in 1796, Oliver Ellsworth in *Wiscart v. Dauchy*[69] in effect rewrote the Judiciary Act so as to provide for such review. He did it by the simple expedient of attributing to the First Congress an intent to use a different meaning in key words than the meaning he himself had carefully sought to convey. He said that the language of Section 22— "And upon like process, may final *judgments* and *decrees* in *civil actions* . . . be reexamined"—covered and included admiralty *causes*.[70]

The Judiciary Act of 1789 carefully distinguished, not only between criminal and civil proceedings, but also between the different types of civil proceedings.[71] The act distinguished between *causes* of admiralty, *suits* in equity, and *actions* at law; it distinguished between *decrees* in admiralty and equity and *judgments* at law; it distinguished between *appeals* in admiralty and causes reviewed by *writ of error* in equity suits and actions at law. The choice of these descriptive procedural words was always meaningful and distinctive.

But in *Wiscart,* to correct what Ellsworth may now have seen as an error, or perhaps because he was now viewing the issue as a Supreme Court justice and not as a legislator, he swept aside this careful use of words in the Judiciary Act:

> Now, the term civil actions would from its natural import, embrace every species of suit, which is not of a criminal kind; and when, it is considered, that the district court has a criminal as well as a civil jurisdiction, it is clear that the term was used by the legislature, not to distinguish between admiralty causes, and other civil actions, but to exclude the idea of removing judgments in criminal prosecutions, from an inferior to a superior tribunal.[72]

The result of this change of meaning of the term "civil actions" was to give the Supreme Court an appellate-review jurisdiction on writ of error over admiralty "causes," which are renamed "actions." Probably done to approve retroactively the practice of the Court in hearing admiralty appeals, the change of meaning had the effect of continuing the creation of a modern appellate-review court. Ellsworth in *Wiscart* ensured that the Supreme Court was now the final appellate authority over every sort of noncriminal case that could be brought in a national court. Its position at the top of a hierarchy was now crystal clear.

The hierarchical structure of a modern appellate court would not fully emerge until *Marbury v. Madison*[73] established the twin notions of judicial review and judicial supremacy. Without such a hierarchical arrangement, choice-of-law decisions as understood by the modern reader of Section 34 could not be made, since without that hierarchy superior courts did not rule solely on questions of law and did not tell lower courts what the law was. Such a hierarchy was only in the beginning stage of contemplation and invention in 1789. Since Section 34 was drafted without any assumption of a hierarchical arrangement of courts, it could not have meant what its modern interpreters say it meant.

"THE LAW" TO BE APPLIED BY THE FEDERAL COURTS

If Section 34 spoke to what was considered an important question of the law to be applied in diversity cases in federal courts, we might expect a debate amongst commentators on the pending legislation, or at least some recognition by the legislators of other aspects of choice-of-law problems. The records do not exhibit a great deal of concern, however. Several of the comments on the Judicial Bill from persons to whom copies had been sent by senators and representatives raised the question, "By what law is the United States to be governed?" These comments were not, however, directed toward some particular branch of the national jurisdiction, but rather to the subject generally, that is, at the whole area of federal jurisdiction. These commentators did not even consider the possibility that "national Law" should apply to some jurisdictional areas and "state law"—whether of the several states or of one of the respective states—to other areas.

Gunning Bedford, Jr., the attorney general of Delaware, wrote Senator George Read of Delaware on June 24, 1789, that it would be "derogatory" to look to the common and statute law of England and thought the bill should refer to the "laws of our own country," but without specifying where those laws were to be found. Bedford wrote:

It will be very difficult accurately to define the jurisdiction of the Federal courts, so as to prevent controversies with the State courts. Indefinite expressions, unavoidably made use of, will create difficulties. Common law and statute law are referred to in the act. Have the States the same accurate and fixed idea of both or either as applied to themselves individually or to the States generally? Do we refer to the common law and statute law of England? This is derogatory. What, then, is the common and statute law of the United States? It is difficult to answer. Yet the dignity of America requires that it be ascertained, and that where we refer to laws they should be laws of our own country. If the principles of the laws of any country are good and worthy of adoption, incorporate them into your own. I think we ought not to refer, at this day, to the law of any nation as the rule of our conduct. This is the moment for legal emancipation; as the foundation is laid so must the superstructure be built.[74]

William Bradford, Jr., of Philadelphia—later the second United States attorney general—writing to his father-in-law, Representative Elias Boudinot of New Jersey on June 28, 1789, saw the same problem, but gave little in the way of answer other than to say, "We ought to know what law it is." Bradford wrote:

The question, "By what law is the U.S. to be governed, under the acts of the Legislature," is a very interesting one. The Lex loci must in many cases govern—but in general matters what is to be the rule.—what form of writs shall be used? What shall be the effect of a judgt in binding lands or of an Execution in binding personal Estate! Is there any limitation of actions in these Courts? What law ascertains the peremptory Challenges in Criminal cases—& what if the prisoner stands mute! Are the rules of the common law respecting the form & certainty of indictments to prevail—A thousand such question [sic] will arise—Amidst the different divisions of the Common law—the Statute law of England—& the laws of the particular states, the Courts will be in a labyrinth of difficulties. The allusion is often made to some law. Thus it is said "if by law the action doth survive."— Does this extend to those actions which survive by the Common Law, or also to those preserved by the Stat. of Edw. Suppose the action were an action of Trover:—this form of action does not survive yet a remedy in another form does. We ought know what law it is is [sic] to give the principles that are to prevail in these new Courts.[75]

Edward Shippen, presiding justice of the Philadelphia Court of Common Sessions, wrote Senator Robert Morris of Pennsylvania under date of

73

July 13 with several comments for improving the bill. Referring to the law by which "we are to be governed," Shippen had these comments:

> It is of the utmost consequence that the Judiciary Law should establish in express terms by what Law we are to be governed. There are some loose Expressions in the Bill concerning the Common Law, but is no where said the Judges should decide according to it. The American states have generally adopted it, either in their Constitutions or by Act of Assembly. The United States should likewise adopt it; and it should not be left to the Judges to make the Law, but only to declare it. Perhaps the common Law alone would not be sufficient; there are many Statutes made in England before our Revolution which amend and improve the common Law; some of these have been long practiced under in America, and are incorporated with the Common Law, which would be imperfect without them. I own it is a difficult and delicate point to fix by any Rule the Extension of the Statutes; and perhaps here there may be a necessity to leave some latitude to the Judges. Such Statutes as do not suit our circumstances, or which have never been at all admitted here, should certainly not be introduced.[76]

This letter would have been received by Morris too late to have been useful in the Senate's consideration of the Judicial Bill, though, as Goebel says, it "may have reflected the opinion of the local bar."[77]

One comment possibly formed the direct source of the phrase "laws of the several states" in Section 34. This is contained in a letter written by Richard Parker of Lawfield, Virginia, to Senator Richard Henry Lee under date of July 6. Parker's comments were directed toward the organization of the courts and to procedural matters. After stating that he has taken notice of everything that occurred to him on reading the bill, he added: "Perhaps upon comparing the Laws of the several States, respecting the practice of the courts a judicious system of Rules may be selected and I really think Rules are necessary and ought to be in the Law establishing each Court."[78]

Senator Maclay's *Journal* shows that he was strongly opposed to permitting the national courts to exercise any part of the jurisprudence of English chancery.[79] Some other senators joined him in this view. But there also were senators who strongly supported giving the national courts an equity jurisprudence, presumably derived from that in effect in England.[80] It is not clear from Maclay's *Journal* whether his antipathy extended to English jurisprudence in general or was limited to equity.

The awareness of the members of the First Congress that there were problems relating to "applicable law" in the government being established is further evidenced by their recognition of the question of what law would be applied in the district that became the seat of government. When it looked like Congress might accede to Morris's desire that a portion of Pennsylvania be selected, Madison secured the adoption of an amendment relating to "Pennsylvania laws being enforced in the district."[81]

One further subject is worthy of comment in this connection. Neither the Constitution nor the Judiciary Act makes any explicit reference to the question of retroactivity, that is, whether the provisions of either are to be applied to controversies existing at the time of adoption of the Constitution or enactment of the Judiciary Act.

This subject was commented upon by Charles Pinckney in a letter to James Madison, dated March 28, 1789, wherein Pinckney posed this question: "Do you not suppose that giving to the federal Judicial *retrospective jurisdiction in any case whatsoever,* from the difficulty of determining to what periods to look back[,] from it's being an ex post facto provision, & from the confusion & Opposition it will give rise to, will be the surest & speediest mode to subvert our present & give it's adversaries the majority?"[82] As posed in this abstract way, the purport of Pinckney's question is unclear. He may have had in mind some specific land speculation claim.[83] A tenable explanation, though, is that Pinckney was asking whether the exercise of federal jurisdiction ought not to be limited to events occurring after the establishment of the federal government. This may mean that when it came to a question of title to land, where one title is necessarily linked to a prior one, title as it existed as of 1787–89 would have to be found in the law as it existed at an earlier relevant time, that is, in English or earlier state law.

The provisions of Section 12 of the Judiciary Act relating to removal to the circuit courts of controversies between citizens of the same state claiming land under grants from different states give no directions as to the law to be applied in these controversies.

If any conclusion can be drawn from these few and scattered materials, it is that the question of what law was to be applied by the national courts was recognized. However, the problem was seen as being applicable to the whole of the federal jurisdiction, not separable depending upon the subject involved. In considering the law to be applied by the national courts, the First Congress had to keep in mind the least common denominator of the eleven states, as it had had to do in organizing the system. It had to keep in mind the status of the law, in terms of accessibility as well as content, in a state such as Georgia as well as in Connecticut and Massachusetts. The sole distinction discussed as to choice of law was to provide for the application of American law rather than English law. In Richard Parker's letter, this was phrased as applying the "Laws of the several states," a phrase actually used in Section 34. Gunning Bedford and William Bradford were both worried about the variety and imprecision of "the laws of the particular states," but neither suggested or implied some crucial distinction between national law and either the law of any state or the "laws of the several states." Even so, there were few queries on the law to be applied. The problem was not a pressing one.

THE PRECEDENT OF THE NORTHWEST ORDINANCE

The Continental Congress had wrestled with the problem of what law should be applied to a new territory belonging to the United States, with settlers of diverse backgrounds, when it developed the Northwest Ordinance of 1787 for the government of the Northwest Territory, adopted on July 13, 1787.[84]

It was first proposed, in a report written by Thomas Jefferson, that the settlers should be authorized "to adopt the constitution and laws of any one of the original states," which laws would then be subject to revision by the territorial legislature.[85] But this gave way to the adoption in the final ordinance of the following provision:

> The governor and judges, or a majority of them, shall adopt and publish in the district, such laws of the original States, criminal and civil, as may be necessary, and best suited to the circumstances of the district, and report them to Congress, from time to time; which laws shall be in force in the district until the organization of the general assembly therein, unless disapproved of by Congress; but afterwards the legislature shall have authority to alter them as they shall think fit.[86]

It was first proposed that the judiciary of the territory should be "a Court, to consist of five Members who shall have a common law and Chancery Jurisdiction"[87] but this was changed to consist of three judges, any two of whom to form a court, "who shall have a common law jurisdiction."[88]

Although it would not have been written in time to have affected the development of the Judiciary Act, a memorial written by Governor Arthur St. Clair to President Washington in August 1789 is useful for its description of how this method of providing laws for a new federal territory operated in practice. St. Clair wrote:

It seems to have been the Intention of Congress that entire Laws of some of the original States, or so much of them as would apply to their Circumstances, should be adopted for the Government of the People. But it was found that the Judges were not possessed of the Codes of the different States—that few of the Laws in the Collections they were in possession of would apply, those made in the earlier Stages, and most likely to suit the present State of the Territory, having been generally repealed as the State of Society had changed.— it therefore became necessary that Laws, corresponding as nearly as possible to those of the original States, should be formed—their first formation was thought to be within the Province of the Judges in their legislative Capacity, the Governor reserving to himself the right to suggest such Alterations & Amendments as he should think necessary, either for the good of the People or the Interest of the united States, and finally to approve or reject them. The Laws that have been published were framed in that manner, and the Governors Observations upon them, in the first Stage, have been recorded with the Secretary of the Territory to be laid before Congress with his other Proceedings.[89]

The method by which the Northwest Territory was provided with laws—by adoption from the laws of the original states—was not satisfactory, a fact that was well recognized at the time. The defects in this procedure were several.

On their early trips to the territory the governor and judges could hardly be expected to pack complete codes of the thirteen original states. This would have been most unlikely, and largely useless, baggage to carry into frontier areas, where hostile Indians were more impressed with lead than paper. Anyway, such codes of laws had not been published at that time for most of the states. A complete collection of laws would have been a conglomerate of codes of various dates and a multitude of session laws, not inappropriately called fugitive laws. At least in the early years, as Governor St. Clair pointed out, the judges simply did not have available the laws of the original states, so as to be able to adopt appropriate laws from these collections.

The laws of the original states most suitable to the frontier character of the territory were those that had been adopted in earlier periods and repealed when the states had reached a more advanced stage of society. Some of these repealed laws would have been more appropriate for the territory than the laws then currently in force.

The laws of the original states had been framed to meet local conditions, so that they were filled with words, phrases, and sections peculiar to certain localities. For example, laws establishing court systems were filled with references to *places* where the courts are established, the *times* when they were to be held, and the *names* of the courts. In adopting such laws for the territory it was necessary to change or delete many of these references. It proved impossible, even with the best of intentions, to adopt literally and without change the laws of any one or more of the original states. Moreover, statute law of the period was not neatly divided into separate laws, suitable for adoption, but instead statutes frequently encompassed diverse subjects under single titles. Another question was how much of a law must be adopted. The adoption of entire acts or chapters could result in the adoption of much unwanted law. On the other hand, partial adoption of sections, clauses, or even phrases and words could result in the creation of entirely new legislation.

Although the Continental Congress paid much attention to the "statute law" to be adopted in the Northwest Territory, it undertook to give no direction to its court as to "the law" that should be used in the absence of a clear direction from a statute. Possibly, the Congress had in mind letting the judges search the statute law of the thirteen states for the most suitable rule and then to adopt that rule as "a law" for the territory.

In any event the court to be established under the ordinance was given a "common-law jurisdiction." Nothing was said about equity. So the question is left unanswered as to whether the territorial courts were denied an equity jurisdiction or whether the ordinance was open-ended so the court could use equity whenever it saw fit to do so. As a common-law court, the territorial court was empowered to act as existing state courts did. While again choice-of-law problems were envisioned, the ordinance gives little aid in dealing with the problem of Section 34 of the Judiciary Act of 1789.

SUMMARY

Choice-of-law problems, and in particular the problem of the law to be applied by the new national courts in diversity cases, do not seem to have been particularly bothersome to the First Congress. In making the multifarious decisions necessary to implement the vague and open-ended constitutional outlines of a national judiciary, that Congress did not seem to be acting within a conceptual framework that assumed the existence either of discrete bodies of definitely ascertainable state law, or of some discrete body of national law as contrasted to state law. The sort of hierarchical judicial structure necessary to a system of modern choice-of-law decisions as envisioned in *Erie's* construction of Section 34 of the Judiciary Act of

1789 was only in the process of being invented—for purposes other than the actualization of such a hierarchical system—in other sections of that act and could not have formed a part of the First Congress's conceptual framework.

While evidence and argument for this point will continue to accumulate throughout the book, sufficient evidence and argument has by now been presented to demonstrate that Section 34 could not possibly have been intended by Oliver Ellsworth and the other members of the Senate and the House of Representatives in the summer of 1789 to have performed the functions that Professors Warren and Goebel, Justices Story and Brandeis, and the Supreme Court majority in *Erie Railroad Co. v. Tompkins* have attributed to it. It would have literally been unthinkable for the members of the First Congress to have directed national courts sitting in diversity cases to apply the law of the states in which they sat. The necessary conceptual framework was only in the early stages of formation.

It remains to be discovered to what purposes Section 34 was to be put. While a definite answer cannot be given, some possibilities can be hazarded. In addition to the information already gathered, we need first to pay close attention to the contemporary usage of some important words and phrases.

CHAPTER V

Word Usage in the Constitution and in the Judiciary Act of 1789

INTRODUCTION

THE LANGUAGE USED in the Judiciary Act of 1789 was carefully chosen and merits careful inspection. This is evident from both the text of the final act and from the handwritten changes made on the drafts prepared by Paterson, Ellsworth, and Strong. It is also evident in the amendments made from the floor of the Senate and by the Judiciary Committee after its recommitment.

Small variations in the style of the individual senators who wrote the bill are evident in the drafts, and some of these stylistic variations are carried into the final act.[1]

Many of the words used in the act had multiple meanings, even as they still do today. Even so, different words are used to draw distinctions. It is worthwhile trying to find the precise meaning of these words in the context in which they were used, recognizing always that 100 percent consistency in usage is not to be expected.

In the discussion below, words and phrases are grouped in order to define both their meaning in isolation, and to show how the different words and phrases were used in the act to draw distinctions. This word usage, of course, is not limited to the Judiciary Act but represents usage during the period, and so examples are also drawn from the language of the Constitution, from the Articles of Confederation, and from other important written documents of the period.

The most dramatic result of this inquiry into usage is the rereading of Section 34. As will be shown below, the phrase "the several states," which is a key phrase in Section 34, had a specialized meaning that differs from that of the phrase "the respective states." The modern interpretation of Section 34 is erroneous in that moderns read the section as though there is no difference between these two phrases. Moreover, Section 34 is not the only part of the act that can be misread because of a lack of familiarity with habits of word usage in 1789. Although it may be the most dramatic example, it is not the only significant example; in the course of this chapter, other examples will be displayed.

THE UNITED STATES, THE SEVERAL STATES, AND THE RESPECTIVE STATES

From the time of the Confederation, and probably even before, there was a need for descriptive terms to distinguish, conceptually, among three different political entities. These were the United States as a single sovereign entity; the "states" as a collective group; and the "states" as individual and distinct political entities. The terms used were the following, and this usage still prevails to this day:

The United States: The single sovereign entity that is recognized as one of the nations of the world.

The Several States: The political entities, otherwise known as "states" collectively, that is, as a group. The emphasis here is on the states as a group, not on each as a separate and distinct political entity.

The Respective States: The states as individual political entities, each different from the other.

The United States

Usage in the Articles of Confederation and the Constitution

Article I of the Articles of Confederation states, "The Stile of this confederacy shall be 'The United States of America.'"

In the articles, the meetings of this political entity were referred to as "The united states in congress assembled." This, too, is the way the meetings are described in the *Journals*. There was no need at that time to distinguish this "congress" from any other congress. The descriptive term "Continental Congress" in this body is a later invention and never was its official name.

This political entity was viewed in Europe as a single nation. For example, Richard Henry Lee, on August 20, 1782, said, "The several states were known to the powers of Europe only as one nation under the style and title of the United States."[2] The Constitution ratified in 1788 speaks as though it were a different Constitution for the very same political entity, describing it by the same name. The preamble says, "We the People of the United States . . . do ordain and establish this CONSTITUTION for the United States of America."

This new, or revised, or old, political entity, since known as the United States, is sometimes referred to by using a plural article as in "these United States." This usage of the term emphasizes the *internal* federalism arrangement, but it can hardly be considered an accurate descriptive term for the United States viewed as a single political entity, from the standpoint of other nations, or as descriptive of the federal government itself, when viewed from an internal standpoint.[3]

The Constitution, the accompanying resolution of the convention, and the letter of transmittal all carefully distinguish the government to be established under the proposed Constitution, which is referred to as "the United States," and the government under the Articles of Confederation, which is referred to as "the United States in Congress assembled." This consistency would naturally lead to usage of the singular pronoun "it" when referring to the United States. Yet in Article III, Section 3, the plural is used: "Treason against the United States, shall consist only in levying war against *them,* or in adhering to *their* enemies giving them aid and comfort" (emphasis added). This may be a calculated ambiguity. If not, one could interpret the phrase so that there is only treason against the states, collectively, and not against *the* United States. (Note also the provision in Article IV, Section 2, relating to extradition of a person "*charged in any state* with treason" [emphasis added].) Thus there are two provisions that recognize the offense of treason against states, but none expressly recognizing the offense of treason against *the* United States, except the ambiguously phrased Article III, Section 3.

Usage in the Judiciary Act of 1789

There is no ambiguity in the use of the phrase "United States" in the Judiciary Act. Section 2 provides for dividing the United States into thirteen districts. The two states, North Carolina and Rhode Island, that had not ratified the Constitution are simply ignored. Naturally, most references are in a judicial context. The courts are not referred to as national or federal courts. They are generally referred to as the supreme court, circuit court, or district court, or courts, as the case may be, and at least in the printed bill, by use of the lower case.[4] The later sections of the act, drafted by Caleb Strong, refer to "the courts of the United States" but this phrase is not used by either Paterson or Ellsworth, except in Section 34.[5]

The Several States versus the Respective States

General

While there is no hard-and-fast rule requiring the use of the phrase "the several states" when referring to the states as a group and the phrase "the respective states" when referring to them individually, at least an effort to use the words "several" and "respective" to draw such a distinction goes back at least to the end of the seventeenth century.

An act of May 6, 1691, establishing the New York Supreme Court of Judicature provided that the court should meet "att the severall & Respective times hereafter mentioned." In the act of November 11, 1692, the justices of this court were required

> once in Every year at the aforesaid times and places in each *respective* County aforesaid goe the circuit, and . . . there hold the Supreme Court, being then assisted by two or more of the Justices of the peace of the *severall Respective* County's where the said Supream Court is to be holden.[6]

The meaning seems clear: As the justices of the Supreme Court move about the state on circuit they are to be joined in each county by different justices of the peace, and the words "several" and "respective" are being used to convey that meaning, even though in this instance the usage could be improved upon.[7]

The distinction being drawn was clear in Maryland in 1698. On November 22 the governor and Council of Maryland "Ordered that the *Severall* Sheriffs doe give publique Notice within their *respective* Countyes."[8]

Many examples are to be found in the *Journals of the Continental Congress.* For example, on October 6, 1777, the Congress: "*Ordered,* That the resolution of Congress of 10th of September last . . . be without delay transmitted to the executive powers of the *several* states, with a request, that they will order the same to be published in their *respective* gazettes for six months, successively."[9] Similarly, on January 13, 1780, the Congress: "*Resolved,* That it be recommended to the executive authorities of the *several* states, to transmit with all possible expedition to General Washington, the names and rank of all officers; and the number of privates belonging to the enemy, held as prisoners of war within their *respective* states, and the places."[10] On May 14, 1781, a committee appointed to devise ways and means to defray expenses recommended: "That the treasurer of the United States be directed to draw orders on the Treasurers of the *several* States *respectively* payable at one month's sight."[11]

On the direction of the Continental Congress the secretary of foreign affairs in 1785 drafted "An Ordinance for the Trial of Piracies and Felonies Committed on the High Seas."[12] This proposed ordinance contained the following provision: "And it is also ordained by the Authority aforesaid that all Accessories to Piracy whether before or after the Fact, shall be considered as principals; but that all Accessories to Felonies committed on the High Seas, shall be considered by the said Judges, as they are considered by the Laws of the State, in which the Offenders shall be tried as aforesaid."[13]

In 1790 when the Massachusetts legislature was considering ratification of the amendments proposed to the federal Constitution, a committee was appointed to report further amendments that might be necessary. Among the committee recommendations was the following: "[e]leventhly, that it be left to the *several* States to make compensation to their Senators and Representatives *respectively* for their services in Congress."[14]

George Washington on June 29, 1791, first wrote in his diary, "The Deeds which remained unexecuted yesterday were signed to day and the Dowers of the *several different* wives acknowledged according to Law" and then changed "of the several different" to "of their *respective*."[15]

A South Carolina statute of 1799 uses parallel construction to define the words. This act of December 21, 1799, provides: "And be it further enacted by the authority aforesaid, That *all and singular* the records of the *several and respective* county courts in this state, shall . . ."[16]

On April 13, 1871, Representative Osborn told the House of Representatives "That the State courts in the *several States* have been unable to enforce the criminal laws of their *respective States*. . . . We are driven by existing facts to provide for the *several States* in the South what they have been unable fully to provide for themselves."[17]

Usage in the Constitution

In the Constitution the words "several" and "respective" are used with contrasting meanings in two different sections.

Article I, Section 2, provides, "Representatives and direct taxes shall be apportioned among *the several states* . . . according to *their respective numbers*." The states are first referred to as a group and then immediately particularized. Article II, Section 2, provides, "The President shall be commander in chief . . . of the militia *of the several states* . . . he may require the opinion, in writing, of the principal officer in each of the executive departments, upon any subject relating to the duties of *their respective offices.*"

The term "several states" is used alone in four provisions:

1. Article I, Section 8, paragraph 3: "To regulate commerce with foreign nations, and among the *several* states, and the Indian tribes" (emphasis added). The report of the committee of style did not have the "and" before "among," this word being inserted by the convention when the report was under consideration.

William Winslow Crosskey reads the word "among" as meaning "within" and concludes that this provision meant that Congress was to have the power to regulate intrastate, as well as interstate commerce.[18] But this is to read "the several states" as though it were "the United States." If the convention did intend, contrary to Crosskey's thesis, to limit Congress's power to regulate commerce to interstate commerce, the language used is as felicitous as can be found. Even stronger doubt is thrown on the Crosskeyian interpretation of the word "among" as meaning "within" by usage in the letter of transmittal that was signed by Washington, on unanimous order of the convention, and accompanied the Constitution when sent to the Congress. This letter says: "It is at all times difficult to draw with precision the line between those rights which must be surrendered, and those which may be reserved; and on the present occasion this difficulty was encreased by a difference *among the several* states as to their situation, extent, habits, and particular interests."[19] The meaning of the word "among" in this sentence is almost synonymous with "between" and it certainly is not synonymous with "within." Another hurdle to the Crosskey thesis is the larger principle embodied in the Constitution that relations between citizens of the same state should be left to the state of their joint citizenship, except where there is some national power given to Congress.

2. Article IV, Section 2: "The citizens of each state shall be entitled to all privileges and immunities of citizens in the *several* states." The choice of words here substantially affects the meaning. As worded, the privileges and immunities referred to are those that are common to a fungible group of states, that is, common to *all* the states. If the word used had been "respective" the privileges and immunities referred to would have been those granted by some particular state, and which very likely would be different from those found in other states.

3. Article V: Amendments are to be proposed by Congress on the application of two-thirds of "the *several* states" and amendments become a part of the Constitution when ratified by legislatures or conventions in "three-fourths of the *several* states." The states are a fungible group. It makes no difference which of the states make application for amendments or ratify proposed amendments, so long as there is the requisite number.

4. Article VI: "the members of the *several* state legislatures, and all executive and judicial officers, both of the United States and of the *several* states, shall be bound by oath or affirmation." The individual state officials of all of the states—the several states—must take oaths or make affirmations to uphold the Constitution.

The word "respective" is used in Article II, Section 1, paragraph 3, which provides that presidential "electors shall meet in their *respective states.*" The word "respectively" is used in Article I, Section 8, paragraph 16: "To provide for organizing, arming, and disciplining the militia . . . reserving to the States *respectively* . . ." The Congress must leave certain functions to the individual states.[20]

In other instances the Constitution uses other words to speak of individualized states, as: "particular state," "each state," "another state," "the state," "one state"[21] or to speak of all the states, as: "no state," "any state," "every other state," "two or more states."[22]

Usage in the Judiciary Act

In the Judiciary Act the words "respective" or "respectively" are used to individualize or particularize the reference, whereas "several" is used to refer to a collection of individuals or entities as a group. At one point in the manuscript bill an improper usage of "respective" is changed to "several." This is at the beginning of Section 10. The language originally written was "that the district courts shall have exclusively of the courts of the respective states." The word "respective" is crossed out and "several" interlined. There are some variations in the sureness of touch with which the different draftsmen used these words. Oliver Ellsworth was the most careful and most successful. William Paterson was less so.

In Section 1, William Paterson provided that the associate justices of the Supreme Court shall have precedence "according to their respective ages." He followed this with references to "the respective districts" in Section 3 and "their respective offices" in Section 8. But in Sections 5 and 7 he used both words, several and respective, apparently in an endeavor to distinguish collective references from an individualized reference, but it is hardly successful.[23]

In the sections drafted by Oliver Ellsworth and by Caleb Strong there are references to the "respective districts,"[24] the "respective courts,"[25] the "courts respectively,"[26] "respective jurisdictions,"[27] in the marshals "hands respectively,"[28] and "in each state respectively."[29]

On the other hand, the word "several" is used to refer to a fungible group, or as a collective reference, for example, "the courts of the several states."[30] In some contexts either word may be appropriate and one may disagree as to which is the most felicitous. But there can be little doubt but that a conscious effort was made by the draftsmen to use the words to draw distinctions, and to do so consistently. Frequently, it may be that the distinction is largely in the mind of the draftsman, but usage of the word "several" does show that the draftsman was thinking in terms of a group whereas use of the word "respective" shows he was particularizing that group into specific members.

To distinguish the courts of the United States from the courts of the states, the phrase "the several states" is invariably used. The district and circuit courts are given jurisdiction either "exclusively of the courts of the *several* states" or "concurrent with the courts of the *several* states." This ordinarily suffices, but when some greater specificity is needed, the language varies, probably with the draftsman. In Section 25, the Supreme Court is given the power to review final judgments or decrees "in the highest court of law or equity of a State in which a decision in the suit could be had." Under Section 33, the act seeks to use the state judicatories to help in bailing persons accused of crimes. It provides that bail "may be taken by any judge of the supreme or superior court of law of such state."

This subject is further discussed with specific reference to Section 34 below in chapter 7.

APPEAL, WRIT OF ERROR, QUESTIONS OF LAW AND FACT

General

Appeals are not limited to judicial proceedings. The word is used now and always has been with a broader meaning, as in "appeal to the people," "appeal to Congress," or even "appeal to the conscience of mankind." Consequently, an appeal "to our Royall Person,"[31] or to the Privy Council or the House of Lords[32] may be an appeal to an executive or legislative body.

"Appeal" in such a context cannot be assumed to be used in the sense of taking an appeal in a judicial proceeding.

In its judicial proceeding usage, appeal derives from the civil law and from equity, that is, from judicial proceedings in which there were no juries. Consequently, on an appeal in admiralty cases and chancery litigation, the whole case is open to review, questions of fact as well as questions of law. Use of appeal in this context carries with it the necessary implication that there may be a new trial on the facts.

Usage in the Constitution

Article III, Section 2 provides that "the supreme court shall have appellate jurisdiction, both as to law and fact, with such exceptions, and under such regulations as the Congress shall make." In this clause, the convention probably intended to make it possible for Congress to arrange the national judicial power so that the Supreme Court had an "appellate jurisdiction" that encompassed both what is now considered appellate review on questions of law and also the eighteenth-century appeal on questions of fact, involving a whole new trial. This would encompass review of proceedings conducted under the civil law, without a jury, where the whole case is open for reconsideration in the superior court. It would also include an appeal of a case tried under the common law in which there would be a trial *de novo* by a jury in the Supreme Court.

With the benefit of hindsight this appears to be an obviously impractical grant of jurisdiction to the Supreme Court, but this is not to say that therefore it was not what the convention intended. The power was given to Congress to tailor the jurisdiction to the practicalities of the situation.

Usage in the Judiciary Act

The Judiciary Act carefully distinguishes review by a superior court by "appeal" and by "writ of error." On an appeal the whole case, including facts, is open to reconsideration. On writ of error only questions of law are open to review.

The result of limiting circuit-court review of civil actions to use of the writ of error, and review by the Supreme Court to the same writ of error, is to eliminate all possibility of a second trial of the facts, by jury or otherwise, on these reviews. The circuit court, however, is given jurisdiction to review admiralty and maritime causes and in these it has power to review the facts.

This aspect of eighteenth-century procedure is almost invariably overlooked, even by authorities on the period. Julius Goebel recognizes that, in the Judiciary Act, "The appeal was apparently conceived as a trial *de novo* in the New England tradition,"[33] yet he seems not to realize that when the term "writ of error" was used this completely eliminated the "trial *de novo*."[34] But instead of recognizing the major significance of the Judiciary Act's requirement that a writ of error was to be used in *all* appellate review by the Supreme Court and the major portion of such review by the circuit court, Goebel sees it as having almost no significance. He writes, "The regulation of appellate jurisdiction by the Committee reveals an intention of placing restraints upon the native zest for pressing a cause through all possible stages of review."[35] And this Goebel sees as being done by limitations on the amount in dispute required for appellate review. Insofar as use of the writ of error is concerned, he considers only its similarity to the elusive "petition in error."[36]

CASES AND CONTROVERSIES

General

Whether in the eighteenth century a distinction was drawn between a case and a controversy so as to explain the choice of language in Article III, Section 2 is not known. Not enough research has been done on the subject.

When one considers the precise language of the Constitution and of the Judiciary Act of 1789, along with some of the other legislation adopted by this and the other early Congresses, it seems probable that such careful research would reveal that there was a difference in meaning in the eighteenth century.

Usage in the Constitution

In defining the extent of the judicial power of the United States, Article III, Section 2 uses both the word "cases" and the word "controversies." Inasmuch as the language of the Constitution was carefully chosen it is probable that these words were intended to carry somewhat different meanings.[37]

Section 2 begins by using the word "Cases," and the jurisdiction is defined by topics—"arising under this Constitution" and "affecting Ambassadors" and "of admiralty and maritime Jurisdiction." The text then switches to the word "Controversies." The transition passage provides for "Controversies to which the United States shall be a Party." The next reference is to "Controversies between two or more states," and thereafter, the word "between" is used and the pattern of specifying two parties is employed.

A reasonable hypothesis is that a controversy involves two parties, that is, a judicial proceeding between parties with adverse interests. On the other hand, a case is a broader term, requiring no controversy.

An example of what the convention might have considered to be a case as distinguished from a controversy is to be found in the well-known 1787 case of *Trevett v. Weeden*.[38] The second part of the title of this pamphlet report is suggestive of the type of questions the convention may have thought were presented by a case, but which would not be a controversy to be resolved in a judicial proceeding. The title is:

> The Case, Trevett against Weeden: On information and Complaint, for refusing Paper Bills in Payment for Butcher's Meat, in Market, at Par with Specie. Tried before the Honourable Superior Court, in the County of Newport, September Term, 1786. Also, The Case of the Judges of said Court, Before the Honourable General Assembly, at Providence, October Session, 1786, on Citation, for dismissing said Complaint. Wherein the Rights of the People to Trial by Jury, &c. are stated and maintained, and the Legislative, Judiciary and Executive Powers of Government examined and defined. By James M. Varnum, esq; Major-General of the State of Rhode-Island, &c. Counselor at Law, and Member of Congress for said State. Providence: Printed by John Carter, 1787.[39]

It does appear that the members of the Second Congress and President Washington thought that the language of the Constitution was broad enough to permit the Congress to impose duties on the courts that did not involve controversies between litigants. This was done by the act of March 23, 1792,[40] which required the circuit court to pass upon the eligibility for pensions of military and naval personnel who had become invalids because of injuries received during the Revolution, and furthermore it required the judges to remain at least five days during court sessions for the purpose of receiving these applications. The judges resisted this duty as involving nonjudicial activity.[41] The point is not so much how this question was ultimately resolved, but whether the First and Second Congresses, whose members had been members of the convention, and the president, who had presided at the convention, could reasonably have understood the Constitution as permitting what we think of as nonjudicial duties by the judges. The fact that they did think the Constitution was broad enough to permit this supports a view that the language of the Constitution is broad enough so as to support this interpretation. The appropriate language must have been that part of Article III, Section 2 that states that "The judicial power shall extend to all *cases,* in law and equity, arising under this constitution, the laws of the United States . . ." (emphasis added).[42]

In this connection it should be kept in mind that in the English and colonial background the legislative, executive, and judicial functions were not separated and clearly differentiated, and in the states a mix continued long after this date. The doctrine of separation of powers is not expressly stated in the federal Constitution as it was for example in the 1780 constitution of Massachusetts. The Massachusetts Constitution in Article XXX expressly prohibited each of the three departments of government from exercising the powers of the other two.[43]

In the Constitution the extension of the judicial power "to controversies to which the United States shall be a party" is the transition passage from subjects described as "cases" to subjects described as "controversies." The conclusion would seem to be that the national jurisdiction extends to controversies between the United States and another party but it does not extend to cases involving the United States. Such a distinction must be found in a difference in meaning between cases and controversies.

Cases to which the United States is a party, but which do not involve controversies, cover the whole range of the legislative and executive functions of the national government. Under a theory of separation of powers, the judicial department is not to interfere with the legislative and executive departments, except when there is a controversy between the United States on the one hand and some other party on the other hand. To a modern eye, it may seem overly technical to rest a fundamental thesis about separation of powers upon a variation in word usage. However, it does not follow from our modern prejudice that this argument is unsound. The eighteenth century was different from the twentieth century.

"Cases" is a broader term than "controversies." All controversies are cases but not all cases are controversies. The second paragraph of Section 2 of Article III dealing with the original and appellate jurisdiction of the Supreme Court speaks only of cases. Inasmuch as all controversies are cases, "all the other cases before mentioned" refers to all the subjects of the judicial power set forth in the first paragraph of Section 2.

Usage in the Judiciary Act

The First Congress did not define the jurisdiction of the national courts in terms of "cases" and "controversies." It appears that the word "causes" is used to refer to the subjects of jurisdiction that the Constitution refers to in terms of "cases" and the words "suits or actions" are used to refer to the subjects that the Constitution refers to as "controversies."

There are two special problems. The first relates to the criminal jurisdiction and the second to proceedings where the United States is plaintiff or petitioner.

Criminal Jurisdiction

The Constitution contains no express language conferring a criminal jurisdiction on the national courts. Conceivably it could be viewed as being encompassed either by the grant of judicial power over "all cases, in law . . . arising under . . . the laws of the United States" or by the grant of judicial power over "controversies to which the United States shall be a party."

The Judiciary Act gives the national courts "cognizance of all crimes and offences that shall be cognizable under the authority of the United States."[44] Section 29 refers to "cases punishable with death" but otherwise criminal proceedings, when referred to at all, are called "causes."

United States as Plaintiff or Petitioner

The grant of jurisdiction in the Judiciary Act is carefully phrased, and differentiated:

Section 9 provides that the district courts "shall also have cognizance, concurrent as last mentioned, of all suits at common law where the United States sue, and the matter in dispute amounts, exclusive of costs, to the sum or value of one hundred dollars."

Section 11 provides that the circuit courts "shall have original jurisdiction, concurrent with the courts of the several states, of all suits of a civil nature at common law or in equity, where the matter in dispute exceeds, exclusive of costs, the sum or value of five hundred dollars, and the United States are plaintiffs, or petitioners."[45]

Section 13 provides that the Supreme Court "shall have exclusive jurisdiction of all controversies of a civil nature, where a state is a party, except between a state and its citizens."

The fact that in all three of these sections the jurisdiction is limited to civil proceedings—suits at common law in the district courts, all suits of a civil nature at common law or in equity in the circuit courts, and all controversies of a civil nature in the Supreme Court—shows that the First Congress thought that the constitutional grant was broad enough to cover criminal proceedings.

When careful attention is paid to the exact language of the Constitution and of the Judiciary Act the implications that arise are large. If the criminal jurisdiction of the national courts rests on the constitutional grant of jurisdiction over "controversies to which the United States shall be a party" then a criminal prosecution by a state of a citizen of another state is also a controversy and within the constitutional grant of national jurisdiction of controversies "between a state and citizens of another state."[46]

CAUSES, SUITS, AND ACTIONS

These words were extensively used in the eighteenth century. But sufficient research has not been done as to show whether they were used precisely so as to draw distinctions between different types of judicial proceedings. It seems that generally "suits" referred to equity proceedings, "actions" to proceedings at common law, and "causes" to admiralty proceedings. Criminal proceedings were occasionally referred to as "causes."

The federal Constitution does not go into sufficient detail so that any of these words are used in the instrument.

Cause

It has already been suggested that Article III, Section 2, draws a distinction between cases and controversies. If this is true then "cause" is the word used in the Judiciary Act to refer to the subjects of jurisdiction that are described as "cases" in the Constitution. The word also is used in the Judiciary Act to cover every type of judicial proceeding, so there is a narrow usage and a broad usage.

Narrow Usage

"Cause" is the only term used to describe criminal proceedings, as in "trial of criminal causes." It is also used to describe proceedings under the admiralty and maritime jurisdiction, as in "causes of admiralty and maritime jurisdiction."[47] Section 26 refers to actions to recover forfeitures as "causes," which may be a recognition that this proceeding is related to the admiralty jurisdiction of the district courts, or it may be that the draftsman of this section, Caleb Strong, used this word differently than Ellsworth did.

Section 9 gives the district courts cognizance "of all causes where an alien sues for a tort only in violation of the law of nations or a treaty of the

United States." This jurisdiction must be a "case" under the laws, Constitution, and treaties of the United States, as distinguished from a "controversy" between a citizen, or a state, and foreign citizens, or states, where the circuit courts have concurrent jurisdiction. The descriptive word used is "cause" not "action at law."

Broad Usage

"Cause" is the broadest term used in the Judiciary Act. In most sections, particularly those drafted by Ellsworth, the word is used with great specificity. It is used to cover different types of judicial proceedings, as in "any civil or criminal cause"[48] or "all causes wherein the marshall or his deputy shall be a party."[49] It is also used to refer to something less than the total, as in "any civil cause,"[50] or "in civil causes."[51]

It appears that the word is used somewhat differently in Section 10 than it is in other parts of the act. Section 10, which relates to the jurisdiction of the district courts in the District of Kentucky and the District of Maine, was not in the bill as introduced into the Senate. Its draftsman is unknown. In the section the word "cause" is used to describe the full range of the circuit court's original jurisdiction.[52]

Suit

The word "suit" is the preferred word used to describe proceedings in equity. Section 16 says, "That suits in equity shall not be sustained." When both equity and common law actions are referred to the language used is still "suits."[53] Once it is clear that both law and equity proceedings are involved, as when Section 11 gives the circuit courts jurisdiction over "all suits of a civil nature at common law or in equity" the term "suit" is used in all subsequent references.

Actions

Proceedings at law, and only such proceedings, are referred to in the act as "actions." No person shall be arrested in one district for trial in another, "in any civil action."[54] Arrest was used only in cases involving private wrongs[55] and not in suits in equity. A citizen of the United States has a right to trial by jury in proceedings in the Supreme Court "in all actions at law."[56] Provision is made for discovery of books and other writings "in the trial of actions at law."[57] Provision is made for further proceedings "upon a verdict in a civil action,"[58] which must be an action at law since it involves a *verdict* of a jury. The act refers to a plaintiff in an action at law as distinguished from a petitioner in equity.[59]

The term "civil actions" is used in later sections to refer to proceedings in the district courts for forfeitures. There is something of a mixture of law and admiralty in the Section 9 provisions relating to the jurisdiction of the district courts, which is reflected later in Section 22 by a reference to "final decrees and judgments in civil actions in a district court." In referring in the same section to the circuit courts, the terms "judgments" and "decrees" are carefully distinguished, the language being "judgments and decrees in civil actions, and suits in equity." Section 26 provides that in these proceedings for forfeitures, etc., where the amount of the judgment is uncertain, the same shall on the request of either party "be assessed by a jury."

In drafting Section 12, dealing with removal from the state courts to the circuit courts, Ellsworth used the word "suit" to refer to removal of diversity cases: "That if a suit be commenced in any state court . . ." But he used the word "action" in referring to the cases in which citizens of the same state are claiming title under grants from different states. "And if in any action commenced in a state court, and title of land is concerned . . ." The choice of language appears to be deliberate, and so the latter cases can only be removed if they are actions at law, such as ejectment cases.

TRIALS AND TRIALS AT COMMON LAW

The word "trial" as used in connection with judicial proceedings has a meaning that is self-evident, and yet it is a word difficult to define so as to distinguish "the trial" from the other parts of a judicial proceeding.

Usage in the Constitution

Trial

The Constitution contains no provision relating to civil proceedings in which it would be natural or appropriate to use the word "trial." It is used to refer to one of the several phases of a criminal prosecution.

Indirectly, the Constitution identifies four distinct steps in the criminal process. This is done in Article I, Section 3, which provides that a party who has been impeached and removed from office "shall nevertheless be liable and subject to indictment, trial, judgment and punishment, according to law." Then Article III, Section 2, paragraph 3, provides, "The trial of all crimes . . . shall be by jury," going on to provide the place where "any such trial" shall be held.

95

Usage in the Judiciary Act

The word "trial" is frequently used in the Judiciary Act with reference to all types of judicial proceedings, criminal and civil. But the word is used only to refer to that part of the proceeding that still today is thought of as "the trial" as distinguished from the proceedings that go before and come afterwards.

In criminal proceedings the circuit courts are empowered "to hold special sessions for the trial of criminal causes."[60] Here, the word "cause" is used to refer to the whole criminal proceeding, and the "trial" is one part of the process. Prisoners in jail are "committed for trial."[61] "The trial" in cases punishable with death is to be had in the county where the offense was committed.[62] Persons charged with offenses are to be "arrested, and imprisoned or bailed, as the case may be, for trial."[63]

"The trial" is that part of the judicial process in which facts are found. Inasmuch as a right to trial by jury was a subject of great concern at this time, the Judiciary Act is very specific as to when there is a right to have facts found by a jury and when it is permissible for the court alone to find facts. It is expressly provided that the "trial of issues in fact" in the district courts is to be by jury "in all causes except civil causes of admiralty and maritime jurisdiction."[64]

Oddly, there is no comparable provision in Section 11, which defines the jurisdiction of the circuit courts. Instead, the last sentence of Section 12, relating to removal of diversity cases to the national courts, provides, "and the trial of issues of fact in the circuit courts shall, in all suits, except those of equity, and of admiralty, and maritime jurisdiction, be by jury." The sentence does refer to *all* suits and excludes those of admiralty and maritime jurisdiction, and so it seems the intent was that this provision should encompass the whole of the circuit-court jurisdiction, and not just the removal jurisdiction.[65]

Section 13 provides, "And the trial of issues of fact in the Supreme Court, in all actions at law against citizens of the United States, shall be by jury." The only application of this provision today appears to be when a state sues a citizen of another state under the Court's original jurisdiction. When put into the bill it would have had a wider application, because under the bill as introduced into the Senate the Supreme Court was given concurrent jurisdiction with the circuit courts of suits of a civil nature, where the amount in dispute was over $500, and in which the United States are plaintiffs or petitioners.

Trials at Common Law

The Judiciary Act uses the phrase, "trials at common law" only once and that is in Section 34.

The phrase does appear, however, as a marginal notation in Ellsworth's draft, marked for insertion at the end of Section 16 limiting national court jurisdiction in equity cases. The notation reads, "And the mode of receiving testimony in suits in equity & in causes of admiralty & maritime jurisdiction shall be the same as in trials at common law, or as is hereinafter specially provided."[66] This marginal notation duplicates a provision contained later in the draft, probably prepared by Caleb Strong, in the section that became Section 30 of the final act. Both in the manuscript draft and in the final act, the provision reads: "And be it enacted by the authority aforesaid, that the mode of Proof by oral Testimony and Examination of Witnesses in open Court shall be the same in all the Courts of the United States as well in the Trial of Causes in Equity and of admiralty and Maritime Jurisdiction as of Actions at Common Law."[67]

There is no way of knowing whether Caleb Strong meant something different by "actions at common law" than Ellsworth meant by "trials at common law" but if there is a difference it would appear that "actions" refers to civil proceedings only, while "trials at common law" refers to either both criminal and civil proceedings, or to criminal proceedings only.

There is evidence here that the phrase "trials at common law" in Section 34 does not refer to the whole proceeding, but only to that part of the proceeding devoted, in Ellsworth's words, to "receiving testimony" and in Strong's words, to "Proof by oral Testimony and Examination of Witnesses in open Court." If this thesis is sound, then it corroborates, albeit rather weakly, the proposition that Section 34 is marginal to the larger purposes of the act; a provision that is limited to the proof process is not a major provision.

However, it is also plausible that the variation is explicable on other grounds. Section 34 was not part of the original draft. As will be shown in a subsequent chapter, the evidence suggests, but does not prove, that this section was not a floor amendment, but instead was added very late in the process, by the committee on recommittal to prepare the engrossed bill. The further in time an amendment is from an original draft, the more likely it is to be inconsistent in language with the original.

97

CHAPTER VI

Criminal Jurisdiction of the National Courts

INTRODUCTION

THERE HAS BEEN a good deal of debate, especially recently, over the possible existence of a federal common law and particularly over the question whether the national government established under the Constitution had the power to exercise a common-law criminal jurisdiction.[1] That is, it has been debated whether the national courts might act as the British and state courts did in 1789 and previously, defining crimes and the punishments therefor in the absence of legislation accomplishing those goals. Interestingly, Charles Warren's article "New Light" entered this debate in the affirmative, as Warren found in his reading of the documents pertaining to the Judiciary Act of 1789 evidence that changes that the Senate made in the draft bill indicated an express enlargement of the criminal law jurisdiction of the federal courts to include common-law crimes.[2]

As this and the next chapter will make clear, this writer's tentative conclusion is to agree with Warren on this point—although not to the sweeping extent of Warren's conclusions—from the standpoint of Section 34 of the Judiciary Act of 1789. The probable purpose of Section 34 was to empower the national courts to exercise a common-law criminal authority, but with a direction to apply American common law rather than British criminal common law, until Congress could draft a national criminal code. A fairly thorough investigation of the subject of the criminal jurisdiction of the United States in the Confederation and early national period is a necessary prerequisite to understanding this conclusion.

THE CONFEDERATION

It would seem elementary that a government must have a criminal jurisdiction in order to protect itself from treasonable activities and to ensure protection for its citizens. Yet the Confederation existed for nearly fifteen years without exercising any criminal jurisdiction. This lack of criminal jurisdiction was not seen as a major defect of the Confederation, or at least no recommendation was ever made to the states to give the Confederation such a jurisdiction, nor was it even debated when the Articles of Confederation were developed.

Under the Confederation, the exercise of a criminal jurisdiction was left to the states, with the Continental Congress, when it saw fit, recommending to the legislatures of the several states the passing of appropriate laws. Two such subjects in which the Confederation made recommendations to the states reappear in the Constitution in Article I, Section 8, in which Congress is given two explicit, but narrowly proscribed, criminal powers: "To provide for the punishment of counterfeiting the securities and current coin of the United States," and "To define and punish piracies and felonies committed on the high seas, and offences against the law of nations." In addition Congress is given a general and exclusive power of legislating for the seat of government and for military facilities and other needful buildings, which had been purchased with the consent of the state. Nothing more in Article I pertains explicitly to crimes.

To determine what these clauses mean in the Constitution, it is necessary to look at their background in the Confederation. There was considerable activity on the second of these topics, and the refusal of the Continental Congress to establish a national court to try crimes committed on the high seas is most instructive.

Courts for the Trial of Piracies and Felonies Committed on the High Seas

The ninth Article of Confederation provided, in part, that the Confederation Congress had the "right and power of . . . appointing courts for the trial of piracies and felonies committed on the high seas."[3] Less than a week after the articles were ratified, on March 6, 1781, Thomas McKean of Pennsylvania, seconded by James Duane of New York, moved that Congress undertake to exercise this power by appointing a committee of three "to devise and report the mode of appointing courts for the trial of piracies and felonies committed on the high seas." Congress approved the motion and named McKean, Duane, and Thomas Bee of South Carolina to the committee,[4] which reported on March 17.[5] Congress considered the report on April 5. On this same day, Congress agreed to an "Ordinance for establishing courts for the trial of piracies and felonies committed on the high seas," the full text of which is set forth for the convenience of readers in the footnote.[6] This ordinance merits close attention, something that it has never received.[7]

Pointing out in a preamble that it was expedient that such courts be speedily erected, Congress declared that "it is reasonable that the same mode of trial should be adopted for offenders of this kind on the high seas as is used for offenders of the like sort upon the land." The "court" was erected solely, however, in terms of the judges, adopting state judges. The ordinance provided: "And the justices of the supreme or superior courts or judicature, and judge of the Court of Admiralty of the several and respective states, or any two or more of them, are hereby constituted and appointed judges for hearing and trying such offenders."

This ordinance did not establish courts for the trial of piracies nor does it even direct the states to establish such courts. It is in the nature of enabling legislation, "appointing" the state officials who are qualified to try pirates. All the justices of the state supreme or superior courts of judicature, that is, the principal state trial courts, and one, but only one, judge of admiralty in each state were so appointed. Having appointed the judges qualified to try piracies, the ordinance left it up to individual states to actually erect the courts.[8]

A week after the adoption of this ordinance, on April 12, 1781, Madison made a motion that related to the Court of Appeals in Cases of Capture, but which also provided:

> That the Judges of appeal in cases of capture be also the Judges for the trial of piracies and felonies committed on the high seas, whose commissions shall be during good behaviour.
> That their sessions be held at the places above mentioned and immediately upon the adjournment of the Court of Appeals.
> That the states be called upon to order their sheriffs and Gaolers to attend the said Court when necessary; and to remove all persons charged with piracy or felony on the high seas to the gaol most convenient for trial.[9]

The motion was referred to a committee,[10] reported and debated,[11] recommitted and reported again,[12] and on June 25 further consideration was postponed.[13]

The purpose of Madison's motion seems evident. He was proposing to establish Confederation courts—the Court of Appeals in Cases of Capture for the trial of persons accused of piracies and felonies committed on the high seas. Since an appeal in the eighteenth century was understood as covering both appellate review in the modern sense and appeal in the sense of a second or retrial,[14] placing the trial of piracies in this eighteenth-century court of appeal involved no mixture of functions, as some modern historians have thought.[15] The Congress refused to establish such a court.

Other Criminal-Law Issues

On May 27, 1780, as a result of an agreement between the minister from France and a committee of the Congress, the committee submitted the following resolution:

> *Resolved,* That it be recommended to the legislatures of these United States to pass laws for the punishment of such persons as shall encourage desertions from the fleets or armies of any foreign power who shall prosecute the war in America in conjunction with these United States, and for recovering such deserters as shall endeavour to conceal themselves among the inhabitants.[16]

On December 6, 1780, the chief executive of Pennsylvania informed the Continental Congress of "a high abuse of office" by James Mease, the late clothier general, and his deputy, in taking merchandise from the inhabitants of Philadelphia and converting it to private use. By resolution Congress deplored this conduct and recommended that Pennsylvania direct its attorney general to prosecute "in the name of the United States, in the ordinary course of law, for the abuse of office and breach of trust complained of."[17] Very probably as a result of this malfeasance in office, a committee on February 16, 1781, reported:

> Whereas all persons who hold or have held offices of trust or emolument under Congress are amenable to them, or to such Judicatures as they shall appoint, for all offences and delinquencies committed by them whilst in office: Therefore
> *Resolved,* That three persons be appointed to constitute a Court of Judicature for the tryal and determination of all causes relative to offences committed against the United States in the civil departments thereof:
> That an Attorney General for the United States be appointed by Congress, whose duty shall be to prosecute all suits in behalf of the United States. To give his advice on all such matters as shall be referred to him by Congress. And when any case shall arise in any of those states, where his personal attendance is rendered impracticable, he shall be authorized to appoint a Deputy or Deputies to prosecute the said suit.[18]

The *Journal* for May 26, 1781, shows that in connection with a plan to establish a national bank, the committee recommended:

Resolved, That Congress will recommend to the several legislatures to pass laws, making it felony without benefit of clergy, for any person to counterfeit bank notes, or to pass such notes, knowing them to be counterfeit; also making it felony without benefit of clergy, for any president, inspector, director, officer or servant of the bank, to convert any of the property, money or credit of the said bank to his own use, or in any other way to be guilty of fraud or embezzlement as an officer or servant of the bank.[19]

Summary

The Confederation itself exercised no criminal jurisdiction. It left this activity to the states, calling upon them when appropriate to prosecute offenders, as well as to adopt appropriate legislation. In providing for the trial of pirates, the Congress drew a distinction between the "order, process, judgment and execution" to be used and the way the offender and the offense were to be defined under the laws of the state where the offender was tried; the latter were to be "according to the course of the common law, in like manner as if . . . committed . . . in one of these United States."

THE CONSTITUTION AND THE FEDERAL CONVENTION

Article III and the National Criminal Jurisdiction

The criminal jurisdiction of the national courts has been assumed to have a constitutional basis, which has gone unquestioned since 1789, yet what is it? Article III, Section 2 of the Constitution makes *no explicit provision* for extending the judicial power of the United States over criminal matters. To find such a grant in Section 2 would require a straining of the jurisdiction covering "controversies to which the United States shall be a Party" beyond any reasonable breaking point.[20] St. George Tucker was in 1803 unwilling to do so, saying that he did "not recollect even to have heard the expression, *criminal controversy.*"[21]

In the absence of any express recognition of criminal jurisdiction in Section 2, what is one to make of the third paragraph in the section:

The trial of all crimes, except in cases of impeachment, shall be by jury; and such trial shall be held in the state where the said crimes shall have been committed; but when not committed within any state, the trial shall be at such place or places as the Congress may by law have directed.

In order to apply this last paragraph in Section 2 to the national courts, it is first necessary to find that the national judiciary *has* a criminal jurisdiction, and the first paragraph of this section does not say anything about the judicial power of the United States extending to criminal matters. If this third paragraph alone is the source of national judicial jurisdiction over treason, it is certainly an odd way of conferring it.

The third paragraph of Section 2 of Article III is easier to understand if it is read as a directive to *state* courts concerning the trial of *state* crimes. The language of the third paragraph does not say that it relates to national crimes. Instead it says it applies to the trial of *all* crimes and so literally applies to the trial of all state crimes, and also to the trial of all national crimes, that is, if there is a national criminal jurisdiction. It surely is logical, if the Constitution is going to deal with state crimes at all, to direct that their trial be "in the state where the said crimes shall have been committed." The trial of criminal offenses at a place other than where the alleged offenses were committed was viewed as one of the grievances set forth in the Declaration of Independence, "For transporting us beyond Seas to be tried for pretended Offences."

When a crime is not committed in any state, this provision of the Constitution gives Congress the power by law to direct the place or places where such trial shall be held, but the express language does no more.

If the judicial power of the United States should be vested in one Supreme Court, no inferior national courts having been established, then the third paragraph of Section 2 would require the Court to ride circuit throughout the nation just for the purpose of presiding at the trial of crimes, if it is found in some source that there is a national criminal jurisdiction. On the other hand, if the trial-by-jury provision in Article III is read as applicable to the states, and not to the national government, then the trial-by-jury provision of the Sixth Amendment ceases to be redundant, and instead extends the right to trial by jury to any national criminal jurisdiction.

Activities in the 1787 Convention

Only a careful reading of the records of the Federal Convention, particularly Madison's *Journal,* gives an answer to the question of whether the convention gave the national judiciary a criminal jurisdiction or whether it was only thinking of giving Congress the power to legislate in certain areas while leaving the actual exercise of criminal jurisdiction to the states.

The convention gave most attention in this regard to the crime of treason.

On June 24, 1776, the Continental Congress had recommended to the legislatures of the several United Colonies that they "pass laws for punishing, in such manner as to them shall seem fit" such persons as "are guilty of treason against such colony." The persons capable of committing treason and the offense were defined this way:

> That all persons, members of, or owing allegiance to any of the United Colonies . . . who shall levy war against any of the said colonies within the same, or be adherent to the king of Great Britain, or others the enemies of the said colonies, or any of them, within the same, giving to him or them aid and comfort, are guilty of treason against such colony.[22]

In the convention the Committee of Detail considered giving Congress the power to declare that treason should be levying war against or adhering to the enemies of the "U.S.,"[23] but in its final report it defined treason in a separate Section 2 of the article devoted to the powers of Congress, not in the judiciary article. In this section the convention defined treason "against the United States, or any of them."[24]

When this part of the report of the Committee of Detail was considered on August 20, there was some disagreement as to whether "giving aid and comfort," as in the British statute and the June 24, 1776, legislation of the Continental Congress, should also be included in the definition. Far more troublesome, though, was the question of whether the same act could be treason committed against both the United States and one or more particular states, and whether an act could be treason against a particular state without being treason against the United States.

Gouverneur Morris and Rufus King wished to give the national government the exclusive or sole right to declare what should be treason, and William Samuel Johnson thought there could not be an act of treason against a particular state, but only against the general government. George Mason thought that since the states retained a part of their sovereignty an act could be treason against a particular state without being treason against the United States. King thought treason against one sovereign would necessarily be treason against the other.[25]

After a motion to define generally was agreed to, the words "agst United States" were struck out by the vote of eight states to two. Then this action was reversed, and the words reinstated by the vote of six states to five. James Madison and Morris were not satisfied, and a motion was made to amend the sentence so as to read, "Treason agst. *the U.S.* shall consist only in levying war against *them,* or in adhering to *their* enemies" (emphasis added), which was apparently agreed to without dissent.

The convention did not resolve the question but sidestepped it by the use of some dubious grammar—a singular noun and a plural pronoun. No question was raised about the section being in the wrong article. It was the Committee of Style that later transferred the section out of what became Article I and into Article III.[26]

The two specific powers as to criminal matters given to Congress in Article I, Section 8, reflect, as we have seen, questions that had arisen during the Confederation and were dealt with by the Confederation by recommending to the states that appropriate legislation be enacted.

The report of the Committee of Detail gave Congress the power: "To declare the law and punishment of piracies and felonies committed on the high seas, and the punishment of counterfeiting the coin of the United States, and of offences against the law of nations."[27] This part of the report was considered on August 17, and the debate centered around the question whether Congress should have the power both to define and punish or only to punish.[28] Finally upon motion of Oliver Ellsworth, agreed to nem. con., Congress was given the power to define and punish all these offenses.[29]

The Committee of Style divided this paragraph in two, one Part covering counterfeiting and the other piracies and other felonies on the high seas and offenses against the law of nations. The Committee of Style then eliminated the congressional power to define counterfeiting. When the report was considered beginning on September 14, apparently no question about this change was raised,[30] and the paragraph went into the final Constitution as reported by the committee: "To provide for the punishment of counterfeiting the securities and current coin of the United States." By this date, Oliver Ellsworth, who had made a motion on August 17 giving Congress the power to define counterfeiting, had left the convention.[31] Perhaps if he had remained, he would have objected to what the Committee of Style had done and Congress would have been given the power to define counterfeiting.

The Committee of Style, this time following Ellsworth's motion, gave Congress the power to define and punish piracy and other felonies on the high seas and offenses under the law of nations. This drew fire and apparently the convention initially agreed to limit congressional power over offenses against the law of nations to that of punishing them, but then on motion of Morris, although opposed by Wilson, it reversed itself by a vote of six states to five and gave back to Congress the power to define offenses against the law of nations.[32] In this form the paragraph became a part of the final Constitution: "To define and punish piracies and felonies committed on the high seas, and offences against the law of nations."

The only other power of Congress encompassing criminal law is found in paragraph 17 of Section 8. Congress is there given power to exercise exclusive legislation over the seat of government and over forts, magazines, arsenals, dockyards, and other needful buildings purchased with the consent of state legislatures. The convention's discussion of this clause and of the necessary-and-proper clause did not touch upon the exercise of a criminal jurisdiction.[33]

There is no clear expression in the records of the federal convention of any intent to establish a national judicial system exercising a criminal jurisdiction. At the same time, there is no clear expression that such a jurisdiction was to be denied. The statements actually made by the delegates are more consistent with a view that the convention was giving Congress the power to legislate on a few specific crimes—piracy and felonies on the high seas; offenses against the law of nations; and counterfeiting—so that the law of these subjects would be uniform throughout the nation, but that the actual prosecution of these crimes would be left to the states. Whether the convention expected the national government to exercise a criminal judicial jurisdiction over the seat of government and military facilities was simply never mentioned.

RATIFICATION

Lack of Debate Over National Criminal Law Powers

The question of whether the national judiciary, under the proposed new Constitution, would exercise a criminal jurisdiction, or whether as theretofore the states would be the only governmental bodies exercising a criminal jurisdiction—although in some limited areas applying laws passed by Congress—went seemingly unnoticed, undiscussed, and undebated during the sometimes heated and contentious debates over ratification.

About the only person raising the question in anything like a clearcut form was "the Democratic Federalist," in the *Pennsylvania Herald* of October 17, 1787. Writing in opposition to the Constitution, he referred to the provision of Article III, Section 2, extending the national judicial power to all cases in law and equity arising under the Constitution and said:

It is very clear that under this clause, the tribunal of the United States, may claim a right to the cognizance of all offences against the *general government,* and *libels* will not probably be excluded. Nay, those offences may be by them construed, or by law declared, misprision of treason, an offence which comes literally under their express jurisdiction.—Where is then the safety of our boasted liberty of the press? and in case of a *conflict of jurisdiction* between the courts of the United States, and those of the several Commonwealths, is it not easy to forsee which of the two will obtain the advantage? [34]

Seemingly in response, James Wilson on December 7, 1787, told the Pennsylvania ratifying convention:

> Whenever the general government can be a party against a citizen, the trial is guarded and secured in the constitution itself, and therefore it is not in its power to oppress the citizen. In the case of treason, for example, though the *prosecution is on the part of the United States,* yet the Congress can neither define nor try the crime. [35]

This may have allayed fears of a national criminal jurisdiction. The United States can only prosecute for treason; it cannot try the crime. But then Wilson may have been saying only that Congress could not try the crime, leaving open the question of whether the national judiciary could do so.

Roger Sherman, in an essay published in the *Connecticut Courant* of January 7, 1788, while the Connecticut ratifying convention was sitting, said:

> The powers vested in the federal government are particularly defined, so that each state still retains its sovereignty in what concerns its own internal government and a right to exercise every power of a sovereign state not particularly delegated to the government of the United States. The new powers vested in the United States are to regulate commerce; provide for. a *uniform practice* respecting naturalization, bankruptcies, and organizing, arming, and training the militia, and *for the punishment of certain crimes* against the United States; and for promoting the progress of science in the mode therein pointed out. There are *some other matters* which Congress has power under the present Confederation to require to be done by the particular states, which they *will be authorized to carry into effect themselves under the new Constitution.* These powers appear to be necessary for the common benefit of the states and could not be effectually provided for by the particular states. [36]

In this paragraph Sherman draws a distinction between the powers given to Congress to pass uniform laws to be administered by the states and the power to deal with "some other matters" that the national government "will be authorized to carry into effect themselves." Among the former is the power to provide for uniform practice for the punishment of certain crimes against the United States.

James Madison in *The Federalist No. 42* commented upon the power of Congress to define and punish piracy and felonies on the high seas, saying, "The provision of the federal articles on the subject of piracies and felonies, extends no farther than to the establishment of courts for the trial of these offences." This was the situation under the Confederation, with no power in the Confederation to actually try cases. Does Madison mean that the national Constitution extends no farther and that there is no power in the national judiciary to try piracy, felony and offenses against the law of nations? Perhaps.

As in the Federal Convention, most comment was on the subject of treason. In *The Federalist No. 43* Hamilton quoted the section of the constitutional provision as to punishment for treason and then commented, "As treason may be committed against the United States, the authority of the United States ought to be enabled to punish it." The principal criticism during the ratification period related not so much to the handling of treason, but in giving the president the power to grant pardons to persons convicted of treason.[37]

Tench Coxe, writing on October 21 as "An American Citizen," found a relationship between the guarantee of a republican form of government and the crime of treason: "[A]ny men or body of men, however rich or powerful, who shall make an alteration in the form of government of any state, whereby the powers thereof shall be attempted to be taken out of the hands of the people at large, will stand guilty of high treason."[38]

The power of Congress to punish counterfeiting was passingly mentioned by Madison in *The Federalist No. 42,* but that was all.

The Demand for a National Bill of Rights

It is more than a little ironic that the recognition of a criminal jurisdiction in the national courts was virtually forced into the Constitution by the opponents of the document, through their insistence of the need for a Bill of Rights.

In the sketchy propositions that might be called a "bill of rights" referred to in the Committee of Style on August 20, but not incorporated into the Constitution, none related to the exercise of a criminal jurisdiction.[39] Neither Edmund Randolph, George Mason, or Elbridge Gerry, in expressing the objections to the Constitution that kept them from signing, referred to any need to protect persons with a national criminal jurisdiction.[40] It was only when the lack of a bill of rights became a rallying cry for the opponents of the Constitution that it became necessary to find that the document gave the national judiciary an extensive criminal jurisdiction. This took considerable doing in light of the complete absence of any extension in Article III of the judicial power to cover a criminal jurisdiction.

Without bothering to find a grant of criminal jurisdiction, the dissenting minority in Pennsylvania pointed out that they had concluded their arguments by offering propositions that embodied the ideas of Articles VIII (devoted exclusively to criminal prosecutions), IX (devoted to bail and punishments), and X (devoted to searches and seizures) of the Virginia Declaration of Rights, proclaiming that these rights ought to apply "as well in the federal courts as in those of the several states."[41]

"Brutus," in his *Essay XIV*, published February 28, 1788, in the *New York Journal*, recognized the lack of a national criminal jurisdiction. After referring to the enumeration of the subjects listed in Article III, Section 2, to which the national judicial power extended, he wrote:

> There is no criminal matter, to which the judicial power of the United States will extend; but such as are included under some one of the cases specified in this section. For this section is intended to define all the cases, of every description, to which the power of the judicial shall reach.[42]

But this provided no basis for being critical of the proposed Constitution, and so he found that criminal cases were within the appellate jurisdiction of the Supreme Court:

> If then this section extends the power of the judicial, to criminal cases, it allows appeals in such cases. If the power of the judicial is not extended to criminal matters by this section, I ask, by what part of this system does it appear, that they have any cognizance of them?
>
> I believe it is a new and unusual thing to allow appeal in criminal matters. It is contrary to the sense of our laws, and dangerous to the lives and liberties of the citizen. . . .
>
> I can scarcely believe there can be a considerate citizen of the United States, that will approve of this appellate jurisdiction, as extending to criminal cases, if they will give themselves time for reflection.[43]

"The Impartial Examiner" told Virginians in a letter published in the *Virginia Independent Chronicle* on February 27, 1788, that the proposed

Congress could pass a law that persons charged with capital crimes shall not have a right to demand the cause and nature of the accusation, and shall not have a right of confrontation, etc., which law would expunge the Virginia Bill of Rights. Rhetorically, the writer asked, "[C]an it be said that they have exceeded the limits of their jurisdiction, when *that* has no limits, when no provision has been made for such a right?"[44]

Patrick Henry, in the Virginia ratifying convention, found it unnecessary in arguing the need for a bill of rights to specify the parts of the Constitution giving the national government a criminal jurisdiction. He asserted that: "Congress from their general powers may fully go into the business of human legislation. They may legislate in criminal cases from treason to the lowest offence, petty larceny. They may define crimes and prescribe punishments."[45]

"Agrippa" (thought to have been James Winthrop) in his Letter of December 11, 1787, published in the *Massachusetts Gazette,* found first that under the Constitution, "Authority is also given to the continental courts, to try all causes between a state and its own citizens."[46] On this dubious foundation it then became easy to sweep under national jurisdiction "the whole branch of the law relating to criminal prosecutions":

> In all such cases the state is plaintiff, and the person accused is defendant. The process, therefore, will be, for the attorney-general of the state to commence his suit before a continental court. Considering the state as a party, the cause must be tried in another, and all the expense of the transporting witnesses incurred. The individual is to take his trial among strangers, friendless and unsupported, without its being known whether he is habitually friendless and unsupported.[47]

Agrippa added to one doubtful proposition, that the national judiciary was to try all cases between a state and its own citizens, a second one, that such a criminal prosecution must be "tried in another" state.

Summary

The question of whether the national courts were to exercise a criminal jurisdiction seems never to have been made an issue during the ratification proceedings. The proponents of the Constitution kept silent on the subject. The opponents argued the need for a Bill of Rights—presumably including guarantees relating to the criminal process—and so premised their argument on the assumption that the national courts under the Constitution did have a comprehensive criminal jurisdiction.

THE FIRST SESSION OF THE FIRST CONGRESS, 1789

Failure to Pass a Crimes Bill

There appears to have been no doubt in the mind of Oliver Ellsworth—and perhaps of most other members of the First Congress—that the Constitution authorized a very considerable national criminal jurisdiction. Ellsworth wrote to Richard Law on April 30 that the Judiciary Committee was contemplating giving the national district courts a criminal jurisdiction over "smaller offences" and the circuit courts the power "to try high crimes."[48]

On May 13, at which time the Senate's Judiciary Committee had been at work on a bill to organize the judiciary for a little over a month, a committee was appointed to report a bill "defining the crimes and offences that shall be cognizable under the authority of the United States, and their punishment."[49] Its membership, like that of the Judiciary Committee, consisted of one senator from each state—being the senator who had not been named to the Judiciary Committee.[50] The work of the two committees must have moved apace, with each committee knowing at least something of what the other was doing and coordinating the two undertakings.

As we have seen, the bill to establish the judicial courts of the United States was reported to the Senate on June 12,[51] and was before the Senate until July 17, when it was finally passed,[52] and on July 20 it was sent to the House for concurrence.[53]

On July 28, according to the *Senate Journal,* "Mr. Johnson, on behalf of the committee appointed the 13th of May, reported a bill for the punishment of certain crimes against the United States."[54] The bill did not purport to define national crimes; thus a significant change had apparently taken place between May 13 and July 28 in the purpose of the Crimes Committee.

This change reflects a change the Senate made in the Judicial Bill. The draft bill of June 12 gave the circuit courts "cognizance of all crimes and offences cognizable under the authority of the United States, and defined by the laws of the same," and there was a comparable provision relating to the criminal jurisdiction of the district courts. The language "defined by the laws of the same" was stricken from both sections by the Senate.[55] It may be that the Crimes Committee changed the title on its bill in light of this action, or more probably, the Senate action on the Judicial Bill reflected a prior decision already taken in the Crimes Committee. Subsequent references to the bill in the *Senate Journal* were all to a bill "for the punishment of certain crimes."

The bill to punish certain crimes was read a second time on August 3 and further consideration was postponed.[56] Consideration was resumed on August 13 and apparently completed, for it was ordered to a third reading.[57] On August 27 the bill was given a third reading and ordered engrossed.[58] The *Senate Journal* never does report that the bill was passed, but the *House Journal* shows that the bill was sent to the House and its concurrence requested on September 1.[59]

The Judicial Bill had been carried to the House on July 20,[60] where it was under consideration from August 24[61] until it passed on September 17.[62] A *Senate Journal* entry for the following day, September 18, reads as follows:

> A Message from the House of Representatives—
> Mr. Beckley, their Clerk, informed the Senate, that the House of Representatives had agreed to postpone the consideration of the Bill, entitled, "An Act for the Punishment of certain Crimes against the United States," which has passed the Senate and was sent to the House of Representatives for concurrence, until the next session of Congress—
> He also brought up a Resolve of the House of Representatives, making it "The duty of the Secretary of State to procure from time to time such of the statutes of the several States as may not be in his office:" To which the concurrence of the Senate was requested.[63]

The *House Journal* contains no entry regarding postponement of the Crimes Bill, but it does show that the resolution relating to state statutes was adopted on September 18 and that the clerk was ordered to carry it to the Senate and ask concurrence.[64]

The Senate concurred in the House resolution directing the secretary of state to procure the statutes of the several states on the same day as it was received,[65] and then on the following Monday, September 21, the following resolution was adopted by the Senate and sent to the House for concurrence:

> That it be recommended to the Legislatures of the several States, to pass laws, making it expressly the duty of the keepers of their gaols to receive, and safe keep therein, all prisoners committed under the authority of the United States, until they shall be discharged by due course of the laws thereof, under the like penalties as in the case of prisoners committed under the authority of such States respectively.[66]

The Congress adjourned on September 29.[67]

The question arises, which crimes were placed within the jurisdiction of the national courts, and whence would derive the national prisoners to be placed in state jails, if no national criminal code existed?

Crimes and Punishments Defined by the First Congress in 1789

Congress was not entirely silent on criminal matters during its first session in 1789. Two crimes were defined, and limits of punishment set, in the act of July 31, imposing duties on tonnage and on goods, wares, and merchandise imported into the United States—the Collection Act.[68] One crime was created by the act of September 1, making provision for registering and clearing vessels—the Coasting Act.[69]

The enforcement of both of these acts was based almost entirely on the use of penalties and forfeitures. The distinction in the legislation between a penalty or forfeiture and a crime does not turn on the nature of the conduct or its blameworthiness, but on the statutory language used. This is well illustrated by Section 35 of the Collection Act, which both made provision for a forfeiture and also created a crime.

A penalty or forfeiture was established by the provision under which any customs officer "convicted" either of taking a bribe or of making a false entry of any ship or of goods shall "forfeit and pay" not less than $200 nor more than $2,000 for each offense and be forever barred from holding an office of trust or profit under the United States.[70] A crime was created by the provision that any master of a ship or owner or consignee of goods who swears falsely shall on "indictment and conviction" be punished by a fine not exceeding $1,000, or by imprisonment not exceeding twelve months, or both.[71] Under the subsequently enacted Judiciary Act, the penalty imposed on the offense resulted in its being within the exclusive jurisdiction of the circuit court.

Section 34 of the Collection Act made it a crime to enter goods for exportation with a view to drawing back the duties, and then to subsequently land the goods in the United States without paying duty. All persons concerned "on indictment and conviction thereof" were to "suffer imprisonment for a term not exceeding six months," and the goods and the vessel used were subjected to forfeiture.[72] This crime would be within the concurrent jurisdiction of the district and circuit courts.

Section 35 of the Coasting Act provided in part

> that if any person or persons shall falsely make oath or affirmation to any of the matters herein required to be verified, such person or persons shall suffer the like pains and penalties, as shall be incurred by persons committing wilful and corrupt perjury.[73]

Here was a statutory crime that made no provision for punishment upon conviction, but the degree of punishment in turn was what determined whether it was within the exclusive jurisdiction of the circuit courts or the concurrent jurisdiction of the district and circuit courts.

The Extensive Provisions Made by the First Congress in 1789 for the Trial of a Few Crimes

When the First Congress adjourned at the end of its first session it had made the following statutory provisions relating to the criminal law of the United States and the exercise of a criminal jurisdiction by the national courts:

The district courts were given jurisdiction of all offenses cognizable under the authority of the United States, committed in their respective districts or upon the high seas, where no other punishment could be imposed than whipping not exceeding thirty stripes, a fine not exceeding $100, or a term of imprisonment not exceeding six months.[74] The circuit courts were given concurrent jurisdiction with the district courts of these offenses, and also exclusive cognizance of all other crimes and offenses cognizable under the authority of the United States, except where the Judiciary Act or some other act provided otherwise.[75] The circuit courts were given the power to hold special sessions for the trial of criminal causes, at their discretion or that of the Supreme Court.[76] All the national judges and justices were authorized to issue writs of *habeas corpus* to make inquiry into the cause of commitment of persons in custody under or by color of the authority of the United States or committed for trial before some national court or to testify in a national court.[77]

Specific provision was made in Section 29 of the Judiciary Act for the selection of jurors and for the trial of cases punishable by death.[78] Quite extensive provision was made in Section 33 of the same act for the arrest, imprisonment, and bailing of offenders charged with committing crimes and offenses against the United States.[79] Section 35 of the act provided for the appointment in each district of a United States attorney who had the duty, among others, of prosecuting delinquents for crimes and offenses cognizable under the authority of the United States.[80]

With this rather extensive, although incomplete, provision made for the prosecution of crimes and offenses against the United States, the First Congress statutorily defined only two crimes, relatively minor ones at that, and named a third, without setting forth a penalty or even pointing to the court with jurisdiction. The two defined crimes were: (1) False swearing by the master of a ship or owner or consignee of goods, the penalty for which was a fine or not more than $1,000 and imprisonment not exceeding twelve months;[81] and (2) Using the provisions relating to drawbacks on goods for exportation to avoid payment of duties, for which the penalty was imprisonment not exceeding six months.[82] The crime for which no specific penalty was imposed was perjury relating to the registering of ships.[83]

Congress also called upon the states to pass laws directing their jailers to receive national prisoners.[84] It had sent to the states a resolution calling for amendments to the Constitution, four articles of which related to the criminal jurisdiction of the national government.[85] It had called upon the secretary of state to procure copies of the laws of the several states,[86] there not being an adequate collection of these laws either at the seat of government or at any other location. And it had considered at length, but had failed to pass, a comprehensive Crimes Bill. The Crimes Bill punished but did not define certain crimes. Moreover, Congress did not defeat the Crimes Bill. Rather, it passed the Senate but was postponed for further consideration to the second session by the House.

The conclusion is irresistible that the national courts were given a broader criminal jurisdiction than that indicated in the Collection Act and the Coasting Act. It must be concluded that the First Congress expected the national courts to exercise—albeit temporarily—jurisdiction over non-statutorily defined crimes.

This conclusion is confirmed by Section 35 of the Coasting Act, which failed to define a punishment for the perjury made criminal thereby. A national court convicting a person thereunder must have ascertained a punishment somehow. There are three possibilities: the court could (1) look to the British common law; (2) look to the law of the state where the prosecution was had; (3) look to the laws of the several states, that is, to American common law.

It was not possible to look to British common law, since there was no such common-law crime as set forth in Section 35. According to Blackstone, this would not be perjury, since the crime was in Great Britain limited to swearing wilfully, absolutely, and falsely in some judicial proceeding a matter material to the issue or point in question.[87]

The necessary implication from the provisions of the Judiciary Act is that the national courts were not to look to the law of the state where the prosecution was had. Section 33 of that act provided for the application of the law of a particular state to some aspects of a criminal proceeding. "The trial" is not one of them. Section 33 provides that "the offender" is to be "arrested, and imprisoned or bailed" by using state procedure—"agreeably to the usual mode of process against offenders in such state." If Congress had intended to use the law of the state where the offender was prosecuted it would have been easy and natural to have included such a provision in Section 33: "The trial of such offenders against the United States shall be agreeably to the usual mode of trial and the usages of law of trial against offenders in such state."

To find the penalties for this crime it was necessary to look to American state law, either using Section 34 of the Judiciary Act or in its absence to judicially create the same rule.

The Inappropriateness of British Common Law

The British common law of crimes was not suited to the American Republic. Treason had been strictly defined in the Constitution so as to avoid the flexible progovernment vagaries of the British common-law courts' definitions of treason. Crimes against the king could hardly be carried over into the law of a nation with an elected president as its executive head, without giving monarchical attributes to the chief executive.

The British law of crimes and offenses against God and religion could hardly be made applicable to the American Republic at the same time that the states were being asked to adopt a constitutional amendment denying to the Congress the power to make any "law respecting an establishment of religion, or prohibiting the free exercise thereof."[88] It was at least not crystal clear that action by the Congress recognizing the English law of seditious libel as in effect in the United States would be compatible with a resolution asking the states to amend the Constitution so as to prohibit Congress from making any law abridging the freedom of speech, or of the press.

The inappropriateness of using the British criminal law in an American state was pointed out by Chief Justice Nathaniel Chipman of the Supreme Court of Vermont in 1792 when he wrote:

> Legal right and wrong, particularly in criminal jurisprudence, have an intimate relation to the constitution, principles, and circumstances of the government. There will be coincidence between the principles of the government, the spirit of its criminal law, and the mode of interpretation and execution.[89]

He pointed out that the monarchial principle in the British government had a silent but uniform influence on the country's criminal jurisprudence, with the result that:

From all these circumstances, their punishments became, in many instances, shockingly severe.—Whether it be owing to the force of habit, to the influence of the monarchial and aristocratical principles in their government, or both, modern refinement of manners, modern delicacy of sentiment has prevailed very little to soften that severity. Their laws, like those of Draco, may emphatically be said to be WRITTEN IN BLOOD. They have about one hundred and sixty capital offences. Blackstone's com. iv. 18. These are, mostly, created, or confirmed by statute; but are some still crimes at common law only.[90]

Turning to the rules to be applied in criminal proceedings in Vermont, Chipman said he considered it an unalterable rule that sentence of death ought never to be pronounced upon the authority of a common-law precedent, without the express authority of a statute. In the provision of the Vermont Constitution requiring fines to be proportioned to offenses, the word "fines" was synonymous with punishments, and taken in this larger sense the clause was consonant with the principles and spirit of the government and laws of the state. Continuing, Chipman said:

> Actions, which are criminal in England, may not be so in Vermont. Civil Crimes become such by a certain relation to the society, where they are committed. From the difference of the relation in different societies, the same action may be either not criminal at all, or criminal in a different degree. Here, *cessante ratione, cessat et ipsa lex,* ought to be applied, whether to determine an action not to be criminal, or to be criminal in a less degree. . . .
>
> May the principles of the common law, which are the true principles of right, so far as discoverable, be competent to decide on the criminality of an action, which shall be, notoriously, and flagrantly, injurious to society in this State; altho' such an action had never been done, or ever heard of in England, and to declare a punishment, but short of death.[91]

THE FIRST SESSIONS OF THE DISTRICT AND CIRCUIT COURTS, 1789–90

President Washington appointed, and the Senate confirmed, six justices of the Supreme Court and eleven district judges in September 1789. Of these jurists five had served in the Federal Convention: three Supreme Court justices, John Rutledge of South Carolina, James Wilson of Pennsylvania, and John Blair of Virginia; and two district judges, David

Brearley of New Jersey and Gunning Bedford of Delaware.[92] In addition, Rutledge and Wilson had served on the convention's Committee of Detail.

When these judges held court they presumably had copies of both the laws passed by the First Congress and the *Journals* of the House and Senate, although there is no evidence that these were provided by the government. The Congress had given the secretary of state the responsibility of keeping the laws, of seeing to their "official" publication in three newspapers, of delivering a printed copy to each senator and representative, and of sending two duly authenticated printed copies to the executive authority of each state.[93] Collections of the *Laws* and copies of the *Journals* were available for purchase from the printers.[94] With these books, and whatever others they chose to carry, the national judges were ready to open court.

The times and places for holding the first sessions of both district and circuit courts were specified in the Judiciary Act. The first district courts were to be held in New York City for the New York District and in Burlington, New Jersey, for the New Jersey District, both on the first Tuesday in November 1789, followed by the District Court of Pennsylvania, to be held at Philadelphia, and so on seriatim through December for the other eleven districts. The first circuit courts were to be held for the District of New Jersey at Trenton on April 2, 1790; for the District of New York at New York on April 4; and so on through April and May for the other nine circuit courts.[95]

Not surprisingly, Francis Hopkinson, district judge of Pennsylvania, delivered the first grand-jury charge that was published.[96] Only the district courts for New York and New Jersey met earlier—on the first Tuesday in November. On the second Tuesday, November 10, 1789, Francis Hopkinson opened the court in Philadelphia, and after telling the grand jury about the establishment of the new government he told them:

> Gentlemen,
> If any crimes or offences, cognizable by the jurisdiction of this Court have come to your knowledge, it is your duty to inquire concerning them, and present them for trial. Should you want any information respecting the law or instruction in points of form, the Court, or the Attorney for the United States, will be ready to give you all necessary assistance.[97]

The first session of the Supreme Court, as provided for in the Judiciary Act, was held on February 1, 1790. At this time the justices assigned the circuits among themselves, in accordance with their convenience, with

Chief Justice John Jay and Justice William Cushing taking the Eastern Circuit, Justices Blair and Wilson the Middle, and Justice Rutledge (who did not attend the session) the Southern.[98] James Iredell was appointed and confirmed on February 10, 1790, receiving official notice of his appointment and his commission on March 3.[99] This gave Iredell time to attend the first session of a circuit court in the Southern Circuit to which he had been "assigned,"[100] and which was scheduled for Columbia, South Carolina, on May 12, 1790.[101]

The first session of the Eastern Circuit was held in the District of New York on April 4, 1790, with Chief Justice Jay, Justice Cushing, and District Judge James Duane present. The two Supreme Court justices then continued on circuit, holding court at Hartford on April 22, at Boston on May 4, and at Portsmouth, New Hampshire, on May 20. At each circuit court, Jay charged the grand jury. In this charge to the grand jury, the Chief Justice said:

> The objects of your enquiry are all offences committed against the laws of the united states in this district, or on the high seas by persons now in the district. You will recollect, that the laws of nations make part of the laws of this, and every civilized nation. . . .
>
> The penal statutes of the united states are few, and principally respect the revenue. . . .
>
> Direct your attention also to the conduct of the national officers— and let not any corruptions, frauds, extortions, or criminal negligence, with which you may find any of them justly chargeable, pass unnotice. In a word, gentlemen, your province, and your duty, extend (as has been before observed) to the enquiry and presentment of all offences of every kind, committed against the united states, in this district, or on the high seas by person in it. If in the performance of your duty, you should meet with difficulties the court will be ready to afford your proper assistance.[102]

At the session held at New York the grand jury reported (according to the *Gazette of the United States*): "The late mutiny on board the brig Morning-Star, Capt. Kermit, being cognizable before this Court, notice was taken of the same; and a grand jury and petit jury ordered to be summoned for attendance on Monday next, to which day the Court stands adjourned."[103] As a consequence, two men, Hopkins and Brown, were convicted of an offense and sentenced to stand in the pillory for an hour, to serve six months' imprisonment, and on the last day to receive thirty-nine stripes each.[104] The grand jury presented one indictment.[105]

The first session of the Middle Circuit was held in Trenton for the District of New Jersey on April 2, followed by a session at Philadelphia for the District of Pennsylvania on April 11, 1790. At Philadelphia, on April 12, Justice Wilson charged the grand jury.

Pointing out that this was the first grand jury assembled in the Circuit Court for Pennsylvania and that there was little business, Wilson took the occasion to instruct it on its functions, as well as those of petit juries. He quoted the Judiciary Act to show the "jurisdiction of the circuit courts in criminal matters" and then continued:

> In describing crimes, and ascertaining their punishment, the attention of the national legislature has been employed, as far as circumstances would permit: and a general law upon that subject will probably be passed in a short time:
>
> Of the offences already known to the constitution and laws of the united states, I shall give you the following very concise account:

He quoted the Constitution as to the definition of treason and its punishment and commented thereon. He then quoted from the revenue acts, both the provisions relating to penalties and forfeitures and the three crimes created by the acts, doing so without drawing any distinctions, concluding that it would be superfluous "to prove or illustrate the necessity and importance of vigilance, vigour, and impartiality, in the collection of the public revenue."

In thanking Wilson for the address, the grand jury said that it took particular pleasure and offered the court its congratulations "that in a district so extensive, and including the first commercial city in the United States, we have found no cause to make even a single presentment." [106]

Although only the views of a few judges are contained in these grand jury charges, there is no indication that anyone challenged the criminal jurisdiction of the national courts. It seems to have been accepted as a matter of course. It is also evident that, accepting the constitutionality of that jurisdiction, the judges also viewed the criminal jurisdiction as extending to nonstatutory crimes. In this connection it is also well to keep in mind that the Judiciary Act of 1789 made no provision for appellate review of criminal cases. In this sense, each district court and each session of the circuit court could act as a law unto itself.

THE SECOND SESSION OF THE FIRST CONGRESS

"An Act for the Punishment of certain Crimes against the United States" was enacted in the second session of the First Congress, on April 30, 1790.[107] When the same bill had been before the Senate in 1789, on August 25, according to Senator Maclay: "Ellsworth had a string of amendments. For a while he was listened to, but he wrought himself so deep in his niceties and distinctions as to be absolutely incomprehensible. He fairly tired the Senate, and was laughed at. I think he may well be styled the 'Endless Ellsworth.'"[108] Maclay never does say whether any of these amendments were adopted. The only other information we have on the Senate debates in 1789 was the comment Senator Maclay made regarding the bill on the third reading on August 27. Maclay wrote:

> The business in the Senate was the third reading on the Penal bill. We had but little debate until we came to a clause making it highly criminal to defame a foreign Minister. Here Izard, King, and Johnson made a great noise for the paragraph. Mr. Adams could not sit still in his chair. It was a subject of etiquette and ceremony. Two or three times did his impatience raise him to talk in a most trifling manner. However, it did not avail; the paragraph was lost.[109]

When the Senate met in its second session, the handling of the Crimes Bill presented a new question of procedure: whether all bills should originate *de novo* each session, or whether the Senate having once passed the Crimes Bill and sent it to the House, this was sufficient and the bill was properly before the House. On January 19, 1790, Ellsworth moved: "That a Committee be appointed to report a Bill defining the crimes and offences that shall be cognizable under the authority of the United States, and their punishment."[110] In his motion Ellsworth returned to the language of the 1789 motion appointing a Crimes Committee: the committee was to report a bill *defining* the crimes and offenses that shall be cognizable under the authority of the United States, and their punishment. After several postponements, and resolution of the procedural questions, on January 26 the Senate ordered the appointment of a committee in accordance with Ellsworth's motion. The committee named was Ellsworth, Johnson, Strong, Paterson, and Benjamin Hawkins from North Carolina.[111]

This 1790 committee consisted of three members from the 1789 committee that brought in the Judicial Bill, and only one member from the 1789 Crimes Committee, plus the new member of the Senate from North Carolina. The naming of William Samuel Johnson of Connecticut, who had reported the 1789 Crimes Bill, seems almost to have been a matter of courtesy. Ellsworth, Paterson, and Strong had been the principal draftsmen of the 1789 Judicial Bill. One can only conclude that the 1789 Crimes Bill was indirectly a product of the committee that drafted the Judicial Bill.

On the same day, January 26, the committee reported the 1789 Crimes Bill as though it were new legislation.[112] On second reading on January 27, Caleb Strong offered an amendment under which judges would issue warrants for execution of criminals, but this was postponed after Maclay raised the objection that this interfered with the president's power of pardon.[113]

Then Hawkins objected to the clause that denied benefit of clergy in capital cases. Maclay sought to clarify Hawkins' comments and added his own:

> I stated that as far as I could collect the sentiments of the honorable gentleman, he was opposed to our copying the law language of Great Britain; that, for my part, I wished to see a code of criminal law for the continent, and I wished to see a tone of originality running through the whole of it. I was tired of the servility of imitating English forms. I could not say whether the bill would be materially injured by leaving out the clause. I wished it should be left out, but I thought at any rate it had better be postponed. It was postponed.[114]

On January 29, Strong's amendment was rejected. One offered by Maclay was also rejected. It was probably a motion to delete the benefit-of-clergy clause.[115] In any event the clause relating to benefit of clergy was not deleted. Before adoption an amendment was made under which courts were given discretion to order dissection of the bodies of executed murderers, instead of this action being mandatory as had been provided in the bill passed in 1789.[116] And then: "Resolved, That this Bill do pass as amended—That the title of the Bill be 'An Act for the punishment of certain crimes against the United States,'—That it be engrossed and sent to the House of Representatives, for concurrence."[117]

There is something of a puzzle here. Under Ellsworth's motion the committee was directed to bring in a bill to define the crimes that shall be cognizable under the authority of the United States. But instead the committee appointed immediately reported a bill only undertaking to fix the punishment of certain crimes, and after the bill was passed, the title was changed to recognize this more limited scope. Under Rule 15, adopted in 1789, all committees were appointed by ballot, with a plurality being sufficient.[118] It thus appears that the Senate in electing the membership of the committee had overruled Ellsworth and elected a committee with a majority that reported the bill previously passed. (Two of the members of this committee, Ellsworth and Paterson, later had the opportunity as judges to

TABLE 6.1
Crimes Established by Crimes Act of April 8, 1790

Constitution	Crime	Section
Art. I, § 8, cl. 6	Counterfeiting and forgery	§ 14
Art. I, § 8, cl. 10	Piracies and felonies on high seas	
	Murder, robbery, etc.	§ 8
	Misprision of felony	§ 6
	Piracy under color of authority of foreign prince	§ 9
	Accessory before fact	§ 10
	Accessory after fact	§ 11
	Manslaughter	§ 12
	Mayhem	§ 13
	Larceny	§ 16
	Receiving	§ 17
	Offenses against law of nations, writs against ambassadors, violating safe conduct, etc.	§§ 25, 26, 27, 28
Art. I, § 8, cl. 17	Seat of government, forts, magazines, etc.	
	Willful murder	§ 3
	Misprision of felony	§ 6
	Manslaughter	§ 7
	Mayhem	§ 13
	Larceny	§ 16
	Receiving	§ 17
None	Administration of Justice	
	Stealing and falsifying court records	§ 15
	Perjury	§ 18, 19
	Subornation of perjury	§ 20
	Bribery of judges	§ 21
	Obstruction of process	§ 22
	Rescue of convicted persons	§ 23
	Rescue of bodies of persons executed	§ 5
Art. III, § 3	Treason	
	Treason	§ 1
	Misprision of treason	§ 2
Punishment		
None	Execution by hanging	§ 33
	Dissection of murderers	§ 4
Art. III, § 3, cl. 2	No corruption of blood, or forfeiture of estate	§ 24
	No benefit of clergy for capital offenses	§ 31

TABLE 6.2
Criminal Procedure under the Judiciary Act of 1789
and Crimes Act of 1790

Procedure	Statute and Section
Prosecution by U.S. attorney	Judiciary Act § 35
Arrest, imprisonment, and bail	Judiciary Act § 33
Indictment, right to counsel	Crimes § 29
Limitation periods	Crimes § 32
Place of trial in capital cases	Judiciary Act § 29
Standing mute	Crimes § 30
Selection of jurors	Judiciary Act § 29
Peremptory challenges	Crimes § 30
Rules of decision at trial	Judiciary Act § 34

consider the authority of the national courts to exercise jurisdiction over nonstatutory crimes.)

The actual provisions of the 1790 Crimes Act are summarized in table 6.1, which shows the crimes established by the Crimes Act of 1790. It must be noted that each crime carried a specific punishment. The crimes are arranged according to the particular article or clause of the Constitution that presumably provides the basis for the statutory provision. In addition, four provisions relating to punishment generally are listed at the end.

Some of these crimes were in no sense "defined" in the act. "Willful murder," "murder," "robbery," and "manslaughter" were referred to only by these names without any further definition of the crime. It thus is obvious that application of the act required looking outside the statute for a definition of these crimes and to ascertain the elements constituting them. Others such as maiming and larceny were probably sufficiently defined so that it would not be necessary to look outside the statute to ascertain the elements of the crime, but the common law of crimes or some other source certainly was to be looked to in order to ascertain what constituted four important offenses.

Table 6.2 shows the "procedural" provisions of both the Judiciary Act of 1789 and the Crimes Act of 1790, arranged generally in the order in which they would have become applicable in the prosecution of a criminal case.

While these two statutes did not cover many aspects of a criminal proceeding, they did contain some provisions relating to the procedures to be followed up until a "trial" begins. They were completely silent as to the many legal questions arising during the trial. The national courts must look somewhere for the rules governing the trial. Again Section 34 of the Judiciary Act gives the direction: look to the laws of the several states, that is, to American state law.

CHAPTER VII

Section 34

INTRODUCTION

SECTION 34 WAS NOT in the Judicial Bill when it was introduced into the Senate; but it was in the bill when passed by the Senate. There is nothing in the records of the Congress to show precisely when the section was added to the bill. There is nothing in the records of the Congress that clearly shows why it was added to the bill. There is nothing in the correspondence of members of the Congress that can be pointed to with assurance that is the source of the section, nor anything that clearly represents a comment on the section.

An analysis of the language of the section, particularly in the context of the development of the Judiciary Act of 1789, insofar as it is known, makes it possible to draw some reasonable conclusions regarding the section. In order to do this, each part of the section will be analyzed, but first the process of amending the bill by the Senate will be more closely looked at, the manuscript amendment itself—contained in the records of the First Congress—will be analyzed, then some comments will be made upon *when* and *where* the amendment was added to the bill and the significance of this timing and location.

THE DEBATE ON THE JUDICIAL BILL IN THE SENATE

As we have seen, on May 11, 1789, a subcommittee of the Senate almost certainly consisting of Senators Ellsworth, Paterson, and Strong was deputed the task of turning the resolutions adopted by the committee on the judiciary into a bill. The subcommittee submitted a handwritten draft on June 12, which the Senate immediately ordered to be printed.[1]

Committee member William Maclay reported that the draft was "somewhat confused."[2] The physical appearance of the manuscript copy that Charles Warren found in the attic of the Capitol supports this conclusion.[3] There is a possibility that the Senate gave the subcommittee or Ellsworth authority to work with the printer to iron out whatever remaining problems might be found. This may explain why there are some discrepancies between the draft bill and the printed bill—although not many of these are of significance.[4]

The printed bill is a quarto imprint of sixteen pages, taken from the handwritten draft of thirty-seven pages. The draft bears printer's marks that conform exactly with the pages of the printed bill. These printer's marks are on the LC 7 Back, marking the division between pages 4 and 5; on LC 12, marking the division between pages 8 and 9; and on LC 16 Back, marking the division between pages 12 and 13.[5]

The draft bill has thirty-three sections; they are numbered, but this numbering may have been added later. The printed bill has thirty-three sections also, of course, but they are unnumbered. The *Senate Journal* uses section numbers, however, and some of the manuscript amendments also bear section numbers, sometimes in the hand of a clerk. In the Senate debate, apparently the provisions were consistently referred to by section number, even though (as will presently be seen) sections were added or deleted at various times. In this book the sections of the bill and act are referred to as they were *finally* numbered in the bill that passed the Senate, unless otherwise specifically noted.

There were two points during the progress of the bill through the Senate debate at which the text of the bill was fixed. The first was at the end of the second reading, on July 6, and the second was at the end of the third reading and when the bill was recommitted, on July 13. Unfortunately, the materials are not available to determine with certainty what parts of the bill as passed by the Senate were in, and what parts were not in, the text at either of these points. The next point at which we have certain knowledge of the text of the bill is on July 17 when it was passed by the Senate. Some tentative conclusions can, however, be drawn from the surviving incomplete records of the debate and from the evidence contained in the manuscript amendments.

Of the two critical intermediate points where the text was fixed, the latter is the more significant, because changes made by the subcommittee after recommittal were not separately voted on by the Senate. Therefore, attention should be directed at ascertaining, to the extent possible, the text of the bill on July 13.

During the second reading of the printed bill, on June 25, what was then Section 9 was deleted.[6] There is no indication that any other section was added or deleted during this reading, so at its end, on July 6, the bill apparently had thirty-two sections. It appears that the Senate renumbered all the sections subsequent to Section 9, and thereafter referred to them by the new numbers.[7] The *Journal* shows that a new Section 19 (as finally numbered) was added during the third reading (and that what became Section 16 was first deleted and was then reinserted),[8] so at the end of the third reading on July 13, the bill apparently had thirty-three sections.[9]

The bill that the Senate passed had thirty-five sections. The sections that had been added at some point after June 12 at unknown dates were Section 10, relating to the district courts in Maine and Kentucky, and Section 34. The evidence would appear to support the conclusion that Sections 10 and 34 were added by the subcommittee *after* the bill was recommitted to it on July 13.

We know more about the addition of Section 10 than we do about the addition of Section 34, and it is instructive to collect the pieces of information on Section 10. It is difficult to trace any particular provision in the bill to some specific comment made by a correspondent; similarly, it is difficult to trace any change in the bill to a particular comment made on the printed bill. However, the thinking embodied in some of these comments clearly shows up in the bill. For example, limiting review by the Supreme Court to the use of writs of error avoids the evil, commented upon by Judge David Sewall of Massachusetts, of putting the parties to two or three trials.[10] Similarly, the establishment of New Hampshire as a separate district in Section 10 well may be a reaction to John Pickering's criticism of putting the Maine part of Massachusetts with New Hampshire into a single district.[11]

By the time the Senate had gone over the bill twice, deleting and adding, and sometimes reconsidering and changing its mind, even the record kept by the secretary could hardly have been in shape to have it engrossed. The logical thing to have done was to recommit the bill to put it into final form for engrossing. The subcommittee could iron out inconsistencies, standardize spellings, and make stylistic and noncontroversial changes. The subcommittee probably was also given the power to draft provisions or even new sections that had been agreed upon in principle by the Senate. This would explain how Section 10 got into the bill.

If both New Hampshire senators had asked the Senate to put New Hampshire in a separate district, instead of along with Maine in a single district, there is no apparent reason why any other senator should have objected. And if there was no objection, the actual drafting could have been left to the subcommittee to do later. The same would have been true of the Kentucky part of Virginia, which was also made a separate district. To create these two new districts, Section 2, establishing the district courts, had to be amended, and the new districts had to be brought into the circuit court system. This was the type of provision best left to a committee and was probably done in a new Section 10.

The only primary source indicating that this was involved in the motion to recommit is to be found in the letter that Senator Wingate wrote to Timothy Pickering on July 11. Wingate wrote: "The Judicial bill has had three readings in the Senate and is now to be committed in order to make some little alterations and amendments and then it will be ready to go to the other house. . . . Six Judges of the Supreme Court are proposed and there is to be a District Judge in each State and one in the Province of Maine and one in Kentucky."[12]

Another clue as to how the text of the bill stood on July 13 is Wingate's annotated copy of the bill. Wingate noted most, but not all, of the amendments set forth in the *Journal* for July 9 through July 13.[13] Of the sixteen manuscript amendments that are not duplicative of amendments reported in the *Journal*,[14] Wingate annotated his bill to reflect six of them.[15] There are no annotations reflecting the other ten amendments.[16] It therefore is not possible to determine with certainty when these last ten manuscript amendments were added. Neither Section 10 nor Section 34 was added to Wingate's copy.

There is some evidence, however, on the manuscript amendments themselves that is helpful in determining when they were added to the bill. The amendments that are *known* to have been made from the floor exactly fit into the language of the printed bill, and this exact language is carried over into the bill as finally passed. The language of other manuscript amendments does not exactly fit into the printed bill,[17] or the language is not exactly the same as was carried into the final bill.[18] This suggests that these amendments were added by the subcommittee when it put the bill into final form after recommittal, the subcommittee not being limited to the exact language of the printed bill, except as the Senate had itself approved exact language in an amendment.

The manuscript of Section 34 does not fit into any of these categories. There is no evidence as to when it was added to the bill. Since it is an additional amendment there is no language in the printed bill being amended, and the language of the section is carried over exactly into the final bill. There is nothing in the evidence to show whether it was added on second reading, on third reading, or by the subcommittee after recommittal.

Section 10 under this analysis represents something agreed upon by the Senate and left to the subcommittee for drafting. But Section 34 may represent either something agreed upon by the Senate and left to the subcommittee for drafting or it may be a clarifying amendment originating in the subcommittee itself. But whichever it was, its purpose was probably the same.

A major difficulty in determining what the Senate did with the Judicial Bill arises out of our ignorance as to how amendments were offered. Apparently they could be offered either orally or in writing.

Rule VII of the Senate, adopted on April 16, provided: "When a motion shall be made and seconded, it shall be reduced to writing, if desired by the President, or any member, delivered in at the table, and read by the President before the same shall be debated." [19] Under this rule it appears that if no member objected to a motion, it would not be debated, and so there would be no need to reduce it to writing. If there was objection, presumably either the president of the Senate or the objecting member would ask that it be reduced to writing so that the Senate would know what it was debating. The result may have been that most amendments were offered orally, and were never reduced to writing. On the other hand, a senator might also for his own convenience and that of the Senate put even an unobjectionable amendment in writing and deliver it to the table. [20]

It may be that the manuscript amendments that have survived are all that were ever put in writing during the Senate's consideration of the bill, or it may be that they are only a part and others have been lost. But it can be said with some confidence that these manuscripts that have survived are such a diverse lot that there appears to be no reason why these particular ones should have survived while others were discarded or lost.

We have then the text of the Judicial Bill as it was introduced into the Senate; we have the text of the Judicial Bill as it passed the Senate. A few of the changes revealed by a comparison of the two are traceable in the *Senate Journal,* in Maclay's *Journal,* and in the manuscript amendments. As to these, when, and to some extent why, these changes were made can be established. But there are a number of changes that are not reflected in any of these sources.

How did these untraceable changes get into the final bill? There are two possibilities. One is that they were made on the basis of amendments offered in the Senate and duly adopted as a result of deliberative action. Maclay did not choose to comment on these amendments, and they were not reported in the *Senate Journal*. If the amendments were originally in writing, instead of oral, they have been lost.

The alternative possibility is that only some of these amendments were made by deliberative action by the Senate. At least those reflected in Senator Wingate's copy of the Judicial Bill came into the bill this way. But the bulk of the untraceable amendments, including all those not reflected in Wingate's bill, were made by the subcommittee after the bill was recommitted. The Senate never adopted these individually, but only as a part of the bill as it finally passed.

Both Charles Warren and Julius Goebel read the history of the Judiciary Act as though all untraceable amendments came into the bill by deliberate Senate action, although Goebel does recognize the possibility that the Judicial Committee made some minor amendments after recommittal.

The writer thinks the likelihood is that these untraceable amendments came into the bill after recommittal. If they were based on explicit directions of the Senate, as Section 10 probably was, they do represent deliberate Senate action. But if intended only as clarification or as amendments of limited duration, as Section 34 well may have been, then they were not thought of by the Senate as being of any particular significance. This conclusion is to some extent confirmed by the appearance of the manuscript of Section 34. There is a clerical notation on the back of the manuscript that simply says "Additional Clause." It does not have any date, or reference to its being a motion, or anything like that. It is simply an additional clause to be added to the bill.

We will now look at the manuscript text of Section 34 more closely.

THE MANUSCRIPT AMENDMENT AND ITS ALTERNATIVE TEXTS

Two versions of the text of Section 34 were discovered by Charles Warren in the attic of the Capitol; both are in the hand of Oliver Ellsworth. The first is much longer than the second. The second was written into the margin of the manuscript of the first. The second was then crossed out and inserted into that manuscript after much language was deleted (see plate on page 133). The alternative texts of the Section 34 manuscript amendment are set forth below in parallel columns:

Texts of Section 34

First Alternative	Second Alternative and Final Text
And be it further enacted, That the Statute law of the several States in force for the time being and their unwritten or common law now in use, whether by adoption from the common law of England, the ancient statutes of the same or otherwise, except where the constitution, Treaties or Statutes of the United States shall otherwise require or provide, shall be regarded as rules of decision in the trials at common law in the courts of the United States in cases where they apply.	And be it further enacted, that the Laws of the several States, except where the constitution, Treaties or Statutes of the United States shall otherwise require or provide, shall be regarded as rules of decision in trials at common law in the courts of the United States in cases where they apply.

Warren assumes that Section 34 had been adopted by the First Congress to apply to diversity cases in the circuit courts. This assumption derives from *Swift v. Tyson*[21] wherein Justice Story's denial that Section 34 applied to common-law decisions appears to be premised on the proposition that it applied only to state statutes. There is not a shred of evidence in its language to support the view that Section 34 had anything to do with the diversity jurisdiction. But Warren's conclusions must be read in light of his premise that there is no doubt of Section 34's applying to diversity cases (and only to diversity cases); for him the only arguable question is whether it applied to statutes only or also applied to judicial decisions.

Warren argues that the changes noted on the manuscript of Section 34 showed that Ellsworth intended to make the section applicable to common-law decisions as well as to statutes. Warren writes: "It seems clear that the word 'laws' was not intended to be confined to 'Statute law,' because Ellsworth expressly and evidently intentionally struck out the words 'Statute law' from his original draft, and broadened it by inserting the word "laws"; having so broadened it, he evidently concluded that the specific enumeration which followed in his original draft was unnecessary."[22]

The very appearance of the draft gives strong evidence that this is not what happened at all. Ellsworth appears to have written out alternative

And be it further enacted, / That the statute laws of the several states ~~...~~ except where the constitution ~~...~~ treaties or statutes of the United States shall otherwise require or provide, shall be regarded ~~as rules of decision in trials at common~~ law in the courts of the United States in cases where they apply—

The manuscript of Section 34.

provisions—one in the body and the other along the margin. The one along the margin was accepted, but mechanically this was done by striking it out and also striking out the necessary words in the body and inserting the single word "Laws." This striking out seems not to have been done by Ellsworth, because the superimposed word "Laws" is almost certainly not in Ellsworth's handwriting. The *L* and the *s* are not characteristic of his handwriting. A conjecture safer than the one offered by Warren is that Ellsworth offered the alternative phraseologies to the Judiciary Committee, which then accepted the "short form" and a clerk made the mechanical changes. The alternatives probably exhibit nothing more than the choice of the more felicitous of two forms of expression, but the change may have been dictated by a preference for the substance of one form rather than the other.

Other scholars have noted that the manuscript of Section 34 does not establish what Warren claimed it establishes. It leads to no clear conclusion. Even Justice Holmes was not wholly convinced of the correctness of Warren's interpretation, for he said only that the Story interpretation "probably was wrong."[23] Judge Henry Friendly, whose view on the merits is expressed in the title of a law-review article, "In Praise of Erie—and of the New Federal Common Law,"[24] says that the change in the manuscript "only demonstrates on what quicksand any attempt to interpret so venerable a statute on the basis of an unexplained change from an earlier draft must rest."[25] Professor William Winslow Crosskey similarly questions the interpretation.[26]

Although the differences in the wording of the two alternatives on the manuscript probably have no substantive significance, the first alternative, or long form, is indicative of the probable reasons the section was added to the Judicial Bill. The long version in the draft of Section 34, which was striken out in favor of the shorter "laws of the several states," is a description of *American law* as it existed in 1789. The national courts are directed to apply American law—probably as opposed to English law—and not the law of any specific state. The section makes no effort to define American law, or even to direct where it is to be found, other than to point to the "laws of the several states." Where else would American law be found? How better to describe American law in 1789?

Also, reference is made in the deleted material to "the Statute law of the several states *in force for the time being* and their unwritten or common law *now in use*" (emphasis added). This is appropriate language for temporary legislation; Congress said: "This is what should be used until we, the Congress, get around to enacting permanent legislation."

THE ENACTING STYLE OF THE JUDICIAL BILL

Some further evidence about the timing of the enactment of Section 34 can be found in the words constituting the enacting style of the various sections. The draftsmen of the Judicial Bill were uncertain as to the most appropriate style to be used for legislation. This uncertainty probably existed in the Senate itself, although there was an effort to develop a consistent style.

William Paterson wrote the draft of the first nine sections of the bill. He introduced the first section with the phrase, "Be it enacted by the senate and representatives of the United States of America in Congress assembled." Paine Wingate's printed bill shows that the Senate amended this by inserting the words "house of" before "representatives," and in this form this section of the bill passed the Senate and was enacted.

"And by the authority aforesaid"

In Section 2, Paterson first wrote, "And be it further enacted That" and then on second thought or later, interlined "by the authority aforesaid" after "enacted." The phrase "by the authority aforesaid" was continued in each succeeding section through Section 8, but in the original Section 9, the last one he drafted, it was omitted. The bill as printed preserved these variations.

Ellsworth consistently began each of the original fifteen sections he drafted with the phrase "And be it further enacted," but his use or omission of the phrase "by the authority aforesaid" is baffling. In Sections 10 and 11 he interlined the phrase and then crossed it out. Beginning with Section 12 and through the rest of the sections he drafted, he included "by the authority aforesaid" in the text as he was drafting it, but then crossed this language out in the original Sections 12, 14, 17, 19, 21, and 22, leaving the language in the other sections. So the phrase is in eight sections Ellsworth drafted and omitted from seven sections. In this form the bill was printed. In his use of this phrase it would appear that Ellsworth was using some organizing principle, but the writer cannot determine what it was.[27]

Caleb Strong omitted the phrase "by the authority aforesaid" in Section 25, which he drafted. In the remaining sections of the bill, all in the handwriting of a clerk, the phrase was used in two sections and omitted from six sections, and the bill was printed in this way.[28] Somewhat mercifully, the Senate on July 10 ordered the phrase expunged from the bill. The *Journal* says: "In Section 31st, line 1st, to expunge the words 'By the authority aforesaid,' So in all cases where the words are redundant."[29] Paine Wingate struck the phrase out only in Section 31.

In the amendment known to have been offered by Ellsworth on the following day, July 11, and which became Section 19 of the final bill, Ellsworth omitted the phrase.

The phrase is *not* in the manuscript of Section 34. This gives some indication that Ellsworth drafted Section 34 after July 10, when the Senate had decided no longer to use the phrase. This though is not conclusive on the point in light of Ellsworth's rather erratic use of the phrase in his drafting of the original bill.

"And be it enacted" or "And be it further enacted"

Another organizing device that appears to have been used in the Judiciary Act of 1789 was to make clear divisions in the act by use of the phrase "And be it enacted" to introduce sections beginning a division, whereas each section within a division was introduced by the phrase, "And be it further enacted."

There are two such dividing phrases in the Judiciary Act of 1789, thus indicating three divisions. The "And be it enacted" phraseology is used in Section 7 and again in Section 31. These dividing phrases are found both in the manuscript and in the printed bill. Although the Senate struck out all of the "and by the authority aforesaid"'s it left the phrases "and be it enacted" and "and be it further enacted" unchanged.

Although it is difficult to see what organizing principle underlay making a division occur with Section 7, the alternative is that the First Congress, both Senate and House, simply made a mistake—failing to insert the word "further" in these two sections.[30] In light of the care with which this bill was developed, error should be the explanation of last resort.

If there is such a tripartite division in the act, Section 34 must be read as in some way related to Sections 31, 32, 33, and 35, and as less closely related to the other sections of the bill, such as Sections 11 and 12.

The latter sections of the act, Sections 31 through 35, all deal with all of the United States courts, and this may be the basis for the division starting at Section 31, which begins, "That where *any* suit shall be depending in *any* court of the United States." Section 32 applies in "*any* of the courts of the United States." Section 33 applies to "*any* crime or offense against the United States" and deals with how the offender is to be handled by "*any* justice or judge of *any* of the courts of the United States" or of any state. Section 35 determines how parties may plead and manage their own causes "in *all* the courts of the United States" (emphasis added).[31]

The significance of Section 34's being placed where it is along with Sections 31 through 35 is thus that it was intended to apply to all the courts of the United States and not just to the circuit courts, and this may be why it was thought appropriate to conclude Section 34 with the essentially redundant "in cases where they apply." Thus there is some strong internal evidence that Section 34 does not have relevance only to diversity cases (dealt with in Sections 11 and 12), as is implied by the current orthodoxy epitomized in *Erie*.

PAGE 15TH

The notation "Page 15th" is written at the top of the manuscript of Section 34 in the hand of Samuel Otis, the secretary of the Senate. The notation refers to the printed bill, as will be shown, but Charles Warren's serious error of assuming that it referred to the manuscript draft must first be dealt with. As we have emphasized, Warren operates under the assumption that Section 34 must have been directed to choice-of-law problems in diversity cases, an assumption he thinks unchallengeable. This assumption leads him to the serious error mentioned.

Warren is clearly in error when he writes: "That [Section 34] was adopted late in the debate is to be seen by its position in the Bill—being inserted next to the last section and between two sections dealing with criminal matters with which it had no connection. Its proper place in the bill would have been after Section 11, dealing with the subject of the Circuit Court jurisdiction." [32] Section 34, rather, was placed in the bill exactly where the Senate wanted it placed. Warren's first assertion that the placing of Section 34 near the end of the bill shows that it "was adopted late in the debate" is absurd, and is belied by both the *Senate Journal* and Maclay's *Journal,* which show that senators made motions to amend any part of the bill at such time as they saw fit.

In support of his second assertion, that the section is out of place, Warren sets forth the following in a footnote: "In the Senate Files, the original slip of paper in which this Section is written bears the notation 'page 15th.' If it had been inserted on page 15 of the manuscript Draft Bill, it would have appeared in its proper position in the bill, for that page contains Sections 11 and 12 as to Circuit Courts." [33] This statement would be correct if the Senate had been using the manuscript bill. However, the Senate was using the printed bill. Section 11 and the beginning of Section 12 of the printed bill are on page 5, not page 15; Section 32 of the printed bill (Section 33 of the final bill) ends at the bottom of page 15, so it is clear that what was finally numbered Section 34 was inserted precisely where the Senate intended to insert it.[34]

Both common sense and his sources should have suggested to Warren that the Senate must have used a printed bill. Admittedly, to expect anything of "common sense" may be too slender a reed to lean on in raising this question. After all, common sense seems not to have caused anyone, even the nation's highest court, to raise the question for some sixty years.

But it defies common sense to think that the First Congress would not have used the printing press to help it in its deliberations. There were printers in New York not only able but eager to do printing for the Congress. Furthermore, the First Congress itself had the taxing power to make it possible to raise the revenues to pay the printers.[35]

How would the Senate have operated if its president (John Adams), the clerk, and twenty senators had to use a single handwritten copy of the judicial bill, as Warren seems to think they did? Warren does not suggest that each senator had transcribed a copy of the bill. What does Warren think the *Boston Gazette* used when it printed the bill on June 29 and July 6, 1789?[36]

But aside from such questions, the sources Warren uses explicitly say that the bill was printed. William Maclay's entry for June 12, the day the bill was reported to the Senate, says, "and a number of copies were ordered to be struck off."[37] Warren quotes the language, "The Judiciary Bill has not yet been published here," from a letter that John Quincy Adams wrote to John Adams, under date of June 28, 1789.[38] Similarly, Warren says that T. Lowther had written to James Iredell on July 1, 1789, that he was "enclosing a copy of the Bill."[39] Warren also uses *Letters and Times of the Tylers*, in which there is a reference to the bill being printed.[40] Why would the Senate have used the handwritten draft after ordering a printing?

There has been considerable bibliographical confusion about these printed bills,[41] and a copy may not have been easy to locate in the early 1920s, but there must have been considerable evidence in the Library of Congress that the First Congress did use the printing press.

Furthermore, Warren does not consistently assume that references to pages and/or lines on all amendments meant the manuscript bill. In all, there are twenty-seven manuscript amendments on twenty-six slips of paper. Seven manuscript amendments have specific section references, while the section to be amended is identifiable by the text in eleven others, either considered alone or in conjunction with the *Senate Journal* or Maclay's *Journal* or both. The nine remaining manuscript amendments bear references to pages and lines, or to pages only, or in one instance to a line only. There is also an amendment with two parts for which there is no manuscript, only the report of the *Senate Journal,* which refers to two separate lines on "page 13th."[42] Warren's methodology with regard to the proper location of the ten amendments locatable in the bill by page or line references only is erratic and haphazard at best.

Warren completely ignores the specific page and line notations on two of the manuscript amendments.[43] He ignores another manuscript, relying instead entirely on a comparison of the bill as passed with the bill as introduced in his discussion of the change made.[44] He ignores yet another manuscript, basing his discussion of the change involved upon Maclay's *Journal.*[45]

In four other instances Warren discusses the amendments, locating them at the proper places in the bill, and citing the manuscript amendments. But again he wholly ignores the page and line notations on the manuscripts. If he had followed them in placing the amendment on the manuscript the result would have been gibberish.[46]

Only with respect to two of the amendments, then, does Warren resort for clarification to the manuscript bill. One of these, as we have seen, was Section 34. The other (the amendment with two parts found only in the *Senate Journal*) is discussed extensively in an appendix.[47] Both such references are clearly erroneous.

Julius Goebel, in his volume of the Holmes Devise *History of the Supreme Court of the United States,* while acknowledging that Warren discovered the important manuscripts,[48] understands but fails to point out Warren's error referring some amendments to the manuscript bill of the Judiciary Act of 1789.

Goebel not only found the printed bills used by the Senate,[49] he also notes that all the *Journal* entries and manuscript amendments must be read as referring to the printed bill. Elaborating upon how a failure to use the printed bill affects all interpretation of what the Senate did, Goebel says,

> [I]t should be noticed that whenever the meagre entries in the Senate *Journal* are specific, the references can be traced to the printed bill alone. This is true also of the chits or slips of paper still preserved on which proffered amendments or alterations were written and "delivered in at the table" pursuant to Senate rule VII. Many of these chits refer to pages—invariably to be found in the printed bill. Since the

latter ran to only fifteen and a half pages and the manuscript draft to thirty-seven, attempts to fix the place of what was offered by reference to the manuscript are meaningless.[50]

Goebel goes no further, however. He offers no examples of how Warren's two efforts to relate amendments, either in the *Senate Journal* or in manuscript, to the manuscript bill yielded a "meaningless" result. This failure to point out a Warren error tends to confirm the interpretation Warren arrived at through error in connection with Section 34. Referring to the section, Goebel says, "Nothing more is known of its genesis than that the text is written out on a chit in Ellsworth's hand and marked for page 15,"[51] and in a footnote says, "The credit for discovering and rescuing this document belongs to Charles Warren."[52] Goebel must have known that the "page 15" on the chit referred to the printed bill, and so was placed in the statute exactly where it was supposed to be, and did not refer to page 15 of the manuscript bill, as Warren had said. But he makes no mention of this.

The amendment that became Section 34 was thus placed on page 15 of the printed bill immediately after what became numbered as Section 33. Section 33 is devoted wholly to criminal matters, and so if Section 34 is viewed as a continuation of the subject matter of Section 33, then Section 34 deals with *criminal* "trials at common law."

On the other hand, the following Section 35 on page 16 of the printed bill is applicable to both criminal and civil matters, inasmuch as it pertains to all of the national courts. And so if Section 34 is viewed as an introduction to Section 35 it applies to both civil and criminal trials at common law. One thing is clear: there is nothing in either Section 33 or Section 35 of peculiar relevance to the diversity jurisdiction.

We will now proceed clause by clause through the language of Section 34.

"THAT THE LAWS OF THE SEVERAL STATES"

The phrase, "the laws of the several states," in Section 34 does not mean that the national courts are to apply the law of a particular state, such as the law of the state where the trial at common law is held. If this meaning had been intended, the word used almost certainly would have been "respective" and not "several." This subject has been extensively discussed above in chapter 5 on word usage,[53] and so will not be repeated here.

The only instance in which the Judicial Bill directs application of the law of a particular state, as distinguished from the law of the several states, is found in Section 29, and relates to the selection and qualification of jurors:

> And jurors in all cases to serve in the courts of the United States shall be designated by lot or otherwise in each State *respectively* according to the mode of forming juries therein now practised, so far as the laws of the same shall render such designation practicable by the courts or marshals of the United States; and the jurors shall have the same qualifications as are requisite for jurors by the laws of the State of which they are citizens, to serve in the highest courts of law of such state. (emphasis added)

By using the word "respectively," the meaning is clear. Thus a comparison of the texts of Section 29 and Section 34 of the Judiciary Act shows, as we would expect, that "respective" is used to refer to the law of a particular state while "several" is used to refer to American law generally.

There is even stronger evidence that the phrase "laws of the several states" in Section 34 does not mean the same thing as "laws of the respective states." During the first session of the First Congress, Ellsworth also drafted a bill to regulate process in the courts of the United States. The manuscript of this bill is preserved in the National Archives. In the Process Act Ellsworth provided that the forms of execution and fees in actions at common law in the national courts should be as near as may be to those of the state where the proceeding shall be had. He had no difficulty in making his meaning clear; he wrote that "the forms of writs and execution . . . and modes of process and rates of fees . . . in the circuit and district courts, in suits at common law, shall be the same in each state *respectively* as are now used or allowed in the supreme courts of the same" (emphasis added).[54]

The draftsmen of the period knew the difference between applying the law of a particular state and applying a general rule, not derived from a particular state. And they had no difficulty in expressing the difference.

"EXCEPT WHERE THE CONSTITUTION, TREATIES OR STATUTES OF THE UNITED STATES SHALL OTHERWISE REQUIRE OR PROVIDE"

If Section 34 is read as applying to crimes against the United States, the exceptions referred to in this part of the statute are easy to find. Article III, Section 3, of the Constitution defines treason and provides for its punishment. This provision obviously prevails over the laws of the several states.

Similarly, there was in 1789 at least one controlling treaty provision applicable to criminal proceedings,[55] but there were none that would clearly apply in a civil proceeding, such as a diversity suit in a national court. However, there were provisions that would control in state courts.[56]

The language of the exception is worded so as to be applicable to then-existing provisions of the Constitution and treaties, as well as to treaties thereafter made and statutes thereafter adopted by Congress. Its language is thus appropriate as a temporary measure covering any situation involving the criminal law until permanent legislation could be enacted.

If Section 34 was intended to have a broader application than just to crimes, the limits of its application become more vague. Would it apply when the Supreme Court reviewed cases coming to it from the highest court of a state under Section 25? Would it be applicable to determine what constitutes a bill of attainder or an *ex post facto* law under Article I, Section 10?

When the question of what constitutes an *ex post facto* law came before the Supreme Court in 1798 in *Calder v. Bull*,[57] if there had been any contemporary understanding about the applicability or even possible application of Section 34, the Court might be expected to have cited the section. William Paterson, who helped draft the bill, was a member of the Court. Neither he nor any other member cited or discussed the section, although Paterson and other members of the Court did examine the provisions in the constitutions of several states, other than Connecticut from which the case came; Paterson looked to legislative developments in Connecticut, and also to constitutional provisions in other states—Massachusetts, Delaware, Maryland, and North Carolina. He concluded that "the framers of the Constitution . . . understood and used the words in their known and appropriate signification, as referring to crimes, pains, and penalties, and no further."[58] But he did not mention Section 34.

"SHALL BE REGARDED AS RULES OF DECISION"

This term was used in the Virginia Act of 1776, which provided for the reception of English law.[59] Otherwise, little can be said about the straightforward language used.

"IN TRIALS"

The phrase "in trials at common law" only appears once in the Judicial Bill as passed by the Senate, in Section 34. However, the term does appear in the margin of Ellsworth's draft of Section 16.

The text of Ellsworth's draft of Section 16 read as follows: "And be it further enacted by the authority aforesaid that suits in equity shall not be sustained in either of the courts of the United States in any case where remedy may be had at law." An asterisk in the manuscript was keyed to a marginal note intended for insertion at this point. This marginal note read as follows: "And the mode of receiving testimony in suits in equity and in cases of admiralty and maritime jurisdiction shall be the same as in trials at common law, or as is hereinafter specially provided."

Although the manuscript does not show deletion of this marginal note, it does not appear in the printed bill. However, the reason is evident. The same substantive provision—but now using the phrase "actions at common law"—was set forth in Section 29 of the draft bill (Section 30 of the final bill), which reads: "And be it enacted by the authority aforesaid, that the mode of Proof by and Testimony and Examination of Witnesses in open Court shall be the same in all the Courts of the United States as well in the Trial of Causes in Equity and of admiralty and Maritime Jurisdiction as of actions at common law."[60] The marginal notation to Ellsworth's draft of Section 16 was not carried into the printed bill, by a process not clear, because it was redundant.

There is evidence here, though, as to what the understanding of Ellsworth, and the Senate, was as to the scope of a "trial at common law." It was that part of a judicial proceeding that was held in open court and when witnesses were examined and their testimony taken. If, as we have no reason to doubt, the phrase was used consistently in Section 34, the application of Section 34 is not to the whole judicial proceeding but only to the "trial" part when testimony is being taken in open court. As we shall see in the succeeding section, this is how Ellsworth consistently used "trial," and there was at least one sort of criminal trial it might refer to.

Although the phrase "trials at common law" in the marginal notation to Section 16 appears to be in Ellsworth's handwriting, when Ellsworth drafted the Process Bill he used the term "actions at common law." If Ellsworth was using the word "trials" in Section 34 to mean civil proceedings he was following a different usage than he followed in drafting the Process Bill. There is a possibility also that the marginal notation to Section 16 was not written by Ellsworth.[61]

If "actions at common law" in Section 30 of the final bill means the same thing as "trials at common law" in Section 34, then Section 30 points to Section 34 to determine the mode of proof and Section 34 points to the "laws of the several states" as providing the mode of proof to be followed.

And this in turn means that American law and not English law is to be looked to for the applicable rules.

"AT COMMON LAW"

The use of the phrase "at common law" in Section 34 shows that the section was intended to apply in proceedings at common law as distinguished from some other type of proceedings. But what were those other proceedings where "the laws of the several states" would not provide the rules of decision?

If the section is read as applying only to *criminal* trials at common law, the proceedings to which the section does not apply are all civil proceedings. But if because of the omission of the word "criminal" the section is read either as applying to all common-law proceedings, both criminal and civil, or only to civil proceedings, then the question arises as to why the section is applicable to civil proceedings at common law but not applicable to civil proceedings in equity, or in admiralty.

While post hoc arguments can be developed that purport to show a rationale for Congress's directing the national courts to apply a different law in equity suits than in common-law actions, such arguments are unsupported by any evidence in 1789, since the debates were directed toward other matters. The First Congress argued about the extent to which the national courts should be authorized to exercise *any* equity jurisdiction, not over the law to be applied in such equity jurisdiction as they were allowed.[62] The overriding consideration involved was *trial by jury,* not applicable law, and so these debates do not shed light on the choice-of-law problem.

The universal character of admiralty law as it was understood in 1789 may provide an explanation as to why the national courts were not directed to apply the laws of the several states in admiralty proceedings, particularly since the national admiralty courts had superseded the state courts of admiralty.

The Judiciary Act of 1789 does not address the question of the trial of pirates, either as to whether such trial should be by jury or as to the place of trial when the pirate is captured on the high seas, unless Section 34 speaks to this issue.

Before 1536, in England, pirates were tried in admiralty according to the course of the civil law, and so were not entitled to trial by jury.[63] This was changed by statute in 1536 so as to provide for trial according to the course of the common law, the same as for offenses committed on land.[64]

Then in 1700 Parliament provided that pirates could either be sent to England for trial or tried in the colonies by a special admiralty commission of seven persons; but the duration of this act was limited to seven years.[65] So after 1707 it was not clear whether pirates tried in the American colonies were entitled to trial by jury or not.[66] At least, Pennsylvania and New Jersey saw fit by statute to require proceedings against pirates to be by jury.[67] Section 29 of the Judiciary Act provides that "in cases punishable with death, the trial shall be had in the county where the offence was committed, or where that cannot be done without great inconvenience, twelve petit jurors at least shall be summoned from thence." Inasmuch as piracy on the high seas is not committed in any *county,* it is necessary to resort to Section 34 unless such piracy is to escape all prosecution and punishment. When Congress passed the Crimes Act of 1790 it closed this gap, providing in Section 8 thereof that the trial of crimes committed "out of the jurisdiction of any particular state, shall be in the district where the offender is apprehended, or into which he may first be brought."[68]

At the time the Judicial Bill was being developed, Ellsworth and the other members of the Senate must have been aware of the special problems presented by the trial of pirates.[69] At least originally they were planning on the adoption of a Crimes Bill covering the situation. It is reasonable to think that Section 34 was put into the Judicial Bill to cover this situation if the Crimes Bill was not adopted by the House, as proved to be the case.

If Ellsworth had intended Section 34 to apply to civil proceedings, and especially if he had intended for the section to have an application to the whole proceeding and not just to the "trial," he almost surely would have used a word other than "trials." He would probably have used "actions at common law," as he did in the draft of the Process Bill, and as was done in Section 29 of the Judiciary Act. He might have used the term, "suits at common law," as he did in Section 9 in setting forth the jurisdiction of the district courts. In Section 9, Ellsworth first wrote "civil suits at common law" and then crossed out the word "civil," probably on the ground of redundancy. In Section 11, Ellsworth gave the circuit courts jurisdiction of "all suits at common law," and someone else interlined after "suits" the phrase "of a civil nature." In Section 12, dealing with removal in diversity cases, Ellsworth invariably described the proceedings as "suits," "causes," or "actions." He used the word "trial" only to refer to the presentation of evidence as distinguished from the whole proceeding. In the last sentence of Section 12, Ellsworth provided, "And the trial of facts in the circuit courts shall, in all suits except those of equity and of admiralty and maritime jurisdiction, be by jury."

145

"IN THE COURTS OF THE UNITED STATES"

The section applies in *all* of the United States courts, not just the circuit courts. It applies as well in the district courts and the Supreme Court. Under the Judiciary Act of 1789, no cases founded on diversity jurisdiction could have been brought to a district court.

"IN CASES WHERE THEY APPLY"

It is difficult to give any substantive meaning to this concluding phrase of Section 34, since it seems to be stating the obvious: the laws of the several states shall be applied as rules of decision in cases where they apply and they apply in the cases where they apply. The phrase provides no clue as to *which* are the cases where they are to be applied.

If this section had been directed at the diversity jurisdiction, and the language of the Constitution had been followed, it should have been worded "in controversies where they apply." But if "cases" has a different and broader meaning than "controversies," or of course if the words are synonymous, the language does not rule out application to diversity cases.

By using the word "cases" instead of "controversies" the language is applicable to criminal proceedings, but not necessarily to those proceedings exclusively.

A TEMPORARY NATIONAL COMMON LAW OF CRIMES

The Senate probably anticipated the possibility that the Congress would fail to adopt a Crimes Bill in the first session. It probably provided, in Section 34, that the national courts should apply an American common law of crimes, as opposed to the British criminal common law, until Congress could get around to passage of a code of national crimes. Should the Congress reverse these expectations and pass a Crimes Bill during its first session, Section 34 could easily have been deleted from the Judicial Bill by either house of Congress. In fact the House of Representatives held both bills (passed by the Senate) until very close to the end of the first session, when all legislators were weary with fatigue and the heat of the summer and adjournment was expected momentarily; then, in almost simultaneous fashion the House passed the Judicial Bill (still containing Section 34) and postponed the Crimes Bill.

The only provision of the Judiciary Act that could possibly have been intended to apply to nonstatutory crimes, within national-court jurisdiction by virtue of the provisions of Sections 9 and 11, was Section 34.

With a fine sense of statutory organization the section was placed immediately following Section 33, which relates exclusively to criminal law matters—the arrest, commitment and admission to bail of persons committing crimes or offenses against the United States.

Section 34 said that the temporary rules of decision for nonstatutory crimes were to be "the laws of the several states," a concise substitute for what Ellsworth had originally written in his draft of this section, that the national courts should look to "the Statute law of the several States in force for the time being and their unwritten or common law now in use, whether by adoption from the common law of England, the ancient statutes of the same or otherwise." The "laws of the several states" meant American law, regardless of the source from which it came, and regardless of whether it was statute law or common law.

In Section 34 the Senate had found a happy formula. It had given the national courts a criminal jurisdiction over nonstatutory crimes defined by American law. It had eliminated undesirable features of the British law of crimes. It had recognized in the exception the constitutional definition of treason; it had provided for future statutory changes such as the expected adoption of the Crimes Act without any necessity of amending the Judiciary Act, and it had adopted a system of criminal-law jurisdiction compatible with any constitutional amendments that Congress might propose. The formula seems to have drawn no opposition from any members of Congress.

This interpretation seems to raise only one problem with Section 34. It did not use the word "criminal" in referring to its application. If one assumes, as is done today, that the Constitution gave the national courts a criminal jurisdiction, this was a mistake. But from the standpoint of Ellsworth and the First Congress it may not have been. To have expressly made this section applicable to a criminal jurisdiction would have been to wave a red flag before opponents of the Constitution, since it would have given to the national courts the power to pick and choose and create national crimes. It could have moved up to 1789 the divisive agitation about whether the national courts had a common-law jurisdiction over crimes, agitation that broke out during the last half of the 1790s and early 1800s.[70] And so the word "criminal" could be read into Section 34 or not as best suited each judge's or politician's purposes.

Ironically, the research of Charles Warren supports this view. Warren

147

notes that the Senate had deleted the language "and defined by the laws of the same" from Ellsworth's draft of Sections 9 and 11, where those sections referred to a criminal jurisdiction of the national courts. Warren considers this deletion to be one of the four great changes made by the Senate in the Judicial Bill, finding it to support his view that the national courts were intended to have a common-law criminal jurisdiction. Warren says: "The only rational meaning that can be given to this action striking out the restrictive words is, that Congress did not intend to limit criminal jurisdiction to crimes specifically defined by it."[71] Warren is persuasive on this point, although the conclusion he drew was not as far-reaching as he thought, since the congressional adoption of a national common law of crimes was likely only intended to be temporary.[72]

CONCLUSIONS

Section 34 is a direction to the national courts to apply American law, as distinguished from English law. American law is to be found in the "laws of the several states" viewed as a group of eleven states in 1789, and not viewed separately and individually. It is not a direction to apply the law of a particular state, for if it had been so intended, the section would have referred to the "laws of the respective states."

The section is directed only at the "trial" part of a judicial proceeding and not at the whole of the proceeding.

The section most probably was intended as a temporary measure to provide an applicable American law for national criminal prosecutions, should national criminal prosecutions be brought in the national courts, pending the time that Congress would provide by statute for the definition and punishment of national crimes.

An alternative possibility, although less likely, is that the section was intended as a direction to the national courts to apply American law in all judicial proceedings at common law, both civil and criminal. This application would have included the diversity jurisdiction.

The one thing that can be said with assurance is that Section 34 was not intended to apply exclusively to diversity proceedings; that it was not intended to direct the application of the law of particular states in diversity proceedings; and that it was not intended to apply to suits in equity. In short, on its historical basis, *Erie* is dead wrong.

CHAPTER VIII

Epilogue: An Outline of the History and Interpretation of Section 34

INTRODUCTION

When the First Congress in its Second Session enacted the nation's first Crimes Act, if Section 34 was a temporary gap-filling measure, its purpose had been served. It should have been repealed. But either because such repeal did not conveniently fit into the legislative agenda, or because the section was thought to continue to serve some useful purpose, or perhaps because they forgot about it, this was not done. But beginning in 1790, Section 34 was a statute without any apparent reason or purpose.

And so it was inevitable that lawyers, as well as courts, sought to find a use for it, or perhaps one should say, to find ways in which it would advance their causes. The attorney general of the United States, Edmund Randolph, used it as a springboard to recommend the codification of national law, a project in which he hoped to participate. Lawyers urged its application in criminal cases, and in civil cases. Finally, of course, those urging its application to diversity cases won the battle.

THE 1790 REPORT OF THE ATTORNEY GENERAL

On the order of the House of Representatives, Edmund Randolph, first attorney general of the United States, prepared a report on the judiciary system, which was read in the House of Representatives on December 31, 1790, and printed.[1] Since the judiciary system had just been established, the report is necessarily a critical analysis of the Judiciary Act of 1789. To the modern eye, the report seems poorly organized, and the obscurities of expression make it extremely difficult to understand what Randolph was trying to say;[2] Randolph was trying to steer a middle course between the Federalists and the Anti-Federalists, between such proponents of national power as Ellsworth and such opponents of national power as Lee; consequently, he tried to state matters discreetly, so as not to offend. Unfortunately, his discretion makes his text obscure to us.

The report itself is in three parts. The first part is a general criticism (nine pages) of the existing act; as noted above, his criticisms are decorously phrased, and so one can be left unsure as to exactly how radical his critique is. The second part is the longest part of the report; it comprises an eighteen-page draft for an entirely new Judiciary Act. The third part contains six pages of notes, which explain several sections of the draft. Most of this report is irrelevant to the topic of this chapter, although it would all be relevant to a larger study of the judiciary in the early Republic. For purposes of this chapter, the questions are: what happens to Section 34 in Randolph's draft? What inferences may be drawn?

One can infer from the way that Randolph treats Section 34 that he did not associate this section with diversity jurisdiction. In part, the inference rests on location. Randolph had an organizational plan for his draft, which he stated as follows: "This bill, although not formally divided into cardinal parts, is yet divisible into four. The first contains all that is peculiar to the organization of the district courts; the second, to that of the circuit courts; the third, to that of the supreme court; and the fourth, what is common to two, or the whole of them."[3]

If Randolph had thought that Section 34 was particularly relevant to diversity, then he would have put it in the circuit-court part of the act; but he didn't put it there; he put it in the fourth and last part of the act. However, this negative conclusion—not limited to diversity—is the only sure inference. The positive sweep of Section 34, rewritten as Section 49 in Randolph's draft, is uncertain.

Randolph's proposed Section 49, described in the margin as covering "rules of Decision," was as follows:

49. Rules of decision.
And whereas the Constitution of the United States, and the laws made in pursuance thereof, and all treaties made under the authority of the United States, are the supreme law of the land.

Be it further enacted, That the laws of the several states, so far as the claim of a plaintiff, or the defence of a defendant may depend thereon, in respect to its merits, evidence or limitation of time, shall, subject to the supreme law aforesaid, be rules of decision: that in all pleadings, except in limitations of time, and in all trials, except in matters of evidence, and in the regulations of the executions aforesaid, such statutes, as were made before the fourth day of July, in the year one thousand seven hundred and seventy-six, for the amendment of the law in those cases generally, shall also be rules of decision: and moreover, that the common law, so far as the same be not altered by the supreme law, by the laws of particular states, or by statutes, shall also be a rule of decision.[4]

Note 26, explanatory of the section, read as follows:

(26.) The constitution, laws and treaties of the United States, are the supreme law; that is, they will controul on federal subjects, every other law.

They will particularly controul the laws of the several states; whether consisting of their own original legislation, the common law, or the statute law, expressly or tacitly adopted.

Such is the extent of mere power. But it may be affirmed, that it will not be exercised, because it ought not, where the claim of a plaintiff, or the defence of a defendant, rests upon a valid law of a state.

This may happen—1. In personal rights; 2. Rights of property; 3. Torts; and 4. Sometimes even in offences, upon the merits, the evidence, or a limitation of time.

But besides these, are three other points, not tinctured by the particular cases, but governed only by the class of actions, to which the individual case belongs: pleadings, with the exception of limitation; trial, with the exception of evidence; and executions.

The common law is confessedly incompetent on these topics. The alternative then is, between the state laws, and the statutes.

The latter have the advantage in uniformity, which the judiciary of the United States ought to cultivate; and without it, a citizen who is a debtor in one state, may, although a creditor to an equal amount in another, possibly be ruined.

But some cases will not be influenced by state laws; to wit, those of a foreign and tramsitory [sic] nature, as a bond executed in Europe. The supreme law may also be silent. The lex loci will then be admitted in its customary degree; and where it ends, the common law and statutes aforesaid will enter into the question.

But the Attorney-General considers these expedients as merely temporary; because he trusts, that the necessity of a federal code is too striking to escape the attention of the House. That it must be a work of time, and difficulty is an exhortation immediately to commence it.

Upon so grand an undertaking, the practice of nations has been variant; some having directed the materials of a code to be reported in the first instance, and others a complete digest. As too much leisure and reflection cannot be bestowed on such a composition, the former mode is preferable; especially since the freedom of correcting the matter, may be fettered by the solemnity of a law, when connected with a great whole.

But arduous as this effort must be, it is not boundless. It would probably be pointed to the following leading objects: 1. The provisions which already exist by the Constitution and the federal laws: 2. Such laws as may still be necessary for the further execution of the Constitution, and the completion of federal policy: 3. The common law, and statutes: And, 4. The laws of the several states, as involved in questions arising therein.

These preliminaries having obtained the sanction of Congress, the reducing of them into laws will become more easy and accurate.[5]

Randolph was recommending a code of laws to govern the national judiciary. Mr. Justice Matthews had the following comment upon this proposal:

The other principal suggestion made by Mr. Randolph is that Congress should provide for its own judicial tribunals a federal code of law. This code, it would seem, was to embrace, 1st, a uniform practice and procedure in the administration of justice in those courts; and, 2nd, a body of law which should constitute a rule of decision upon the rights of litigants in those courts. Of course this was not intended to interfere with the operation of the principle that the Constitution, laws, and treaties of the United States were the supreme law of the land, and that in many cases the laws of the States, and sometimes the laws of foreign States, according to the nature of the transaction, would, upon the principles of private international law, be looked to as fixing the rights of the parties.[6]

Randolph would apply "the laws of the several states" to civil proceedings but it is hardly clear whether he is speaking of the law of a particular state or more generally of American law. If he is speaking of the law of a particular state it is difficult to understand what he means by providing that the amendments to those laws made before July 4, 1776, shall also be rules of decision. Why are amendments made after July 4, 1776, ignored, or why is it necessary to specifically mention amendments made before that date? Moreover, Randolph would provide that "the common law, so far as the same be not altered by the supreme law, by the laws of particular states, or by statutes, shall also be a rule of decision."[7] According to the explanatory note, the Constitution, laws, and treaties of the United States are the supreme law and particularly control the laws of the several states. "Such is the extent of mere power. But it may be affirmed, that it will not be exercised, because it ought not, where the claim of a plaintiff, or the defence of a defendant, rests upon a valid law of a state."[8] According to this statement, national law can override all state law, but the power may not be exercised. If Randolph had the diversity jurisdiction in mind, he seems to be saying that national law can be applied, but it probably would not be wise to apply it; however, there is no reason to assume that he is limiting his discussion to diversity cases.

Charles Warren says that Randolph's report shows that he understood Section 34 to include the common-law decisions of the states, as well as the statutes.[9] But this conflicts with Randolph's own statement: "It is conjectured that the common law was omitted among the rules of decision, as having been already the law of the United States. Most probably this will be seldom if ever controverted."[10] In other words, Randolph would have the national courts use the common law (an American common law?), but he did not understand Section 34 to be the vehicle through which such use was commanded.

Although he did not develop the point, Randolph did take notice that the national courts would be called upon to consider conflict of laws or private international law cases. He referred to cases "of a foreign and transitory nature, as a bond executed in Europe." Such a case will not be influenced by state laws and on it, "The supreme law may also be silent." In which situation, "The lex loci will then be admitted in its customary degree; and where it ends, the common law and statutes aforesaid will enter into the question."[11]

But as to conflict-of-laws cases internal to the United States it does appear that Randolph envisioned application of a uniform law, at least after "a federal code" had been developed to cover all the law to be applied by the national courts.

It is most probable that Randolph saw himself as the person to whom Congress should confide the task of developing a federal code.[12] But nothing seems ever to have come of Randolph's ambition to prepare a federal code, nor, for that matter, to Randolph's report.

THE JUDICIARY ACT OF 1801

A strong indication that Section 34 was a temporary provision that soon served its purpose is provided by the Judiciary Act of 1801.[13] Section 34 and all vestiges of it were simply dropped from this act, showing that in 1801 it was understood to have outlived its usefulness.

EARLY APPLICATION TO CRIMINAL PROCEEDINGS

Edmund Randolph wrote James Madison in 1799 that he had considered Section 34 to be applicable in the 1793 prosecution of Gideon Henfield for illegally enlisting on a French privateer.[14] No further record has survived as to Randolph's understanding; from his letter it appears that he considered Section 34 to support this prosecution under the common law.

The relevant paragraph in the letter reads as follows:

> 5. This must have been the idea, if I meant to say that he was triable at common law in the Federal court; that the treaties by stipulating for peace with the U.S., in substance prohibited the citizens of the U.S. from engaging in a war against the nations with whom the treaties subsisted: that treaties being the supreme law, and the judicial act (p. 74) having provided that the laws of the States should be the rule of decision, that they should apply;[15]

In context the reference to the Judicial Act quite clearly is to Section 34, which is confirmed by the fact that Section 34 is found on page 74 of the then-current printing of *The Laws of the United States of America*.[16]

In 1797 Alexander Dallas as defense counsel argued in *Commonwealth v. Schaffer*[17] that Section 34 vested the exclusive jurisdiction of certain offenses in the United States courts. This was a prosecution in the Mayor's Court of Philadelphia for the forgery of papers relating to federal land donations to soldiers who served during the Revolution. The judge, Recorder Wilcocks, sustained his own jurisdiction by rejecting Dallas's argument, saying that Section 34 "plainly refers to trials of a civil nature, according to the course of the common law, and not to the trial of crimes by the rules of the common law."[18]

In the succeeding cases in which an effort was made to use Section 34 in criminal proceedings, the effort was to obtain the application of the law of the state in which the criminal proceeding was taking place rather than the more vague "law of the several states."

In the 1800 prosecution of James Thompson Callender for a seditious libel,[19] defense counsel William Wirt argued that Section 34 provided "that the practice of the courts of Virginia shall be observed in this court."[20]

When Justice Samuel Chase was impeached, Article VI charged Chase with violating Section 34 in that he ordered Callender to trial at the same term at which he was presented and indicted, which it was alleged was contrary to the law of Virginia under which a defendant could not be held to answer until the next succeeding term of court.[21] Chase's defense was multifaceted. He was, he argued, wholly ignorant of the Virginia law at the time of the trial, and it was not called to his attention by counsel for Callender or by District Judge Cyrus Griffin of Virginia, who presided with him at the trial, and it was they, and not he, who would be expected to know of the law and call it to his attention. Also, he argued, there was no Virginia law stating in express terms what the Article of Impeachment alleged, and the Virginia statute from which it was inferred was subject to interpretation. An error of interpretation of the Virginia statute was not an impeachable offense. Furthermore, on the merits, the true interpretation of Section 34 was that it only applied to "civil rights acquired under the state laws," which are to be governed by the laws under which they accrued when questions about them arise in the courts of the United States. If he was incorrect in these opinions, it was an honest error, and could not be considered an offense liable to impeachment.

The prosecution was unable to support this Article of Impeachment, as the testimony of Callender's trial counsel supported Chase, being to the effect that the issue of continuance was raised only in general terms and neither Section 34 nor any Virginia statute was specifically cited and relied upon.[22] In end result, Chase was acquitted on this Article of Impeachment by a vote of thirty to four.[23]

District Judge Pierpont Edwards may have used Section 34 in the District of Connecticut in a series of seditious-libel suits that were begun in 1806, so as to apply a Connecticut statute allowing truth as a defense.[24]

Because of the absence of any type of appeal in criminal proceedings, questions about the application of Section 34 to criminal trials were slow in reaching appellate courts. In 1789 the states did not allow a defendant in a criminal case to appeal, and thereby to obtain a trial *de novo,* as was allowed in some states in civil cases. Nor was there any appellate review on questions of criminal law. The Judiciary Act of 1789 does not provide for any review in criminal cases, either from the district to the circuit court, or from the circuit court to the Supreme Court. A criminal proceeding began and ended in the trial court.

In 1802 an act was passed authorizing the circuit courts to certify questions to the Supreme Court, when the judges were opposed in their opinions.[25] It was not until 1852, however, that the Supreme Court considered the applicability of Section 34 to a national criminal trial. This was in *United States v. Reid,*[26] which came to the Court on a certificate of division between the judges of the Circuit Court for the District of Virginia. Reid and Clements had been jointly indicted for a murder committed on an

American ship on the high seas. They were separately tried. Upon the trial of Reid, he called Clements as a witness in his behalf, but the testimony was rejected on the ground that a co-indictee was not a competent witness. Reid was convicted and moved for a new trial arguing that Clements's testimony was improperly rejected.

On behalf of Reid it was pointed out that an 1849 Virginia statute provided that only a person "jointly tried" with the defendant was incompetent to testify by reason of interest. It was argued on his behalf that Section 34 made this statute applicable to this criminal prosecution and so Clements should have been allowed to testify for Reid.

A unanimous Supreme Court, in an opinion by Chief Justice Taney, rejected the argument that Section 34 applied, saying: "The language of this section cannot, upon any fair construction, be extended beyond civil cases at common law, as contradistinguished from suits in equity. So far as concerns rights of property, it is the only rule that could be adopted by the courts of the United States, and the only one that Congress had the power to establish."[27] Having rejected the applicability of Section 34, the Court went ahead and found by necessary implication from the statute that the "rules of evidence in criminal cases, are the rules which were in force in the respective States when the Judiciary Act of 1789 was passed."[28]

This decision gave impetus to the growing inclination to interpret Section 34 as applying to civil proceedings, particularly to those arising under the diversity jurisdiction. Insofar as the criminal law was concerned, the Supreme Court was not given any power of direct review of federal criminal cases until 1889, and then only of federal convictions where the death penalty had been imposed.[29]

EARLY APPLICATION TO CIVIL PROCEEDINGS

The first reported civil case citing Section 34 is *Brown v. Van Braam*.[30] This was a decision in the Supreme Court on writ of error from the Circuit Court for the District of Rhode Island, in a suit to collect on a bill of exchange protested in London for nonacceptance and nonpayment. Although the facts would indicate that the case arose under the diversity jurisdiction, this is not stated in the report. One of the points at issue was whether the suit had been discontinued in the trial court so that no judgment should have been entered. Counsel for both parties cited Section 34 and argued that under this section the issue should be decided in accordance with the practice and procedure followed in Rhode Island, although they, of course, disagreed as to the result that should be reached under Rhode Island law. Dallas reports that at February Term 1797, Justice James Wilson delivered the opinion of the Court, "We are unanimously of opinion, that under the laws, and the practical construction of the courts, of Rhode Island, the judgment of the Circuit Court ought to be affirmed."[31] And then Dallas adds a note contradicting his report of Wilson's assertion of unanimity in the rationale of the decision. In the note, Dallas says, "Chase, Justice, observed, that he concurred in the opinion of the court; but that it was on common law principles, and not in compliance with the laws and practice of the state."[32] Chief Justice Ellsworth was absent from this term of Court, and so we do not know what he would have said about the applicability of this section of the Judiciary Act that he had drafted.

In the early years of the nineteenth century, Section 34 was cited in civil proceedings, but only infrequently. And when it was, the cases either were not based on the diversity jurisdiction, or at least this basis was not mentioned.

Some cases involved both interstate compacts and lands claimed under grants from two different states,[33] or involved claims deriving from the Northwest Ordinance.[34] In others the United States was plaintiff[35] or a federal land register was the defendant.[36] Others involved executions, but without any indication in the report of the basis of the jurisdiction of the proceeding that led to the judgment.[37] The facts in *M'Niel v. Holbrook,*[38] decided in 1838, are strongly suggestive that this was a diversity case, but the basis of jurisdiction is not stated.

In fact, *Swift v. Tyson,*[39] decided in 1842, appears to be the first case in which the Supreme Court both expressly stated that diversity of citizenship was the basis of jurisdiction and considered the applicability of Section 34 to the substantive merits of the case, although one must soften this conclusion by noting that the express statement in *Swift* was dictum.[40]

In *Swift v. Tyson,* suit had been brought in the Circuit Court of New York by a citizen of Maine to recover as a holder in due course on a bill of exchange from the drawer of the bill, who was a citizen of New York. The defendant claimed that the bill had been obtained from him by fraud and that he had this as a defense against the holder who had taken the bill for a preexisting debt. The Supreme Court had itself twice held that taking a negotiable instrument for a preexisting debt was a giving of value that was sufficient to make the holder one in due course and cut off the drawer's defenses. However, there was a court decision in New York holding that

157

such a taking was not for value, or at least it was arguable that under New York judicial law it was not. The defendant argued that Section 34 required application of this New York rule.

In rejecting this argument, Justice Joseph Story said:

> In the ordinary use of language it will hardly be contended that the decisions of Courts constitute law. They are, at most, only evidence of what the laws are, and are not of themselves laws. . . . In all the various cases, which have hitherto come before us for decision, this Court have uniformly supposed, that the true interpretation of the thirty-fourth section limited its application to state laws strictly local, that is to say, to the positive statutes of the state, and the construction thereof adopted by the local tribunals, and to rights and titles to things having a permanent locality, such as the rights and titles to real estate, and other matters immovable and intraterritorial in their nature and character. . . . And we have not now the slightest difficulty in holding, that this section, upon its true intendment and construction, is strictly limited to local statutes and local usages of the character before stated, and does not extend to contracts and other instruments of a commercial nature, the true interpretation and effect whereof are to be sought, not in the decisions of the local tribunals, but in the general principles and doctrines of commercial jurisprudence.[41]

Somewhat ironically, even if the plaintiff had prevailed on the argument that Section 34 required the application of state law to this civil suit based on the diversity-of-citizenship jurisdiction of the federal courts, it would not have followed that the plaintiff would have won the case. The events surrounding the plaintiff's becoming a holder of this bill of exchange occurred in Maine, not in New York, and insofar as appeared under the law of Maine, plaintiff was a holder in due course.[42]

THE PATH TO ERIE

The question of whether Section 34 applied to diversity cases, or whether it required the application of state statutes in some cases, was not presented for decision in *Swift v. Tyson*. All that Story said about Section 34 requiring the application of state statutes was dictum, uttered in support of the holding that Section 34 did not require application of state judicial decisions.

Nevertheless, when this dictum from *Swift v. Tyson* was viewed along with cases in which the federal courts applied state statutes, whether citing Section 34 in support or not, the thinking developed that Section 34 did require the application of a particular state's statutes to some diversity-of-citizenship cases.

Following upon *Swift v. Tyson* the doctrine came to be accepted that the First Congress actually intended Section 34 to apply to diversity-of-citizenship cases, and that it was intended to apply at least to state statutes. This construction of the section must have influenced the *Reid* decision a decade later, in 1852, when the Supreme Court for the first time said that Section 34 did not apply to criminal cases, but without citing *Swift v. Tyson*.[43]

During the last half of the nineteenth century, legal thinking was gradually changing from a view that judges only find the law, their decisions only being evidence of the "unwritten law," to the view that judges do make law and that their decisions are as much "law" as the statutes passed by the legislature. At the very end of the century, in 1899, Howard M. Carter published a book under the title *The Jurisdiction of Federal Courts, as Limited by the Citizenship and Residence of the Parties*,[44] in which *Swift v. Tyson* is not even listed in the table of cases.

But by 1909 this shift in legal thinking had advanced so far that when John Chipman Gray published *The Nature and Sources of the Law*[45] he argued that since judges make "law," it followed that Congress in Section 34 intended the word "laws" to encompass judicial decisions as well as statutes. And this, Gray argued, must have been the intent of Congress "because in many of the States the statute Law was meagre."[46]

Gray thus exhibits the kind of presentism widely prevalent today, viewing 1789 as though it were a mirror image of 1909. Inasmuch as in 1909 the law consists of many statutes and many judicial decisions, he seems to assume, it must also in 1789 have been similarly as comprehensive, and if the statute law was meagre the decisional law must have been abundant, so Congress in 1789 must have done what a Congress, given the same situation, would be expected to do in 1909.

In the next year, 1910, the Supreme Court decided *Kuhn v. Fairmont Coal Co.*[47] A citizen of Ohio sued a citizen corporation of West Virginia for damages arising out of a coal mining operation on West Virginia land. The Supreme Court of West Virginia had, after the action was brought, decided another case in a way that favored the defendant corporation, which urged application of the West Virginia decision. The plaintiff, on the other hand, argued that the court should decide the case on general principles in order not "to sacrifice truth, justice or law."[48]

The question presented was whether the federal court in a diversity-of-citizenship case was free to decide the case in accordance with its independent view of justice, or was required to follow the law of the state in which the court was sitting. This question had been considered by the Supreme Court many times since 1789, without any hard-and-fast, automatic rule having been developed.

The majority of the Court, in an opinion by Mr. Justice Harlan, held that on the facts the lower federal court should "exercise its own judgment," the Supreme Court itself expressing no opinion on the rights of the parties.[49] Mr. Justice Holmes, with the concurrence of two other justices, dissented, fully embracing the view that judges make law. Holmes said;

> I admit that plenty of language can be found in the earlier cases to support the present decision. That is not surprising in view of the uncertainty and vacillation of the theory upon which *Swift v. Tyson,* 16 Pet. 1, and the later extensions of its doctrine have proceeded. But I suppose it will be admitted on the other side that even the independent jurisdiction of the Circuit Courts of the United States is a jurisdiction only to declare the law, at least in a case like the present, and only to declare the law of the State. It is not an authority to make it. *Swift v. Tyson* was justified on the ground that it was all that the state courts did. But as has been pointed out by a recent accomplished and able writer, that fiction had to be abandoned and was abandoned when this court came to decide the municipal bond cases, beginning with *Gelpcke v. Dubuque,* 1 Wall. 175. Gray, Nature and Sources of the Law, §§ 535–550.[50]

In *Kuhn,* Holmes stated the developing positivist or realist judicial thinking in this way: "The law of a State . . . called the common law . . . is the law as declared by the state judges and nothing else."[51]

When Louis Brandeis joined the Court another adherent to this way of thinking was added.

In 1928 the Supreme Court decided what has come to be the leading attraction in the chamber of horrors attributed to *Swift v. Tyson.* This was *Black and White Taxicab and Transfer Co. v. Brown and Yellow Taxicab and Transfer Co.*[52] Brown and Yellow was originally a Kentucky corporation with an exclusive contract with the Louisville and Nashville Railroad Company to solicit business at the railroad's depot in Bowling Green, Kentucky. In order to seek to avoid the application of certain decisions by the Court of Appeals of Kentucky, Brown and Yellow reincorporated as a Tennessee corporation, and then in the federal court under the diversity jurisdiction sought to enjoin its competitor, Black and White, from having access to the depot. Applying general law, as distinguished from Kentucky law, the federal courts held in favor of Brown and Yellow.

Holmes again dissented, joined by Brandeis and Stone:

> [T]he question is important and in my opinion the prevailing doctrine has been accepted upon a subtle fallacy that never has been analyzed. If I am right the fallacy has resulted in an unconstitutional assumption of powers by the Courts of the United States which no lapse of time or respectable array of opinion should make us hesitate to correct. Therefore I think it proper to state what I think the fallacy is.— The often repeated proposition of this and the lower Courts is that the parties are entitled to an independent judgment on matters of general law. By that phrase is meant matters that are not governed by any law of the United States or by any statute of the State—matters that in States other than Louisiana are governed in most respects by what is called the common law. It is through this phrase that what I think the fallacy comes in.[53]

Holmes again emphasized that judges make law and that Story was wrong when he said in *Swift v. Tyson* that the word "laws" in Section 34 only meant statutes. The decisions of courts, in Holmes's view, were "laws" as much as the statutes passed by legislators. And in support of this argument that Story had been wrong in his interpretation of Section 34, he referred to "An examination of the original document by a most competent hand" citing, but without identifying, the article by Charles Warren, "New Light on the History of the Federal Judiciary Act of 1789," published in 1923.[54]

In this 1928 dissent, Holmes fully developed the argument for overruling *Swift v. Tyson* and for requiring the federal courts in diversity cases to apply state-court decisions. The only thing remaining to be done was to convert a majority of the Court to this jurisprudential view.

Brandeis had long sought to limit the diversity jurisdiction of the federal courts, being persuaded that the Court had more important things to do than handle this type of case. His view was shared by Professor Felix Frankfurter, who with James Landis had written a book on the history of the jurisdiction of the Supreme Court,[55] also writing articles and promoting research directed at improving the federal judicial establishment. A principal thrust of these "reform" efforts was the abolition or restriction of the diversity jurisdiction.[56] Brandeis actively promoted, through Frankfurter, legislation by Congress to restrict the diversity jurisdiction.[57]

The efforts by Brandeis and Frankfurter, among others, to get Congress to act to limit the diversity jurisdiction were unsuccessful, but by 1909—

10 the theoretical underpinnings for the *Erie* decision had been developed, by John Chipman Gray in *Nature and Sources of Law* and by Holmes in his dissent in *Kuhn v. Fairmont Coal Co.* Historical support for the thesis was added in 1923 when Warren published his article "New Light." By 1938 Holmes had retired but Brandeis had garnered enough support in the Supreme Court to modify the diversity jurisdiction by overruling the "supposed rule" of *Swift v. Tyson. Erie Railroad Co. v. Tompkins*[58] was used as the overruling vehicle.

Erie involved a routine controversy without any unusual features. On a July night in 1934, Tompkins was walking along the railroad right-of-way in Hughestown, Pennsylvania, when he was hit and injured by what he claimed was an open swinging door on a refrigerator car of a train coming toward him. He retained the services of a New York lawyer, and in September suit was filed in the United States District Court for the Southern District of New York. Inasmuch as Tompkins was a citizen of Pennsylvania and Erie Railroad a citizen of New York, the federal courts provided a forum for this suit, which could also have been brought in a state court, either in Pennsylvania or New York.

The railroad raised various defenses including one that under a decision of the Supreme Court of Pennsylvania, there could be no recovery without proof of wilful and wanton negligence on the part of the railroad. But the federal district judge held the Pennsylvania decision inapplicable and sent the case to the jury, which returned a verdict for Tompkins for $30,000.

The judgment for Tompkins was affirmed on appeal to the Court of Appeals for the Second Circuit.[59] The Second Circuit found the case easy to dispose of, inasmuch as the railroad conceded that the great weight of authority in other states was contrary to the Pennsylvania decision. "This concession is fatal to its contention, for upon questions of general law the federal courts are free, in absence of a local statute, to exercise their independent judgment as to what the law is; and it is well settled that the question of the responsibility of a railroad is one of general law."[60]

The railroad petitioned the Supreme Court for *certiorari* and the Court took the case. The railroad did not ask the Court to overrule *Swift v. Tyson,* but instead sought an interpretation of the rule that would lead to application of the Pennsylvania decision. At oral argument, led by Brandeis, the Court directed the discussion to the continuing validity of *Swift v. Tyson.*[61] At the Court conference, according to Hughes's biographer, the Chief Justice in laying the case before the conference said, "If we wish to overrule *Swift v. Tyson,* here is our opportunity."[62] And, according to the biographer, "Every judge except Butler and McReynolds agreed that the time for a change had come."[63] The writing of the opinion was assigned to Brandeis.

On April 25, 1938, the Court announced its decision in *Erie*. Brandeis's opinion for the Court was joined by Hughes, Stone, Roberts, and Black. Reed concurred in the judgment only, writing a separate concurring opinion. Butler, joined by McReynolds, dissented. Cardozo did not participate.

An avalanche of comment followed, which still continues. At first, there were criticisms, along the lines of the Butler dissent and the Reed concurrence. But the decision has never been seriously questioned, and it has become "accepted" law. Congress continues to consider abolishing the diversity jurisdiction, and while from time to time the jurisdiction is modified, it still remains a significant part of the federal-court caseload.

No one, it seems, has ever questioned the historical basis of the decision, whether Congress intended for Section 34 to apply to diversity at all, and if it did, whether there was any historical support for the "supposed" *Swift v. Tyson* rule that Section 34 requires the application of state statutes but not judicial decisions.

While Warren's article provided what seemed to be a sound historical basis for overruling *Swift v. Tyson,* even if the historical facts had been known to the Court, the result would probably have been the same, the only difference being that the opinion for the Court would not have relied upon history for support.[64]

The First Congress did not write Section 34 into the Judiciary Act of 1789 for the purpose of giving the national courts directions as to the law to be applied in diversity cases. Furthermore, no court said that the First Congress did so for that purpose—until years after *Swift v. Tyson* had been decided.

There is no historical support for either the *Erie* decision, for the supposed rule of *Swift v. Tyson,* or for the current view of the work of the First Congress relating to this subject.

Charles Warren and the Judiciary Act of 1789

INTRODUCTION

THE ACCURACY OF Charles Warren's article, "New Light on the History of the Federal Judiciary Act of 1789,"[1] has gone virtually unchallenged for sixty years. While Professor Julius Goebel does call attention to some of Warren's errors and misinterpretations, he does so in such an indirect way that the force of his critical comments are dissipated and leave little impression on the reader. As a result Warren's article is currently the "accepted" history of this act, which established the national judiciary.

The time is long overdue for a critical examination of Warren's article. This book has undertaken to do this with respect to Warren's principal subjects and conclusions. Such examination reveals this article to be riddled with demonstrable errors, as well as mythologizing many questionable interpretations of the primary source materials. A rewriting of the history of the Judiciary Act of 1789 requires discarding most of the interpretations embodied in Warren's article, although Warren should be given credit for the many primary sources he located and used in the article, and for the interpretations that still stand up to modern inspection.

THE WRITING OF "NEW LIGHT"

Warren's three-volume history of the Supreme Court was published in May 1922.[2] The work begins, appropriately, with Washington's appointment on September 24, 1789, of the first justices of the Supreme Court.[3] There is no discussion of the development of the Judiciary Act of 1789.

In this work, Warren leaves no doubt as to how he felt about *Swift v. Tyson*.[4] He writes, "This decision . . . introduced a novel and original doctrine into Federal law. . . . Probably no decision of the Court has ever given rise to more uncertainty as to legal rights . . . and the adverse criticisms by Judges and jurists, which have continued to the present day, have had much justification."[5]

The next month, on June 23, 1922, Judge Louis Brandeis, who had known Warren for years,[6] wrote Warren a highly congratulatory letter about the work. "Since I joined the Court no book has given me so much instruction or more pleasure." He continued with a suggestion: "Have you ever thought of writing on the lower Federal courts? A consideration of their functioning in the past would be interesting and it would help in determining their province for the future. My impression is that it should be abridged—particularly in criminal cases."[7]

In researching his history of the Supreme Court, Warren would have run across the statement by Henry Flanders that a draft of the Judicial Bill in Oliver Ellsworth's handwriting was "still preserved in the archives of the Government."[8] An assiduous researcher into primary sources, Warren's effort to locate the draft thus seems probable, even inevitable. But if he had not already begun this research, the letter from Brandeis could not but have stimulated his interest.[9]

The published materials do not show that at this early a date Brandeis was interested in upsetting the *Swift v. Tyson* decision. But it is certain that in the later twenties both he and his friend Professor—later Justice— Felix Frankfurter were very much interested in limiting the diversity jurisdiction of the federal courts.[10]

It is hardly too much to say that, in researching the history of the Judiciary Act of 1789, Charles Warren found what he very much wanted to find, and Justice Brandeis liked what he found. Although Warren's article purports to be a scholarly historical inquiry, the most charitable view that can be taken is that his bias against *Swift v. Tyson* so colors his views that he is unable to use his materials with anything approaching objectivity.

In a way his scholarship was doomed from the beginning by his failure (already detailed in chapter 7) to realize that the Senate used a printed bill during its deliberations and not the manuscript bill that he had found. In fitting amendments, both manuscript and from the *Journal,* into this manuscript bill, Warren simply ignores page and line directions that showed that the technique he was following was wrong.

A little more understandable is the fact that Warren reads some of the material on the manuscript bill, intended for inserts into the draft, as being amendments made by the Senate,[11] but surely it was unrealistic to think the Senate recorded amendments on the manuscript.

If one ignores how fast and loose Warren plays with page and line references in order to substantiate his views of *Swift,* it must be admitted that the results he obtains do make some sense. For sixty years, his findings have remained orthodoxy. But Warren's failing is a common one. Everyone tends to find what he is looking for. Everyone views new evidence as tending to support arrived-at conclusions, rather than throwing doubt on them. This inquiry into Warren's failings is not only a criticism of Warren, but also a warning, for this writer as well as others, to beware of finding what one is looking for.

Attention will now be turned to an examination of the validity of Warren's interpretation of the history of the Judiciary Act of 1789. The defects in his history of Section 34 have been detailed in chapter 7, but other significant aspects of the act will be looked at here.

THE MANUSCRIPTS

About 1922 Charles Warren discovered in the attic and basement of the Capitol some manuscripts on which he based his famous article, "New Light," published in 1923 in the November issue of the *Harvard Law Review.* The article has strongly influenced the interpretation and application of the federal judicial statutes.

Warren says of the bill: "While statements have been made by various historians that the original Draft Bill was preserved and that it was in the handwriting of Oliver Ellsworth, no one has apparently ever consulted it, and the existence of the other papers has not been known, hitherto." Warren goes on to describe how he "discovered" the manuscripts:

> Through the aid and courtesy of the Secretary of the Senate, the Draft Bill and the amendments were located in the Senate Files in the attic of the Capitol; the Bill as passed by the Senate was discovered in a cellar room, under a heap of miscellaneous papers of confused and intermingled dates and subject.
>
> At the same time with the discovery of these papers, the writer has also found that a copy of the Draft Bill originally introduced into the Senate was published in full in the *Boston Gazette,* of June 29, and July 6, with the interesting omission, however, of the diverse citizenship jurisdiction granted to the Circuit Courts by the Bill.[12]

Warren does not further describe the "Bill as passed by the Senate" that he found in the cellar, but it presumably is the engrossed bill.[13] After Warren finished using the manuscripts he left them with the Library of Congress. It appears that the manuscripts again became "lost,"[14] but were found again and are now in the National Archives.

Warren gives this description of the manuscripts:

It now appears upon examination, that the original Draft Bill is in several different handwritings. Sections 1 to 9 inclusive are in the handwritings of William Paterson; Sections 10 to 23 are, in all probability, in the handwriting of Oliver Ellsworth; Section 24 is in the handwriting of Caleb Strong; and the succeeding Sections are written by a recording clerk. On this original document comprising the draft Bill as introduced into the Senate, the changes, additions, insertions and deletions made during the process of construction by the Committee and before its introduction into the Senate, appear in handwriting in the body of the draft, and on its margin, and on slips of paper pasted or affixed by sealing wax upon it. The amendments offered in the Senate are contained in various handwritings and on odd, loose slips of paper of different sizes and shapes, preserved in a bundle, in the Senate Files. The Draft Bill, as amended and adopted by the Senate, is in the handwriting of a recording clerk.[15]

There are sufficient samples of the handwriting of Paterson, Ellsworth, and Strong to remove any reasonable doubt about the accuracy of Warren's identification of these draftsmen. The "in all probability" in the identification of Oliver Ellsworth as the draftsman of Sections 10 through 23 should be deleted. The manuscript "Judicial Bill" that Warren found is the "copy" that was given to the printer on June 12, or very soon thereafter, after the manuscript had been reported by the subcommittee to the Senate.

Warren, in the preparation of his article, used the manuscripts, the Senate and House *Journals,* Maclay's *Journal,* and some of the correspondence, newspaper accounts, and similar items. He did not use the printed Senate and House bills.

MYTHICAL CHANGES IN THE DEVELOPMENT OF THE JUDICIAL BILL

Warren writes that the new evidence that he had found in the way of manuscripts made it possible "to write, for the first time, an accurate history of the progress of the Act through the Congress, and of the variations of the final Act from the original Draft Bill."[16] Such an accurate history, he continues, "makes it certain that Madison was wrong in stating, in 1836 (when he was eighty-five years of age and probably of failing memory), that 'it was not materially changed in its passage into a law.'"[17] While opinions may differ as to what constitutes "material changes" it would appear that Madison was correct and that the bill was not materially changed in its passage into a law. With one exception the material changes that Warren points to were illusory. It is surprising how very little the bill was changed during its passage through the Senate committee, the Senate, and the House; most of the changes made were stylistic rather than matters of real substance.

Quite naturally, Warren's coverage of the development of the Judicial Bill is not limited to a discussion of the manuscripts he had found. He undertakes to cover the whole story from the time the Senate Judiciary Committee was named. The result is that he blends together into "New Light" the newly found manuscripts and information derived from other sources, particularly from correspondence.

It is not always easy to determine the exact stage at which Warren is saying that some particular development took place. Essentially, Warren seeks to identify six distinct stages in the development of the Judiciary Act. These are:

1. The thinking of the Judiciary Committee three weeks after its appointment, as shown by a letter written by Ellsworth under date of April 30. Warren says this letter probably outlines "the first or an early draft" prepared by Ellsworth for the consideration of the committee,[18] but it seems doubtful that Ellsworth had prepared what in present-day terminology would be called a "draft."
2. The thinking of the Judiciary Committee at some unspecified later time, after April 30 but before June 12, as shown by a letter published in the *State Gazette of North Carolina* of July 30.[19]
3. The bill as introduced into the Senate on June 12.
4. Changes made in the bill by the Senate during its consideration, from June 22 to July 17. (To a very limited extent Warren distinguishes between changes made during second reading and those made on third reading.)
5. Changes made in the bill by the House.
6. Changes made by the conference committee.

Although the manuscripts Warren found cast "new light" only on the bill as it existed at stages three, four, and six, some of Warren's major conclusions are drawn from his comparison of the bill at stages one, two, and three, and it is here that Warren begins creating myths.[20] Because of the sweeping conclusions Warren draws from very slender sources, it is necessary to reexamine all the sources Warren used in some detail.

Development of the Judicial Bill in the Committee

Warren finds "three strikingly different provisions" in the second stage of the development of the bill from what it had contained at the first stage, and then he finds that "the Bill which was finally agreed upon and reported to the Senate markedly differed from both of these early drafts."[21] While Warren does not clearly distinguish between these stages, it is possible to determine what he had in mind.

To show the thinking of the Judiciary Committee as regards the organization of a federal judicial system when the bill was in its first stage, that is, as of April 30, Warren quotes from the aforementioned letter of Oliver Ellsworth, written to Richard Law under that date. In describing the circuit court, Ellsworth wrote (according to Warren): "This Court to receive appeals in some cases from the District Court, to try high crimes, to have original jurisdiction in law and equity, in controversies between foreigners and citizens and between citizens of different States, etc., where the matter in dispute exceeds five hundred dollars."[22]

The second stage of development Warren discovers in a letter written "from a gentleman in New York to his friend in Winchester, Virginia" and published in the *State Gazette of North Carolina* on July 30, 1789. In light of the importance Warren attaches to this letter, the text as published in the *State Gazette* is set forth below in full:

EDENTON, July 30.

Extract of a letter from a gentleman in New York, to his friend in Winchester, Virginia.

The Senate have had the judiciary system before them. No bill is yet brought in, but the Committee have agreed to the following principals [*sic*].

That there shall be a Court of Admiralty in each state, to consist of one judge; who, besides his admiralty jurisdiction, shall have criminal jurisdiction in smaller offences.

That the Supreme Court shall consist of six Judges.

That the states shall be divided into circuits, and each circuit into districts.

That Inferior Courts shall be held twice a year in each district, which courts shall consist of two of the Supreme Judges and the Admiralty Judge, and shall take cognizance of all cases of federal jurisdiction, whether in law or equity, above the value of 500 dollars (inferior matters to be left to the State Courts) and of all criminal cases, not within the jurisdiction of the Admiralty Judges.—This court shall act as a *nisi prius* Judge, in cases originating in the Supreme Court, and as a Court of Appeals from the Admiralty Court; and from this Court no appeal shall lie, except the matter in dispute be of the value of 2000 dollars; and in common law cases in points of law only. In cases of concurrent jurisdiction, the plaintiff may sue either in the State or Federal Court, but having made his option, he shall abide by it. A defendant sued in a State Court, in a matter of federal jurisdiction, may remove the cause to the Federal Court, before trial, but will not be allowed to appeal.

Warren's interpretation of these two parts of these two letters is as follows:

[The] latter letter, while confirming the general scheme in Ellsworth's letter, sets forth three strikingly different provisions; while Ellsworth stated the civil jurisdiction of the Circuit Courts to be only of controversies between foreigners and citizens and between citizens of different States in cases involving over five hundred dollars, the New York letter stated that the Circuit Court was "to have cognizance *of all cases of federal jurisdiction, whether in law or equity* above the value of five hundred dollars"; and while Ellsworth's letter stated that appeals were to lie "*except as to facts,*" the New York letter stated that "no appeal shall lie, except the matter in dispute be of the value of two thousand dollars and *in common law cases on points of law only,*" and the New York letter stated that a defendant in a State Court presenting a Federal Question was to be allowed to remove before trial, but not to appeal, to a Federal Court.[23]

The "three strikingly different provisions" are:
1. The second stage gives the federal courts a federal-question jurisdiction, whereas the first stage did not;
2. The second stage allowed appeals "in common law cases on points of law only," whereas the first stage allowed appeals "except as to facts"; and
3. The second stage provided for removal of diversity cases from the state courts to the federal courts "before trial, but not to appeal."

While interpretation of these letters must be undertaken with considerable caution, under a reasonable interpretation they are describing the *same* judicial plan. In referring to "all cases of Federal jurisdiction" the New York letter was not referring to what has come to be known as "federal-question" jurisdiction, but instead was referring to the "diversity" jurisdiction. The supposed difference in appeals to the Supreme Court is semantic only, there being no difference between an appeal on points of law only and an appeal except as to facts. While the New York letter does refer to removal of diversity cases and Ellsworth in his April 30 letter did not, it does not follow that removal was not in the contemplation of the committee when Ellsworth wrote, but even if it was added it is hardly a "strikingly *different* provision" unless it had been contemplated at the first stage of the bill that the state courts would be barred from exercising jurisdiction in diversity cases, something that seems never to have been contemplated.

The letter published in the *State Gazette of North Carolina* on which Warren leans so heavily is a slender reed. It was a letter from an unknown gentleman in New York sent to an unknown correspondent in Winchester, Virginia, and which reached the *State Gazette* by some unknown means. Moreover, the date the original letter was written is unknown, and so its dating as having been written later rather than earlier than Ellsworth's letter of April 30 is pure conjecture.

Reported Bill as Compared with Bill in Earlier Stages

When Warren compares the bill as reported to the Senate on June 12 with the earlier versions, as he understands them to have existed, he reports finding the following differences:

> The Bill as reported, as appears now from the Senate Files and as published in the *Boston Gazette,* eliminated entirely the jurisdiction of the Circuit Court over "all cases of federal jurisdiction"; it also contained a much restricted jurisdiction over cases between citizens of the different States; it limited appeals, not only "in common law cases" but in all other cases, to appeals purely on questions of law, on writ of error; and—a very important change—it allowed a defendant sued in a State Court in a case involving a Federal question, not only to remove the case before trial into a Federal Circuit Court, but also to appeal, after trial to the Supreme Court on writ of error.[24]

The reported bill made none of these changes. There is no indication that the Judiciary Committee ever intended to give the federal courts an *express* "federal-question" jurisdiction, but this is different from saying that the committee did not intend for the federal courts to have such a jurisdiction. The reported bill did not restrict the diversity jurisdiction. The reported bill did not change the subject of "appeals" to the Supreme Court. The reported bill did not change the provisions relating to removal of diversity cases.

Changes Made by the Senate in the Judicial Bill

Warren says that, on the basis of the manuscripts he found, "It is clear now that very important and, in some instances, vital changes were made from the Draft Bill before it became law."[25] If these changes had been known to the Supreme Court, "several of the leading cases before that court might have been decided differently." Warren refers specifically to three cases:

United States v. Hudson,[26] *United States v. Coolidge,*[27] and *Swift v. Tyson,*[28] with the last drawing most of the attention. Warren says, referring to his discovery of the manuscript Section 34, "Had Judge Story seen this original draft of the amendment, it is almost certain that his decision would have been the reverse of what it was."[29]

Warren refers to four great changes having been made in the Judicial Bill by the Senate before it was passed: (1) the criminal-law jurisdiction of the lower federal courts was enlarged to include common-law crimes; (2) the diversity jurisdiction of the federal courts was restricted; (3) Section 34 was added to the bill as an amendment, not being in the draft bill; and (4) a change on the manuscript of the amendment showed that Section 34 was intended to apply to common law as well as statute law.

The present writer draws the following conclusions about Warren's great changes: (1) The first great change rests on a comparison of the draft bill and the bill as passed by the Senate, there being no record of when or why the change was effected. Warren's conclusions in this regard seem accurate, if a bit expansive, and a discussion of this matter can be found in chapter 6. (2) The second change is nonexistent, growing out of nothing more than Warren's placing a manuscript amendment at the wrong place in the bill. This has been discussed in chapter 4. (3) While it is true that the third change came into the bill by an amendment, this book shows that such reduces rather than magnifies its importance, and further that Warren's interpretation of the action is marred by his locating the amendment at the wrong place in the bill. (4) Warren's interpretation of the manuscript is pretty much an example of the wish being father to the thought. The third and fourth "changes" have been discussed in chapter 7. While each of Warren's so-called great changes has been discussed in the text where appropriate, and three of them have proved illusory, Warren makes other important errors in his explication of the 1789 act.

WARREN INVENTS TRIAL BY JURY IN NATIONAL EQUITY SUITS

Warren's failure to recognize that it was the printed bill and not the manuscript bill that was before the Senate leads him into an error regarding equity and trial by jury. He writes: "The next change made by the Senate was one which, if retained, would have completely altered the Federal judicial procedure in equity trials. . . . Now, the Senate took the extraordinary and radical step of amending the Draft Bill, so as to require jury trials in all suits in equity. Luckily, at a later date, the Senate reversed its action."[30] Later, Warren explains this action a little more fully: "This provision which would have revolutionized equity procedure, the Senate now voted to expunge, not being willing to yield any further to the anti-equity faction."[31] In footnote 79, Warren explains:

> See Senate Journal, July 10. The entry reads: "On motion it was agreed to reconsider the amendment, page 13th, line 35, 'or on any hearing of a cause in equity in a circuit court.'" Until the recent discovery of the original Draft Bill, it was impossible to locate the point in the bill where this amendment had occurred. It now appears to have been at the end of Section 10 of the Draft Bill (Section 9 of the Act) relative to the jurisdiction of the District Courts.[32]

The last sentence of Section 9 provides: "And the trial of facts in both cases last mentioned shall be by jury." Warren apparently thinks that the deleted phrase came after the words "last mentioned." Warren does procrustean tailoring on both the amendment and the manuscript bill to get the fit leading to his conclusion. First of all, he quotes only a part of the motion to reconsider. The full text of the amendment, as reported in the *Senate Journal* is as follows: "On motion it was agreed to reconsider the amendment, page 13th, line 35th, 'Or on any hearing of a cause in equity in a circuit court'; and in line 39th, to reconsider 'Or supreme court, as the case may be—' So the words were struck out."[33] Warren discusses the two parts separately, as though there were distinct amendments. He inserts them into the manuscript bill on page 14, not on page 13, and for the line count for the first part he used the section, and not the page, arriving at a dubious count at that. And for the second part, he simply ignores the reference to line 39, there being no line that can be so numbered by any count.[34]

Lines 35 and 39 on page 13 of the printed bill refer to portions of Section 30 where the deleted language fits comfortably. It is obvious that the Senate was dealing with something very different from what Warren thinks was involved.

A major concern of the Senate was to deal with "appeals" that resulted in trials *dé novo*. We have seen that a criticism of the Constitution made in the ratifying conventions was that by the use of appeals litigants would be dragged to far parts of the country to go through a second, and perhaps even a third trial. Section 30 was originally designed merely to *alleviate* the problem by providing for the use of depositions and other techniques, including the one involved in this amendment. If a party told the district court he probably could not produce a witness to testify at a later trial in court he probably could not produce a witness to testify at a later trial in the circuit court, or, when the proceeding was in the circuit court, if a party told the court he probably could not produce a witness to testify at a later trial in the Supreme Court, then the testimony would be taken down in writing for use at that later trial in the circuit court or the Supreme Court, as the case might be.

But then the Senate amended the bill so as to eliminate rather than to alleviate this problem. The Senate decided that civil actions in the district court could be taken up to the circuit court only by writ of error, and that all actions in the circuit court could be taken to the Supreme Court only by writ of error. Since this provided only a review of law, and not of fact, it eliminated the possibility of having second trials in the reviewing court. It was therefore unnecessary to take down in writing the testimony in the first trial court for use at a second trial, because there would be no second trial. Thus the alleviating provision in section 30 had been nullified. Consequently the motion to reconsider and to strike.

And so the amendments made by the Senate make good sense, but they have nothing to do with jury trials in equity suits. The Senate never added jury trials in equity suits, so it never subtracted them either. Instead the result of the overall Senate action is reflected in Section 21 of the final act, which allows the circuit court to review admiralty cases by appeal, but under Section 22 it can review civil actions only by writ of error. Thus in the circuit court admiralty cases can be tried a second time, but civil actions cannot be tried a second time. Similarly, all review by the Supreme Court was limited to use of a writ of error, and so all possibility of having second trials in the Supreme Court was eliminated. Consequently, the Senate struck the language from the bill that provided a means of preserving testimony for use in a second trial in the Supreme Court.

WARREN CONFUSES WHO'S FOR AND WHO'S AGAINST EQUITY

Section 16 of the Judicial Bill, as introduced, contained the following restriction on the equity jurisdiction of the federal courts: "That suits in equity shall not be sustained in either of the courts of the United States, in any case where remedy may be had at law." This is the language that Ellsworth used on page 20 of the manuscript bill. Later he added and struck out some additional language.[35]

The section received a good deal of attention from the Senate. At some point, probably before July 11, the word "complete" was inserted before "remedy." Many senators still opposed the restriction on equity that the section embodied.

According to Maclay, on July 1, on second reading, "Dr. Johnson rose first against the clause [Section 16]. Ellsworth answered him, and the following gentlemen, all in turn, Lee, Reed, Bassett, Paterson, and Grayson. Strong spoke in favor of the clause. The lawyers were in a rage of speaking."[36] Johnson and the other proponents of equity lost on this day, for Maclay reports, "The clause stood on the question."

On Saturday, July 11, on third reading, the Senate changed its mind and voted to expunge Section 16.[37] The leaf in Maclay's *Journal* containing most of his comments for this date has been destroyed, but from what is left it appears that some, perhaps most, of the lawyers who had been in the convention, but not including Ellsworth, viewed this as a triumph.

Maclay also says that there was something of a confrontation between himself and Johnson as they came down the stairs after the session ended. Maclay said, "Doctor, I wish you would leave off using these side-winds, and boldly, at once, bring in a clause for deciding all causes on civil law principles, without the aid of a jury." Johnson demurred, saying that "the civil law is a name I am not very fond of." But Maclay rejoined, "You need not care about the name, since you have got the thing."[38] Maclay, an opponent of equity with Ellsworth and Strong, disliked a broad equitable jurisdiction without restraints.

On the following Monday, July 13, Maclay reports that he asked Ellsworth if he would not join in an attempt to regain the clause "we had lost on Saturday," and he agreed to do so.[39] "Mr. Elsworth rose and spoke long on the subject of the necessity of a discrimination or some boundary-line between the courts of chancery and common law. He concluded with a motion nearly in the words of the clause we had lost," there being an addition of the words, "plain, adequate, and" before "complete."

In supporting the Ellsworth motion, Maclay reports that he said:

As the bill stood, chancery was open to receive everything. In England, where by the letter of the law no suit could be brought in chancery if the common law afforded a remedy, yet such was the nature of that court, and so advantageous had it been found to the practitioners, that it encroached greatly on the common law. Gentlemen would not consider this as an inconvenience. So high were their ideas of English jurisprudence they said all the world admired it, and every member of this House must admire it.

He goes on to describe the evils of the chancery system in England, as he saw it: "The present bill before you has been considered as enjoying perfection in proportion as it approaches the British system." Noting that with some people "English features will be no recommendation of the bill," he concludes:

> The bill, however, before you, as it now stands, is not chancery. It is something much worse. The line between chancery and common law is broken down. All actions may now be tried in the Federal courts by the judges without the intervention of a jury. The trial by jury is considered as the birthright of every American. It is a privilege they are fond of, and let me add, it is a privilege they will not part with.

The Senate voted to accept the amendment proposed by Ellsworth and restored Section 16 to the bill.

The Wingate copy of the printed bill reflects this action. It is marked to reflect the addition of the word "complete" and also the later addition of the words "plain adequate &."

Warren simply misreads the *Senate Journal* in interpreting this account of the development of Section 16. He concludes that the supporters of equity were seeking to retain the section in the bill, while the opponents were seeking to delete it. He misses the fact that the section was expunged on July 11 and then restored on July 13, with the addition of a couple of words.[40] And so Warren also says that the section was only amended on July 13 with the addition of the "plain, adequate &" phrase, instead of its being actually restored on that date.[41] According to Warren, "When this Section was taken up, the batteries of those who opposed all equity jurisdiction were at once opened."[42] Warren has the wrong side firing. It was the batteries of those who *favored* equity that were firing, since by striking the section, the equity jurisdiction would be enlarged.

The circuit courts had been given jurisdiction in Section 11 of cases of both common-law and equity jurisdiction. Section 16 is meaningful only if it is viewed as placing restrictions on that grant, not so much in the sense of what cases the federal courts could entertain but rather on whether they could treat them as common-law cases, requiring trial by jury, or as equity cases, with no right to trial by jury. It was this fear of the effect on trial by jury that led senators such as Maclay so strongly to oppose the federal exercise of equity.

THE CONSTITUTION, SECTION 13, AND *MARBURY V. MADISON*

In drafting Section 13 of the Judiciary Act of 1789, most particularly in extending to the Supreme Court the power to issue writs of *mandamus* in an original proceeding, Ellsworth did exactly what John Marshall later said the Constitution did not permit.

The language of Ellsworth was carried unchanged into the printed bill and into the act, except for changing an ampersand to "and." Yet in *Marbury v. Madison* John Marshall, referring to this provision in Section 13, said: "If congress remains at liberty to give this court appellate jurisdiction, where the constitution has declared their jurisdiction shall be original; and original jurisdiction where the constitution has declared it shall be appellate; the distribution of jurisdiction, made in the constitution, is form without substance."[43]

Although Warren points out that five members of the Judiciary Committee had been members of the Federal Convention[44] and by a footnote citation implied that this provides weighty evidence of the true meaning of the Constitution,[45] Warren has nothing to say in "New Light' about Section 13 and how it fared in *Marbury v. Madison*.[46] However, in *The Supreme Court in United States History,* Warren has the following to say about this decision and the statute involved:

> It seems plain, at the present time, that it would have been possible for Marshall, if he had been so inclined, to have construed the language of the section of the Judiciary Act which authorized writs of mandamus, in such a manner as to have enabled him to escape the necessity of declaring the section unconstitutional. The section was, at most, broadly drawn, and was not necessarily to be interpreted as conferring original jurisdiction on the Court.[47]

But if the provision of the statute was to be interpreted in accord with the intent of the draftsman and his colleagues on the committee and in the Senate, it almost surely did mean that the Supreme Court was given original jurisdiction to issue writs of *mandamus* to a national official. That is what the section says.

If the plain language of this part of Section 13 standing alone is not sufficient to show that, contrary to Warren, the First Congress felt it had power to arrange the original and appellate jurisdiction of the Supreme Court, the history of another part of the same section does so in unmistakable fashion.

Section 13 of the Judicial Bill was subjected to debate in the Senate on June 30. The debate was not about the provision involved in *Marbury v. Madison;* instead the Senate was concerned about which national court should exercise jurisdiction over ambassadors, public ministers, and consuls.[48] In end result Section 13 was amended, by a provision, again drafted by Ellsworth, by which the exclusive original jurisdiction of the Supreme Court in this regard was limited to suits *against* ambassadors, other public ministers, and their domestics. As regards suits brought by them, or to which consuls were parties, the amendment provided that the Supreme Court should not have exclusive jurisdiction. This left the subject to be governed by the general provisions of Sections 9 and 11 relating to suits in the district and circuit courts involving foreigners.[49] Ellsworth had converted the Supreme Court's constitutionally given original jurisdiction over suits by ambassadors, other public ministers, or consuls into a *concurrent* original jurisdiction, and so at least in part a jurisdiction appellate in the Supreme Court. On July 1, the Senate considered the provision and went further than Ellsworth's amendment, eliminating entirely the Court's original jurisdiction over consuls and vice-consuls.[50] In light of this action, Ellsworth rewrote this part of Section 13,[51] and this rewriting was carried into the final act.

While Warren mentions this action, and quotes Ellsworth's rewriting in a footnote, he has no comment other than to say in the footnote that "Section 13 and the Constitution are in accord," telling the reader to look at three Supreme Court cases. The cases referred to do not so much as mention the part of Section 13 relating to ambassadors, but deal only with the part relating to the Supreme Court's jurisdiction when a state is a party.

If Congress has the power under the Constitution to regulate the jurisdiction of the entire judicial department, the language of the Constitution is broad enough to authorize Section 13 as finally written, including the *mandamus* and the foreign-minister provisions. In Section 13, the First Congress showed that it understood the Constitution to be broad enough to permit it to regulate the original jurisdiction of the entire judicial department. Viewed from the 1789 standpoint, then, it is only the *Marbury v. Madison* interpretation of the Constitution that is untenable.

The Sources for a History of the Judiciary Act of 1789

THE MANUSCRIPTS

What is known today about the work of the First Congress and the development of the Judiciary Act of 1789 is based on the manuscripts and printed documents of the period that have survived. A surprisingly large amount of materials from the period of the First Congress has survived, particularly manuscripts. At the same time it appears that many manuscripts and printed documents have not survived. Of course there is no way of knowing the full extent of what has been lost. The nearly two hundred years of "interpretation" that have followed upon the events of 1789 cannot add to the record of primary sources. Later interpretations are useful but they cannot supersede or prevail over the primary sources. While, as James Hutson has recently pointed out, the sources are biased and somewhat untrustworthy,[1] that is a problem pervading all historical source material. It is the historian's job to make the best judgments possible based upon the available sources.

What do we have in the way of primary source materials, manuscripts and documents written in 1789 or at least thereabouts? What can we discover to be missing? The extant materials, with particular reference to the Judicial Bill, are listed below by more or less chronologically related categories, and then the materials in each category are evaluated.

1. Manuscript senate Judicial Bill and related manuscripts, including twenty-eight documents.

2. Senate Judicial Bill printed and delivered about June 16 (five known copies, including Senator Paine Wingate's copy).

3. Senate Judicial Bill printed and delivered about June 23.

4. Senate engrossed bill.

5. House Judicial Bill printed and delivered about July 23.

6. Enrolled bill.

7. Manuscript report by the Senate of the results of a conference with the House.

8. Certified copies and slip laws.

9. Senate and House *Journals*.

10. Newspaper accounts.

11. Letters, diaries, and other unofficial materials, including especially Senator William Maclay's diary.

Manuscript Senate Judicial Bill and Related Manuscripts

These are the manuscripts that Charles Warren found about 1922 in the attic of the Capitol, as described in appendix 1. There are forty-nine separate manuscript leaves, most of them written both front and back. Subsequent to the time Warren examined the documents, the Library of Congress stamped each leaf on the front (as the library understood the front) lower lefthand corner with a number, 1 through 47, and later added two more numbers, in handwriting, 33a and 44a. In this book these manuscripts are referred to by "LC" and these numbers, as "LC 7" or "LC 7 Back." Warren had no convenient way to cite the individual manuscripts and simply describes them and cites the "Senate Files."[2] Julius Goebel did use the Library of Congress numbers, citing individual manuscripts in the style of "Chit stamped 22."[3]

Handwritten on the first nineteen of these manuscript leaves of eight-by-thirteen-inch paper is the earliest known version of the Judicial Bill. The leaves are written on front and back (with one back wholly blank). The first eighteen leaves are stamped on the front 1 through 18. The nineteenth leaf was torn in two, and the separate parts were stamped by the Library of Congress with the numbers 19 and 20. LC 44a is the text of a change intended for insertion on the LC 15 leaf of the manuscript bill, and which was originally wafered to the bill, but which became loose sometime after I inspected the bill in 1956. Another such slip, not stamped with an LC number, is still wafered to LC 20. Thus, the manuscript Judicial Bill consists of twenty-one sheets of paper, containing the provisions the subcommittee set before the whole committee plus two amendments, one of which is still wafered on.

LC 1 through LC 6 are in the handwriting of William Paterson and contain the first nine sections of the bill as later printed. Paterson numbered his sections, 1 through 9, and he also numbered the fronts of the leaves on the lefthand margin, 1-3-5-7-9-11. He did not number the backs. Paterson's draft ends on the back of LC 11, which also contains a clerk's endorsement.

LC 7 through the top of the front of LC 14 are in the handwriting of Oliver Ellsworth and contain Sections 10 through 23 of the printed bill. Ellsworth did not number his sections. He did, however, number the leaves 1 through 9 on the front in the upper left-hand corner. Someone, very possibly Paterson, picked up the numbering from the Paterson leaves, and continued it through leaves 13-15-17-19. But then the numbering shifts to the top middle of the page, and continues throughout the rest of the manuscript, with the numbering (page numbers 20 through 39) being placed on both the front and back of the leaves.

The front of LC 14 also contains, in the handwriting of Caleb Strong, Section 24; the back of LC 14 is blank. LC 15 through LC 20 are in the handwriting of a scribe, and contain Sections 25 through 33 of the printed bill. The first thirteen lines on LC 15 have been hatched out; much of the substance is incorporated in Section 11. The sections are not numbered, but what would be Section 25 begins underneath the crossed-out portion. The pages are numbered 29 through 39, as described previously. The back of LC 20 contains a clerk's endorsement. It is reasonable to assume that these latter Sections 25 through 33 were drafted by Caleb Strong. They follow the one section that is in his handwriting; they represent an appropriate tripartite division of the work of a subcommittee of three members. Strong is also known to have had an interest in criminal prosecutions as shown by the manuscript "Mr. Strong's amendment" to the 1790 Crimes Bill.[4]

A more recent hand, perhaps that of Warren, has also numbered some of the pages and sections.

There are twenty-eight other leaves of paper of varying sizes and shapes, now stamped LC 21 through LC 47 plus LC 33a. Some are simply slips of paper torn off some larger sheet that happened to be handy. LC 38 and LC 41 are two slips containing writing on both sides, the writing on one side apparently being a false start, the writer changing his mind about the wording, turning the slip over, and starting again. LC 43 apparently also contains a false start. LC 36 contains writing largely unintelligible and that probably has nothing to do with the Judicial Bill.

LC 26 relates to Senate action on the House amendments. LC 47 is the conference committee report. The remaining twenty-six leaves of paper contain twenty-seven identifiable changes or proposed changes in the bill. Some are identifiable as having been made from the floor of the Senate. Others, however, may well have changes made by the Senate committee after the bill was recommitted on July 13. Without some other evidence, such as a *Journal* entry, it is impossible to determine precisely when and how these changes were made.

LC 28 is unusual. It is the proposition offered by Richard Henry Lee on June 22 under which the lower national judiciary would have been limited to an admiralty jurisdiction.[5] Unlike the other manuscripts, it bears no clerical notations, and the language differs somewhat from the motion as quoted by Maclay.[6]

Senate Judicial Bill Printed and Delivered about June 16

The Printing History

A Bill to Establish the Judicial Courts of the United States 16 p. 34 cm. [Bracketed colophon at page 16 reads: New York, Printed by Thomas Greenleaf. There is no date.] It is Bristol B7, 153 and mp. 45,657. Microcard 45,657 reproduces the DLC copy. In addition to the DLC copy, there are other copies in MB (Adams Papers), MWiW-C, NN, and NhD (Paine Wingate).

Information on printing for the Senate during its first session is to be found in James B. Childs, *Senate Documents*.[7] Childs reports that sometime between June 3 and June 12 the secretary of the Senate entered into an agreement with Thomas Greenleaf, printer of the *New-York Journal* and *Weekly Register,* to do printing for the Senate.[8] Under the Senate authorizing resolution, paper was supplied to the printer at government expense. A manuscript titled, "Acct. of paper expended for the Senate of the United States by Thomas Greenleaf" provides information on the bills and number of copies printed. This manuscript begins:

1789			*sheets*
June 12	100	Tonnage Acts	50
16	250	Judicial Bills	1000
23	120	do do	480

Although the account rendered by Greenleaf dated the printing of the Judicial Bill as June 16, Ellsworth had copies on June 15, or else he misdated two letters he wrote on that date, claiming to enclose copies. One letter was addressed to Richard Law[9] and the other to Oliver Wolcott.[10] Senator George Read of Delaware sent a copy to John Dickinson on June 16.[11] William Maclay on June 17 mailed four copies, and jointly with his Pennsylvania colleague Senator Robert Morris sent two more.[12]

The Printer's Copy

There have been mistaken assertions made about the copy from which Greenleaf printed the June 16 version. At the risk of some repetition, the proof that Greenleaf used the extant manuscript bill will be set forth here.

The manuscript "Judicial Bill" that Warren found is the "copy" that was given to the printer on June 12, or very soon thereafter, after the manuscript had been reported by the subcommittee to the full committee, and that same day by the committee to the Senate. Because of some discrepancies between the manuscript and the printed bill, Goebel concluded that the manuscript was "no more than a working draft of the Committee in a late stage of its deliberations." [13] That it is the actual "copy" is shown by the presence of printer's marks on the manuscript.

The printed bill is a quarto imprint of sixteen pages. The manuscript bears printer's marks that conform exactly with the pages of the printed bill. These printer's marks are on LC 7 Back, marking the division between pages 4 and 5; on LC 12, marking the division between pages 8 and 9; and on LC 16 Back, marking the division between pages 12 and 13.

In setting a handwritten manuscript into type the printer is expected to read the handwriting correctly, to correct misspellings, to rationalize punctuation and generally to use a consistent style. [14] All this, of course, must be done without changing the sense or meaning of the text. In setting the manuscript of the Judicial Bill into type the printer, probably without direction, expanded "&" into "and"; eliminated dashes used to emphasize stops already marked with periods; and corrected or changed the spelling of several words. [15]

But there are discrepancies between the manuscript and the printed bill that cannot be explained this way. [16] If the manuscript is the copy used by the printer, then how are the substantial discrepancies between the printed bill and the manuscript to be explained? [17]

Maclay gives this account of the reporting of the bill on June 12: "Attended the Judicial Committee and had the bill read over. It was long and somewhat confused. I was called out; they, however, reported it soon after the Senate met, and a number of copies were ordered to be struck off." [18] By referring to the manuscript as being "somewhat confused" Maclay probably did not mean it was "substantively" confused, but rather that the pages and provisions were mixed up. This is a conclusion adequately supported by the physical appearance of the manuscript, with its hatchings-out, interlineations, transfers of provisions, and wafering-on of insertions. While the Senate may have given the subcommittee or even Ellsworth alone specific authority to work out problems with the printer, such authority must have been tacitly assumed to rest with the secretary of the Senate or the committee. Provisions that were garbled or did not accurately reflect what the committee intended would show up in the page proofs of the bill. Corrections and changes would be made on the page proofs, not on the manuscript. A final printed bill will be a corrected version of the copy given to the printer, not an exact replication of that copy.

Senator Wingate's Annotated Bill

Inasmuch as the writer is relying a great deal on Senator Paine Wingate's annotated copy of the printed Judicial Bill, which was not used by Warren and Goebel when they wrote their accounts, a few words regarding it may be appropriate.

This copy of the bill is now in the library of Dartmouth College. It is unique in that it is the only known copy actually used by a senator during the deliberations of the Senate and on which the senator kept track, more or less, of changes made in the bill. While the copy owned by John Adams, or presumed to be his, is in the Boston Public Library, it bears no annotations. The provenance of the other three extant copies is unknown.

Since Wingate's annotated copy is a unique record of the deliberations of the Senate, the question arises as to how complete and reliable it is. The *Senate Journal* indicates that Wingate was present every day that the Senate had the Judicial Bill under consideration.[19] Although Wingate was a minister, not a lawyer, it would be easy to understand his interest in legal matters. He later served for a number of years as an associate justice of the Superior Court of New Hampshire.

Many of the changes that Wingate made on his copy of the bill directly reflect amendments reported in the *Senate Journal,* or reported by Senator Maclay in his diary, or extant among the manuscripts. His copy of the bill reflects the last amendment made by the Senate, as shown by the *Senate Journal* for July 13, just before the bill was recommitted.[20] Wingate's copy also shows all deletions from the bill that are known to have been made from the floor of the Senate. Wingate did not note on the bill all of the amendments known to have been made from the floor of the Senate.[21] Nevertheless, it appears that Wingate tried to keep an accurate record of all changes made on the floor.

Professor Goebel did not know of Wingate's copy of the bill, for he writes that there were at the time of his writing three known copies in existence and it is not listed as one of them.[22] Of the five copies of the bill now known to exist, only the Paine Wingate copy bears annotations. For purposes of comparison it would be most useful if another copy, owned and marked by another senator, would come to light.

Judicial Bill Printed and Delivered about June 23

No copy of this bill that is distinguishable from the bill printed about June 16 is known. Its printing is shown by the manuscript account set forth above.[23] Childs, however, misconstrues this account and says that the June 23 printing was of "120 copies printed, as amended on the third reading with sections numbered."[24] This is impossible, because the third reading did not begin until July 7 and was completed on July 13.[25] Nor is there any basis for thinking that the sections were numbered.

The reason for the second printing must have been simply that more copies were needed. Nothing had happened that would have called for a reprinting because of changes in the text.[26] Although it is not known how many copies each senator was entitled to, at least Senator George Read of Delaware felt restricted in this regard. In writing to John Dickinson, president of Delaware, on July 16, on behalf of himself and Senator Bassett, enclosing a copy, Read wrote: "And we must beg the favor of you to give the attorney-general, Mr. Bedford, an opportunity to peruse and consider this copy, expecting his observations also. We are so restricted in our number of copies that we could not afford one to each of them."[27] Members of the House were also distributing copies. The dittos in Greenleaf's account should be read literally, as referring to a reprinting of the same bill, and not as a new printing of a different bill with the same title.

The Senate's Engrossed Bill

An engrossed version of the June 16–23 bill, titled "An Act to establish the judicial Courts of the United States," and consisting of twenty engrossed leaves, fifteen-by-nineteen inches, with an endorsement on the last page, is now in the National Archives. This is probably the document that the secretary of the Senate carried to the House on July 20, in asking for its concurrence. Whether it or a copy was sent to the printer as copy for the July 23 printing is unknown. *Documentary History of the First Federal Congress* (the project providing a full published record of the First Congress, more fully described later in this appendix) has identified the underlinings on the engrossed bill as being the points at which the House proposed amendments.[28]

House Judicial Bill Printed and Delivered about July 23

A Bill to establish the Judicial Courts of the United States. [Bracketed colophon at page 12 reads: New-York, Printed by Thomas Greenleaf. There is no date]. 12 p. 34 cm. Pages 1 through 4 set in 10-point type, with sections not numbered; pages 5 through 10 set in same size type but with sections numbered; pages 11 and 12 set in 8-point type, sections numbered. This is Evans 21511, although incorrectly dated as having been printed in 1788. It also is Bristol B7, 155 and mp. 45,683. Microcard mp. 45,683 reproduces the copy in DLC. Another copy is at NhD.

Information on printing for the House is found in James B. Childs, *House Documents.*[29]

On July 20, the date the House received the engrossed Senate bill, the House ordered, according to a report in the *New York Journal* of that date, that "100 copies be printed for the accommodation of the House."[30] No mention of this is made in the *House Journal.* The copies were delivered on July 23, as is shown by a letter of that date written by Thomas Hartley to Jasper Yeates, in which he begins, "I enclose you a copy of the Judiciary Bill—as it this day came from the Printer—under the Direction of the House."[31]

There is considerable bibliographical confusion about this version of the bill. Evans 21,511 describes the bill accurately, but incorrectly dates it as having been printed in 1788. The Readex microcard says the entry is "apparently a ghost of a later Federal Act." It reappears in Bristol as B7,155, mp. 45,683, correctly dated but described as "Senate Bill [1] in the House." The microcard, mp. 45,683 and *Short-title Evans* both incorrectly describe it as a "Senate" bill.

Childs describes the House bill as having the title "An act . . ." and refers to the *New York Journal* report about its printing, but then concludes that the bill is "Not located." Apparently Childs was doubtful about identifying the extant bill with the bill the House ordered printed because of the discrepancy between use of the word "Act" in the engrossed Senate bill, and the use of the word "Bill" in this imprint.[32] There can be no reasonable doubt about the bill described above being the bill that the House ordered printed on July 20.

Enrolled Bill

This is the manuscript enrolled bill, "An Act to Establish the Judicial Courts of the United States," which was signed by the president on September 24, 1789. Upon signature it became the Judiciary Act of 1789.

*Manuscript Report by the Senate of the Results
of a Conference with the House*

This is one of Warren's discoveries numbered later as LC 47, and mentioned briefly above.

Certified Copies and Slip Laws

Congress of the United States, begun and held at the City of New-York, on Wednesday, the fourth of March, one thousand seven hundred and eighty-nine. An act to establish the judicial courts of the United States. Approved, September the 24th, 1789. [No other date of publication, printer, or place of publication.]
12 p. 34 cm.

The Judicial Bill became law on September 24, and so an act passed September 15 was applicable to its publication. Under that act, the secretary of state is directed to cause "two printed copies duly authenticated to be sent to the Executive authority of each State."[33] Two of these authenticated copies of the Judicial Bill are known.[34]

The act also required the secretary of state to deliver one printed copy to each senator and representative. These are the same as the certified copies sent to the executives of the states, except not authenticated by signatures. Of these there is no known copy of the Judicial Act.[35] These acts were printed by Childs and Swaine of New York, a fact established by Childs.[36] Bibliographical sources do not clearly distinguish between the certified copies sent to the states and the uncertified copies printed for distribution to congressmen.[37]

Insofar as state officials needed copies, it apparently was left to the states, using the official certified copy sent to the executive authority, to print such additional copies as were needed. One example is known. On June 23, the governor of Virginia laid before the council the letter he had received from the president enclosing a copy of "An Act to regulate the time and manner of administering certain Oaths." The council ordered that two hundred copies of the act be struck, and two sent "to each of the Superior and County Courts within this State." This was done, the act so reprinted being the unsigned certified copy.[38]

However, the national government itself made some distribution of newly enacted legislation to its officials. At least this was done for members of the judicial department. According to an entry made by George Washington in his *Diary* for October 5, 1789: "Dispatched the Commissions to all the Judges of the Supreme and District Courts; & to the

Marshalls and Attorneys and accompanied them with all the Acts respecting the Judiciary Department." [39]

There is no indication of what imprints these were, and while the diary entry does show that there was governmental distribution of information about the judiciary to judges, marshals, and United States attorneys, the entry also carries the negative implication that these officials were not provided with information about the *other* laws passed by the First Congress.

Aside from the possibility of state reprinting of the United States laws, the provision of copies for the public, including the bar and even the judges, was left to the printers as a matter of private enterprise.

They quickly began printing the laws for sale to the public, both as separates and as session laws. Childs and Swaine, for example, announced in the *New York Daily Advertiser* issue of September 28 the availability of "An Act to establish the Judicial Courts of the United States." No copy of this imprint is known. [40] Considering the printing situation with regard to the bills and Acts of the First Congress it is frequently difficult to identify the imprint to which a bibliographical source is referring. [41]

After the session ended, a bound volume was issued that contained all the acts and resolutions adopted by Congress in its first session. [42]

Senate and House Journals

Both of the houses of Congress kept journals, which record much but not all of the official business. The *Journals* were actually printed during the session and distributed periodically in parts. These parts were corrected and gathered together after the session ended, and were published as bound volumes.

On May 19, 1789, the Senate accepted a committee report, which called for the printing of 120 copies of the legislative journal each month, commencing June 1, and said that each member should be furnished with a copy. [43] Apparently, though, publication did not begin that early, for it was not until July 3 that the *Daily Advertiser* offered subscriptions to the *House Journal*. [44] This was for a volume to be published at the end of the session, the advertisement also saying, "For the early information and accommodation of such subscribers as wish to have them in sheets as they are printed, they will be forwarded to them without delay." Another announcement followed in the July 9 issue, asking that subscribers "be speedy in their application, in order that the Printers may ascertain what number of copies may be wanting." [45]

The availability of the *Senate Journal* was first announced by Greenleaf in the July 9 issue of the *New-York Journal* on terms similar to those on which the *House Journal* was available. The first part was not published until sometime after July 22, and in all at least three parts were issued.[46]

The *Senate Journal* contains for the latter part of the third reading of the Judicial Bill the text of amendments proposed, whether accepted or rejected.

Newspapers, Congressional Register, and Annals of Congress

The Senate met in closed session during this period, and so neither the public nor the press could attend. Thus there are no significant newspaper reports regarding its proceedings.

The House was open to the public, and "reporters" regularly attended. Thomas Lloyd was given a preferred seat and took notes on the basis of which he published the *Congressional Register*. These notes are discussed in an article by Marion Tinling: "In many respects what Lloyd published bears only slight resemblance to the literal transcript of his own notes."[47] And again, "In preparing copy for publication, Lloyd chose only 'the most interesting speeches.' These he subjected to a good deal of embellishment."[48] When Joseph Gales and W. W. Seaton, beginning in 1834, published the *Annals of Congress*, they reprinted the *Congressional Register* "almost in its entirety."[49] Tinling points out that there were two editions of the first two volumes of *Annals*, each bearing the publication date of 1834, but with different running heads and pagination. Citations herein are to the edition with the running head "History of Congress."

The *Annals* does not identify the sources used in the publication, but simply says, "Compiled From Authentic Materials, By Joseph Gales, Senior." The proceedings for the Senate for its first session are based solely on the *Senate Journal*, with the omission of some entries that Gales thought were unimportant.

There were also reporters other than Lloyd attending the sessions of the House, and their reports appeared in other newspapers. These reports were ignored in the printing of the *Annals of Congress*. According to *Documentary History of the First Federal Congress*, which plans to publish these other newspaper reports, the relevant newspapers were: *Gazette of the United States*, published in New York by John Fenno; *New York Daily Advertiser*, published by Francis Childs; and *New York Daily Gazette*, published by J. and A. M'Lean.

Inasmuch as the major development of the Judiciary Act was in the Senate, these newspaper accounts do not cover the major events in the development of the act. Both the *Annals* and the other newspapers gave only spotty coverage of the House debates on the Judicial Bill.

A copy of the Judicial Bill as it came from the subcommittee and was printed by the Senate on June 12 was printed in the *Boston Gazette*'s issues of June 29 and July 6, 1789.

Letters, Diaries, and Other Personal Materials

The most important item under this heading is the diary or journal kept by Senator William Maclay of Pennsylvania. Aside from scattered, very incomplete notes taken during the Senate's debates by its president (John Adams), Senator William Paterson of New Jersey, Senator Rufus King of New York, and Senator Pierce Butler of South Carolina, this is the only source of its kind extant. Senator Paterson's notes of the debate on the Judiciary Act have been published,[50] but too late to have been of aid in the writing of this book.

There is a great deal of private correspondence that deals with matters pertinent to the First Congress in the Library of Congress and National Archives, in several state historical societies, and in other manuscript repositories. Important and almost definitive collections of this correspondence have been made by *Documentary History of the First Federal Congress,* which grants access upon permission and presentation of credentials, and by *Documentary History of the Supreme Court,* which at this writing is closed to scholars.

We must return to Maclay's *Journal* because its value as a source has been severely questioned by modern historians, particularly Charles Warren and Julius Goebel. This writer places more trust in Maclay's observational veracity.

Any discussion of William Maclay's *Journal* and its credibility must take note, first, that until recently there were two different editions of the *Journal,* one that is complete and one that is not. The first edition of the *Journal* was published in 1880 under the title *Sketches of Debate in the First Senate of the United States in 1789–90–91;* it was reprinted in 1969. It is incomplete and the editorial comment it includes is sometimes indistinguishable from the actual text of Maclay's notes. This edition was used by Warren.[51]

In 1890 a "complete" edition of the Journal was published, reprinted in 1927, under the title *Journal of William Maclay, United States Senator from Pennsylvania, 1789–1791.* This edition was used by Goebel.[52] Apparently not noting the differences in the contents of the two editions, Goebel implicitly and somewhat unfairly criticizes Warren for overlooking entries in Maclay's *Journal,* entries that in fact were not in the *Sketches* edition that Warren used.[53]

There is a leaf missing from the Maclay's manuscript journal and it is said by the editors of the *Journal* to have been "destroyed," but with no indication as to who destroyed it. It concerns July 10 and 11, 1789; the surrounding pages show that it related to the debate on the Judicial Bill. Apparently someone thought that Maclay's comments on the debate over equity were so caustic it was best to destroy them.[54]

Neither Warren nor Goebel think that Maclay was wholly reliable. Warren writes, "[H]ere as elsewhere, the dates given in Maclay's journal are not reliable, as the matters mentioned as acted on do not always coincide with the officially printed Senate Journal."[55] Somewhat similarly, Goebel points out that Maclay's *Journal* does not show an amendment made on July 9.[56] However, when Maclay is checked on the dates he used that are verifiable, he is found to be accurate *in all instances*. The so-called dating errors referred to by Warren and Goebel are actually errors in their own interpretations of the sources, not errors made by Maclay.

Both Warren and Goebel also comment, unfavorably, on the subjects Maclay saw fit to cover in his notes. Warren says that Maclay "treats only of amendments in which he was interested, and often in a form impossible of understanding."[57] Goebel is even more caustic. Referring to the Senate debates, he writes: "For this stage of the proceedings Maclay's journal is a prime source but inadequate in this, that the Senator, understandably enough, was mainly concerned with magnifying his own little triumphs and ignoring particulars which did not interest him. Consequently one receives the impression that the bill was not gone through systematically but was subjected to a species of grasshopper visitation."[58]

But Wingate's annotated bill shows that Maclay in his notes did reasonably cover everything that the Senate debated. While naturally taking notes more fully on subjects of interest to him, perhaps even "magnifying his own little triumphs," the indications are that he did not overlook anything of true significance that was debated in the Senate. Warren and Goebel are criticizing him for not taking notes on what *they think* the Senate *should* have debated, and which therefore *they assume* the Senate did debate. But both Maclay's *Journal* and Wingate's annotated bill are consistent in showing that most of these subjects were probably not debated.

In fact, most of the Senate debate on the Judicial Bill involved nitpicking or, at least in modern ways of thinking, dealt with matters of stupendous insignificance. Maclay accurately reflects this debate in his *Journal*. Warren and Goebel would restage the Senate proceedings so as to consider the subjects that, from a more modern viewpoint, the Senate ought to have been debating in 1789. But surely Maclay cannot be criticized for not taking notes on debates that never took place. On all the evidence, properly evaluated, Maclay was an accurate notetaker and his *Journal* is a credible source of information on the First Congress.[59]

[Another, thorough edition of Maclay's diary, usefully and capably edited by Kenneth Bowling and Helen Veit, has recently been published as Volume 9 of *Documentary History of the First Federal Congress*. It was unfortunately seen neither by the author nor by the editors before this book went to press.]

SOURCES IN PRINT

Most of the primary sources used by Warren and Goebel, even during the quarter century when this writer was researching these subjects, were not easily available to the public. Projects now under way have resulted and will continue to result in the publication of a great deal of this material, some of it in facsimile. Soon it will be possible for judge and lawyer, scholar and layman to have a fair chance of testing and determining for themselves the validity of the histories set forth by Warren, Goebel, and this writer.

The sources relating to the first session of the First Congress that are generally available in print are described below. The *Early American Imprints Project,* through which access to other printed materials can be obtained, is also described.

Two important publication projects are currently in the process of publishing almost all of the documents that might be used in a study like this one. Each will contain the Judiciary Act of 1789 and pertinent documents and correspondence. Three other projects have published or will publish some of these materials. These projects are described next.

First Congress Documentary History

The Documentary History of the First Federal Congress 1789–1791, sponsored by the National Historical Publications Commission and George Washington University, is issuing a series of publications that will soon provide a full record of the debates, actions, and documents of the First Congress. The present editor is Charlene Bangs Bickford. The Johns Hopkins University Press, Baltimore and London, is publishing the series, seven volumes having now appeared.

Documentary History of the First Federal Congress divides the materials into two parts. The first, with six volumes published to date, presents the official papers of the Congress. The second part will present all unofficial materials, such as the correspondence to and from congressmen, newspaper accounts, shorthand transcriptions of debates, other accounts of debates, and diary entries. The only volume of this part to be published so far is a fresh edition of Maclay's journal, as just noted. Extensive editorial aids provide glossaries, biographies, maps, chronologies, tables, and extended explanatory notes. The original sources, to date, are being reprinted and are not reproduced in facsimile. Consequently, the pagination, as in the reprinting of the House and Senate *Journals,* varies from that of the original imprints.

Volumes 1 and 3 of *Documentary History* are new editions of the Senate and House *Journals,* respectively. These will be noticed more thoroughly below. Volume 9, the new edition of Maclay's *Journal,* will also be treated below.

Volumes 4 through 6 present the legislative histories of all bills and resolutions introduced in the First Congress, including amendments to the Constitution, but excepting private legislation, which will be reproduced with petitions to Congress in the remaining unpublished volumes of official papers. All extant evidence of all stages in the development of all pieces of legislation are set forth, from motion to bill to amendments to final action. In addition, a skeletal chronological calendar of the events in the passage of each bill through Congress is provided. Volume 4 contains the proposed constitutional amendments, and the Collection Act and the Coasting Act referred to in chapter 6, while volume 6 contains the Crimes Bill (called therein the Punishment of Crimes Bill).

Volume 5 contains the Judiciary Act. In addition to the chronological calendar, three versions of the act are set forth. First is the manuscript bill, dated June 12, containing in footnotes and sometimes in the text all changes made by the Senate before passage (two manuscript amendments that failed of passage are also set forth); it has been compared to the June 16–23 printed version of the manuscript bill contained in the National Archives, in order to restore passages presently illegible due to water stains. Next is the engrossed Senate bill, as passed by the Senate on July 17. Finally of course is the enrolled bill as signed by the president on September 24.

Supreme Court Documentary History

The second project is *The Documentary History of the Supreme Court, 1789–1800,* edited by Maeva Marcus and others, two volumes of which will have been published by Columbia University Press by 1990. *Documentary History of the Supreme Court* is designed to present an accurate and comprehensive record of all cases heard by the Supreme Court before 1801. It will incidentally publish selected correspondence, newspaper accounts, and public and private records concerning the Court, its establishment and duties, the justices, and their work. As with *Documentary History of the First Federal Congress,* the volumes of this project are replete with extensive editorial aids. For our purposes the most valuable portion of this work will be the proposed volume 4 containing Article III of the Constitution and the various Judiciary Acts establishing federal-court jurisdiction during the period 1789–1800, and the correspondence pertaining thereto. The documents will also not in general be reproduced in facsimile, however. Volumes 2 and 3 will contain the records, correspondence, newspaper reports, and other material pertinent to the judges' circuit-riding duties, including their grand-jury charges, but they will appear too late to be of any use in the preparation of this book.

The Founders' Constitution and Other Projects

A third project, which has been completed, is *The Founders' Constitution,* edited by Philip B. Kurland and Ralph Lerner. Much less comprehensive in scope than the two previous publications, the five volumes of this project collect documents pertinent to the meaning of the Constitution and contain a scattering of items useful to the early history of the national-court system and the Judiciary Act of 1789 (particularly volume 1, dealing with the preamble, and volume 5 insofar as it treats of Article III).

The Documentary History of the Ratification of the Constitution and the First Ten Amendments (seven volumes published to date) and James Hutson's one-volume *Supplement to Max Farrand's The Records of the Federal Convention of 1787* (published by Yale University Press in 1987) should also be consulted.

Micropublication, Facsimile Publication, and Bibliographies

Michael Glazier, Inc., of Wilmington, Delaware, is presently engaged in publishing, in facsimile, the *National State Papers Of The United States Series, 1789–1817.* While the publications are not annotated, significant additional information to that contained in the facsimiles is included in the form of notes, directories, rosters, and the like. Whether this publication undertaking will publish the text of manuscripts, and if so, in facsimile or in print, or in some combination, is not clear. So far, it has published in facsimile the *Journals of the Houses of Congress.*

The extant papers generated by the First Congress have also been reproduced on microcard as a part of the *Early American Imprints Project* of

Readex Microprint Corporation of New York City and the American Antiquarian Society. The project reproduces the comprehensive list of all extant pre-1801 American publications found in the fourteen volumes of Charles Evans, *American Bibliography* (1903–1959), and in Roger P. Bristol, *Supplement To Evans's American Bibliography* (1970). Bristol's *Supplement* lists some papers found after the Readex microprinting project had begun, for which Bristol gives no microprint numbers. Those entries are not being reproduced on microcard. Moreover, the project is a continuing one, and microcards still are not available for some of the Evans/ Bristol entries. A consolidated list of the publications being reproduced on microcard is given in Clifford K. Shipton and James E. Mooney, *National Index Of American Imprints Through 1800. The Short-Title Evans* (1969). This index gives for each publication a microcard number that is the same as the *Evans* entry number or is one of the two entry numbers used in Bristol's *Supplement.*

These bibliographies of American imprints have been extended from 1801 through 1819 by Ralph R. Shaw and Richard H. Shoemaker in separate volumes for each year (*American Bibliography,* 1958–63). *Early American Imprints, Second Series,* is reproducing these imprints on microcards. In addition, the bibliographies, although not the microprinting, have been continued under the title *A Checklist of American Imprints,* by Richard H. Shoemaker, for the years 1820 through 1829 (1964–71); by Gayle Cooper for 1830 (1972); and by Scott and Carol Bruntjen for 1831 through 1833 (1975–79).

Beginning with *Evans,* there is considerable confusion in bibliographical sources relating to the printed documents published by the First Congress, a confusion that has unfortunately carried forward into Bristol's *Supplement,* the *National Index,* and the *Early American Imprints Project.* The most authoritative study of these documents is in two articles by James B. Childs.[60]

The House and Senate Journals

The original *Journal Of The First Session Of The Senate Of The United States Of America, Begun And Held At The City Of New-York, March 4th, 1789,* was printed by Thomas Greenleaf in New York as a book of 172 pages. This is *Evans* 22,207. The microcard reproduces the copy in the American Antiquarian Society.

By order of the Senate, this *Journal* was reprinted in 1820 by Gales and Seaton in Washington, D.C., as a volume of ninety-five pages. This is *Shoemaker* 3762.

Documentary History of the First Federal Congress in 1972 published the 1789 *Senate Journal* as volume 1 of its series. In 1977 Michael Glazier published its facsimile reproduction of the *Senate Journal* as volume 1 of Part 1 (The Congressional Journals of the United States) of *National State Papers.*

Documentary History of the First Federal Congress points out that Samuel Alyne Otis was elected secretary of the Senate on April 8,[61] and he assumed the responsibility of keeping the *Journal.* He attended each session, keeping the minutes in his own hand. On the following day, this "rough journal" was read to the Senate and corrected, in accordance with Rule I.[62] The corrections were incorporated by Otis, who then inked in directions to his clerks, who copied out a "smooth journal" in a fine round hand. The "smooth journal" was signed by Otis and sent to the printer. (On one occasion the smooth journal was water-damaged, and had to be redone.) By a joint resolution effective June 3, Otis was authorized by Congress to make the necessary arrangements for printing the *Senate Journal,* and the work was contracted out to Thomas Greenleaf. *Documentary History* has reprinted the *Journal* as printed by Greenleaf, annotating the reprinting as appropriate with references to the rough journal, which sometimes contains additional information, such as the name of the senator making a motion.[63] This reprinting of the *Senate Journal* covers 210 pages and has a different pagination than is found in the original.

The original *Journal Of The House Of Representatives Of The United States* was printed in New York in 1789 by Francis Childs and John Swaine. It is a document of 177 pages. It is *Evans* 22,208. The microcard reproduces a copy in the American Antiquarian Society. It was also printed in Richmond in 1790 in an edition of 145 pages, *Evans* 22,980, but no copy is known to be extant.

By order of the House, the *Journal* was reprinted in 1826 by Gales and Seaton in Washington, D.C. This is *Shoemaker* 27,139. This reprinting is included in a nine-volume reprinting of all the House journals from the First through the Thirteenth Congresses.

In 1977 *Documentary History of the First Federal Congress* published *House of Representatives Journal* as volume 3 of its series. The introduction points out that the "rough journal" has not survived, as it has in the case of the Senate, and that there are several variant printings of the *House Journal.* However, the substance of all the variant printings is the same, and so the text published in *Documentary History of the First Federal Congress,* with the aid of silent editing, is the same as that of all of the variant printings.[64]

Also in 1977 Michael Glazier issued its facsimile reprint. This reprint contains no clue as to which of the variant printings of the *House Journal* is being reproduced, although it apparently is a copy in either the Library of Congress or the National Archives, and is "the best preserved and most legible."[65]

The pagination of the *House Journal* as reprinted by *Documentary History of the First Federal Congress* is different both from that of any of the variant printings on which it is based, and from the pagination in the Michael Glazier facsimile reproduction of an unidentified printing.

Evans 22,207 of the *Early American Imprints Project* reproduces a copy of the *House Journal* that is in the American Antiquarian Society, without further identification, so it is not clear whether this is the same as or different from the journals used by *Documentary History of the First Federal Congress* or the one reproduced by Michael Glazier.

The Annals of Congress

Information on the debates of Congress during the First Congress is found in volume 1 of *The Debates and Proceedings in the Congress of the United States*.[66] The source on which the *Annals* (as this work is usually known) is based, and the other newspaper accounts, are discussed above.

Maclay's Journal

A personal account of the proceedings of the Senate during the First Congress is found in the journal of Senator William Maclay of Pennsylvania. The journal begins with an entry for April 24, 1789, and continues through March 3, 1791, when Maclay's term ended.

Several editions of this journal have been published. Until the most recent publication, these editions have given no satisfactory explanation of the contents in relation to the original or to other editions.

In 1880 a first edition, edited by George W. Harris and published by L. S. Hart of Harrisburg, was privately published for limited distribution. It was an abridgment of the journal. The title was *Sketches of Debate in the First Senate of the United States in 1789–90–91.*

The complete text of the journal was published in 1890 as *Journal of William Maclay, United States Senator from Pennsylvania, 1789–1791.* This has a preface by Edgar S. Maclay, in which it is pointed out that there had been an earlier reluctance to publish the complete journal because of "the severity of the criticisms made on prominent personages" by Maclay. This edition was published in New York by D. Appleton.

The *Journal* was reprinted in 1927 in New York by A. and C. Boni, with an added introduction by Charles Beard. In 1965, Frederick Ungar Publishing Co., New York, reprinted the 1927 edition, but with different pagination.

In 1969, Burt Franklin of New York City reprinted the 1880 edition of *Sketches and Debate;* this publication makes no reference to its being an "abridged" printing.

Just as this work was being prepared for the press, there has appeared a fine and comprehensive edition of Maclay's diary making up volume 9 of *Documentary History of the First Federal Congress.* The other editions, above, have been completely supplanted.

Letters to and from Caleb Strong During May 1789

THE ORIGINAL of the letter from David Sewall to Caleb Strong is in the Forbes Library, Northampton, Massachusetts. The exchange of correspondence between R. T. Paine and Caleb Strong is in the Massachusetts Historical Society. Sewall, a member of the Supreme Judicial Court of Massachusetts and the first national district judge for the United States district court established in Maine, was a thoughtful and astute critic of the plans for a national judiciary. The letters here transcribed are a part of a larger correspondence between Sewall and Strong dealing with the impending organization of the new national judicial system. Two earlier letters are Sewall to Strong, March 28, 1789, also in the Forbes Library, and Sewall to Strong, April 6, 1789, in the South Natick Historical Society, South Natick, Massachusetts. See also Sewall to George Thatcher, April 11, 1789, in the Chamberlain Collection, Boston Public Library. Unfortunately, the important letters of Strong to Sewall, April 18 and April 22, 1789, to which the letters of Sewall and Paine (another high judge of Massachusetts) are in response, have not come to light. Strong wrote these letters just after the Judiciary Committee had adopted an outline of the new judicial system, and several senators on the committee simultaneously wrote to friends at home asking for advice and help. See especially Ralph Izard to Edward Rutledge, April 24, 1789, in the South Caroliniana Library at the University of South Carolina; and Oliver Ellsworth to Richard Law, April 30, 1789, at the Connecticut Historical Society.

LETTER WRITTEN FROM NORTH HAMPTON, MASSACHUSETTS, BY
JUDGE DAVID SEWALL TO CALEB STRONG, MAY 2, 1789

North Hampton 2d May 1789
Saturday Eve

Dear Sir:

I Wrote you last from Worcester, since which yours of the 18th. and 22d. have come to hand. The Scetches or rather Scratches therein Suggested, Where such Ideas as arose in my mind at the Time on the Subject of the Judicial System, some of Which I think were in some Instances Simular to those contained in the System now Communicated, in Contemplation. A maritime Judge its probable will be expected in Each State, and perhaps it may be difficult if not Inexpedient to have them otherways appointed—my meaning is, that it may Create a Jealosy in the members of the Smaller States if the Continent should be divided into an equal Number of Maritime Districts, without having Regard to the Boundarys of particular States that it might Tend to a Consolidation—especially if this Judge of the District is to have the authority named in the *Sixth* paragraph of the Paper transmitted before I forget it let the Act for appointing the District Judge declare that He shall be a Person *Learned in the Law* as a Necessary qualification.

The objections you mention in yours of the 22d. to the making the S. J. Courts of the respective states the Inferiour federal Judicial Strike me foreceably and as having great Weight at this Juncture Especially. The hurry of a Court, especially when pinched in time, is an unsuitable Season to arange ones Ideas especially upon so intricate and Important a Subject, and this must appollogize for omissions respecting your request at this Time. My Ideas heretofore communicated were partly to expedite the operation of the Revennue System—to make the Judicial Business as cheap and as little expensive to the Revennue as possible, and to make an Experiment, that might be easily amended, at some future day when Congress should have more time and leisure to digest this Business. I have communicated your last to the Chief Justice & Judge Sumner the only Judges that have attended here. The chief Justice has copied out the *Sixth,* and I have requested him to consider it particularly, & write you on the Subject but Whether he will or not he has made me no particular Promise. The Business of the Circuit Court as chalked out in the Sixth seems so large that some doubts may be raised, whether they will be able to perform it and to meet twice a year in the Center and there dispatch the grand Business of the *Supreme Judicial.* Perhaps a concurrent Jurisdiction in some matters in the State Courts Where the parties Shall incline to make use of them, may afford some relief, in this Respect. My Original Idea with respect to the Admiralty Judge was for him to decide without a Jury and maritime matters had best perhaps be there decided agreable to the usage of all Nations I believe, The Court for this Purpose should be had upon Emergencies that the decisions should be Spedy. But if he is to have the cognizance of such Common Law matters as are Cognizeable in the Infr. Judiciary, Some provision must be made for a Jury in these matters at least and I think at present that He must Conform to the Rules of the State in which he is placed—and this mode will give the least umbrage to the Cytizens thereof. If they have the same mode of obtaining Jurors in a Federal Court as in their own State Court, and a Short Bill on that head may be made to answer the purpose without going into the minutia. A Fee Bill will also be necessary, possibly that reported by the revising Committee last fall to our general assembly might afford some relief as to the article. I presume the Clerk of the House of R. has it and a Copy from thence might be procured. But this matter of Fees being a Mony Bill will come into the other House I presume first. The power of granting new Trials should be placed in every Court. This is perhaps a part of the Judicial Power, and in their Original formation it may be best to expressly make it such under certain modifications and restrictions, and this method may answer all the purposes of Reviews, or Appeals with power to determine the Facts, in the Court appealed unto. We in Massachusetts have been used to various Trials of the same Facts by different Jurys of Course. But the time will come when the Ill consequences of this mode will appear—and if no Review were now had, but such as upon the particular Cause in question Justice and Equity required it would be pro bono in the opinion of some. Appeals therefore in the nature of a Writ of Error in some matters in the federal Courts may be more expedient. The Provision for a Writ of Error *from the "ultimate determination of a Cause in the highest Court of Law or Equity of a State,"* as mentioned in the Scetch to the S. Fed. Judicial is a necessary, and usefull Provision. Upon reviewing the Powers of the District Court I do not find that Impost and Revenues matters are expresly made Cognizeable therein, unless it is couched under the Claim of "When the united [States] Sue". I conclude such matters are to be made cognizeable then. What provision is to be made for Causes under the Value of 100 Dollars? having been up last night until after one upon a Capital Cause I can ad no more but that I am

Your obedt. huml. Servant
David Sewall

LETTER WRITTEN FROM BOSTON BY R. T. PAINE
TO CALEB STRONG, MAY 18, 1789

Boston May 18th 1789

My dear Sir

I have been much gratified with the sight of Sundry Letters you sent Judges respecting the forming the federal Judicial System—from the first proposal of the new Government, that part Struck my mind as attended with peculiar difficulties; I wish it was in my power to throw any light on the Subject—as the Administration of Justice is one of the main Pillars of Government & perhaps the point on which every other part of a free Government turns & is supported, it therefore is indispensibly necessary that it grow from the same Root from which the whole Govt. Springs, otherwise the Questions of Justice & the *Extent* of the Laws that arise in the new Govt. would be determined in a foreign Jurisdiction, & therefore there must be federal Courts to try all matters that are of a federal nature, but I must confess I do not at present see the necessity of carrying the trials of disputes between Citizens of different States to the length some do vizt. to enable them to sue in a third State where neither party lives. I have always considered that as a very important part of the Machinery, as also the right wch. foreigners may have to sue in any State where the Deft doth not live; the vexations of carrying a Deft to answer at a distance may amount to a greater Oppression to individuals than any we expect the Resolution to deliver us from: great care has always been had in our Laws to prevent this Evil & I do but hint it for consideration whether the same regulation should not now take place; for to suppose that a partiality in common causes would take place in the State where a man lives is contrary to our continual observation & supposes such a corruption of morals in all the States as would render it unsafe to go any where for Justice. Undoubtedly there may be exceptions of important popular causes, for wch. provision may be made by some special Application. With regard to the forming the Federal Infr. Courts I find there is a difficulty in the minds of many in Constituting States Supreme Jud. Courts for that purpose; it is said the regulation must be general & that the S. J. Court of every State do not hold *quam die;* it certainly would save much expence of time & money if such a regulation could take place, & those are very great objects in every point of View; but if this can't be done, & it became necessary to have distinct Fed. Inf. Courts, the Expence must then be lessened by reducing the number of the Judges; there must be a Court to determine all Matters of Revenue Seizures etc. and also all Admiralty matters; Quere, is there a real inconsistency in Vesting these powers in one, two or three persons by the name of fed. Infr. Court, or must there be an Admiralty Jurisdiction distinct? And then where will you vest the Jurisdiction of Revenue questions Seizures etc? In the Admiralty or Infr. Court? must there then in each State be an Admiralty Court and an Infr. fed. Court beside the S. J. Court of the State? This complicates the Machinery too much, and how will it be Supported? These are but hints of enquiry; I presume not to propose, I have too long been acquainted with public life to Suppose an Individual by himself can propose and determine such questions as well as a collection of Sages who bring together all the matter to be considered, & ripen each others Judgment by mutual Observations. I think there is much less difficulty in for[ming] the fed. Supr. Jud. Court, as you may construct it from first principles and are not fettered with the hard Circumstances of particular States, who will unavoidably feel offended perhaps embarrassed & lessened or burthened by the Infr. fed. Court. I think the fed. Sup. Jud. will be itinerant & the trial of Appealed Causes so regulated as to prevent as much as may be the expence and burthen of going far from ho[me] for Justice. I find you have sent for a copy of the System of Laws for new forming our Courts which was reported to our Genl. Court; the Law for Establishing the Sup. J. Court is the part which I drafted. I wish the System had taken place with us, whether it will throw any light on your Consultation you will best judge. You will have to consider the great Question of Appointing Jurors. I suppose a Similarity in this respect doth not take place in the several States, & if you make one general regulation, wch. I consider necessary, hard then will be the task to procure a facility of Execution, for this matter laying with the *Lay Gens* it will be hard to make them alter their old habits—you'll excuse these bare hints, & attribute them to a hearty desire to promote the common Cause of a well regulated Judiciary System; if you should see fit to make me acquainted with the great Subjects of Enquiry & alterations & what progress is making in forming the Machine & setting it to work I shall Consider it as a favour, mean time I wish you Success & happiness & rest with great Esteem.

Yr most
R. R. Paine

LETTER WRITTEN FROM NEW YORK BY CALEB STRONG
TO R. T. PAINE, MAY 24, 1789

New York Sunday Evening, May 24, 1789

Dear Sir:

I thank you for your Favour of the 18h. Inst. which I recd. the last Evening. I believe the Evil which would arise if Foreigners might sue in a State where the Defendant does not live, will be guarded against. I stated to Judge Sewall in a Letter which you saw the Inconveniences of giving to the State Courts federal Jurisdiction. There is another which at that time I forgot to mention, the State of Virginia by a Law passed since their adoption of the Constitution, have prohibited their officers from holding offices under the United States, and their Courts from having Jurisdiction of Causes arising under the Laws of the Union; by such laws every State would be able to defeat the Provisions of Congress if the Judiciary powers of the Genl. Government were directed to be exercised by the State Courts.

I sent to Judge Sewall at Northampton the Outlines of the System agreed on by the large Committee which consisted of a Member from each State, the Business was then committed to a Sub Committee to carry it on to detail and prepare a Bill or Bills. they have been employed some time and will not be able to report the Bill untill the later part of this or the beginning of the next Week—when it is reported the Senate will probably order a Number of Copies to be printed. Should that be the Case, I shall endeavor to furnish the Court when at Ipswich with a Copy.

We propose that the Supreme Court shall consist of one Chief Justice & 5 other Justices who shall hold two Sessions annually at the seat of the Government one on the 1st Monday of Feby. & the other the 1st Monday of August four Justices to make a Quorum.

That there be 11 Districts one to consist of Newhampshire & the Province of Main to be called Newhampshire District one of the remainder of Massachusetts to be called Massachusetts District etc etc. That there be a Court called a District Court in each District to consist of one Judge who shall hold 4 Courts annually, and special Courts at the Discretion of the Judge. The Courts in New Hampshire District alternately at Portsmouth & Portland, in Massachusetts District at Boston, etc.

That the Districts be divided into 3 Circuits, the eastern to consist of New York & all east of that State, the southern of Carolina & Georgia & the middle of the rest of the States, that a Circuit Court to consist of two Justices of the Sup. Court and the District Judge be held twice in a year in each District any two to be a Quorum, the first

Session to commence in the several Districts as follows in New Jersey the 2d. New York the 4h. Pennsylvania the 11h. Connecticut the 22d. So. Carolina 25h. Delaware the 29h. Days of April next in Massachusetts the 2d. Maryland the 7h. Georgia the 10h. Newhampshire the 20h. & Virginia the 22d. Day of May next and subsequent sessions on like Days of every 6h. Calendar month afterwards, except Sundays, in such Case on the next day, the Session in Newhampshire at Portsmouth, Massachusetts at Boston, Connecticut Middletown, etc etc.

The District Court to have Cognizance exclusive of State Courts of all causes cognizable under the Authority of the United States & defined by its Laws committed in the District or on the high seas when the Punishment cannot exceed 30 stripes, 100 Dols. fine or 6 months Imprisonment, except offences against the Law Marshall the trial to be by Jury—and to have exclusive original Cognizance of all Causes of Admiralty & maritime Jurisdiction except high Crimes of Seizure made under Laws of Impost & Navigation of the U.S. when made on waters navigable from the Sea with Vessels of 10 Tons burthen, saving to suitors the common Law remedy when the common Law is competent to give it. & have Cognizance concurrent with the State Courts or the Circuit Courts as the Case may be of Causes when a foreigner sues for a tort only in violation of the Law of nations or a Treaty of the U.S. and of all civil Causes when the United States or a common Informer as well for himself as the U.S. shall sue and the Matter in Dispute amounts to 100 Dolls, the trial of Facts in the last mentioned Causes to be by Jury.

The Circuit Court to have Cognizance concurrent with the Courts of the States, or the Sup. Court as the Case may be of all Causes at Common Law or in Equity amounting to 300 Dols. when the United States are Pltffs or Petitioners or a State is Pltff and the Suit is against a Citizen of another State—and when it exceed 500 Dolr. and a foreigner or Citizen of another State than that where the Suit is brought is a Party—and when a Suit is brought in another Court against a Citizen of another State than that in which the Suit is brought or against a Foreigner, and the Matter in Dispute exceeds 500 Dolr. and such Citizen or foreigner shall at his first appearance file a motion that the Cause may be removed into the Circuit Court and give Bond to [illegible] the Action of the Circuit Court and appearance etc. the State Court shall proceed no further, and the Circuit Court have cognizance—and if in any Action in a State Court the Title of Land is concerned and the Parties are Citizens of the same State, and the Matter in Dispute exceeds 500 Dolr. and the Deft. in his plea sets up a Title under the Grant of another State than that where the Suit is brought, and moves that the Pltff set forth his Title, the Pltff shall set forth his Title in his Replication and if he founds it on a Grant of a State different from that under whose Grant the Defendt. claims the Deft. may then on Motion have the Cause removed to the Circuit Court, and the Deft. shall abide by his Plea—the Circuit Court also to have Cognizance of all Crimes cognizable under the Authority of the United States the Trial of Facts in all Actions at Law to be by Jury; No Person to be arrested for Trial in any civil Action before any other Circuit or District Court than those within the District where the arrest shall be made. The Circuit Court to have appellate Jurisdiction from the District Court in all Cases except Criminal above [blot] Dolr., but the Appeal shall not submit Facts to a Revision unless in maritime Cases when the parties will not be entitled to a Jury trial, and the Court appealed from not to issue ex[ecuti]on.

The Supr. Court to have exclusive jurisdiction of all Causes of a civil nature when any of the United States or a foreign State is a party except between a State and its Citizens and except also between a State and the Citizens of other States or Foreigners in which latter Case it shall have original but not exclusive Jurisdiction, and that original but not exclusive Jurisdiction of all Suite for Trespass by Ambassadours other publick Ministers or Consuls & their Domesticks—the Trial of Facts in the Supreme Court in all actions at Law against the Citizens of the U.S. to be by Jury—to have appellate Jurisdiction from the Circuit Court when the Value is 2000 Dollrs. but no Revision of Facts.

The Supr. Court may grant Writs of prohibition to the District Courts in admiralty proceedings & Writs of mandamus to any Court appointed or Persons holding office under the authority of the United States. Writs of Error may be brought to reverse the Errors in the district, at the Circuit Courts, in Causes not criminal and between 50 & 200 Dollrs. value but Ex[ecuti]on not to be issued and double Costs if no reversal.

Writs of Error from the Circuit to the Supr. Court in all Causes not criminal of which the Circuit Court has original Cognizance and the Matter in Dispute does not exceed [sic] 2000 Dollrs.

If in a Cause in a State Court the Question is whether a Law of the State or of the United States is constitutional and the judgment is in favour of the State Law or against the Law of the U.S. a Writ of Error will lie to have *that Question & that only determined* in the Supreme Court. *No other power in the Federal Courts to revise Judgment in the State Courts.*

That all the Courts have power in the Trial of Actions at Law on Motion and due Notice to require the Parties to produce Books &

Papers and the Defendant to disclose on oath in Cases & under circumstances where such power has been usually exercised in Chancery, and if the Pltff refuse to produce Books &c to render Judgment as in Cases of nonsuit and if Deft. refuses to produce Books &c or to answer on oath to render Judgment by Default.

That a Marshall be appointed to each District with power to execute Writs issuing under the Authority of the U.S. to appoint Deputies who may be removed by the District or Circuit Court at Pleasure.

The Mode of appointing Jurors is not yet agreed.

I have been obliged to abridge this plan but hope you will understand it, if you do be kind enough to mention it if you have an opportunity to the Judges or to any of our Brethren who will give themselves the Trouble to reflect on this Subject, if you or they would write me any objections that occur to you I should be greatly obliged for it will be much easier to effect alterations now than at a future stage of the Business—I don't know that Judge Sullivan or Brother Parsons have heard any thing of this plan be kind enough to state it to them. the mail will soon be closed.

I am Sir with great respect
your most obedt Servt
Caleb Strong

Table of Short-Form Citations

Annals

The Debates and Proceedings in the Congress of the United States (Washington: Gales and Seaton, 1834). This is the predecessor to the *Congressional Record*. See appendix 2.

Blackstone

There are numerous editions of Sir William Blackstone's *Commentaries on the Laws of England,* so we have followed the standard legal practice of citing to a "star-page" (indicated by an asterisk). The star-page is the page in the first edition; all subsequent editions preserve the original pagination.

Childs, *House Documents*

James B. Childs, "Disappeared in the Wings of Oblivion: The Story of the United States House of Representatives Printed Documents at the First Session of the First Congress, New York, 1789," 58 *Papers of the Bibliographical Society of America* 91 (1964).

Childs, *Senate Documents*

James B. Childs, "The Story of the United States Senate Documents, 1st Congress, 1st Session, New York 1789," 56 *Papers of the Bibliographical Society of America* 175 (1962).

Correspondence of George Read

William Thompson Read, *Life and Correspondence of George Read* . . . (Philadelphia: Lippincott, 1870).

Crosskey, *Politics and the Constitution*

William Winslow Crosskey, *Politics and the Constitution in the History of the United States,* 2 vols. (Chicago: University of Chicago Press, 1953). Volume numbers are not cited herein since the volumes are paginated consecutively.

Diaries of George Washington

Donald Jackson et al., eds., *The Diaries of George Washington,* 6 vols. (Charlottesville, Va.: University Press of Virginia, 1976–1979).

DocHistConst

Merrill Jensen et al., eds., *The Documentary History of the Ratification of the Constitution,* 9 vols. to date (Madison: State Historical Society of Wisconsin, 1976 to date).

DocHistFirstFedCong

Linda Grant DePauw et al., eds., *Documentary History of the First Federal Congress of the United States of America,* 7 vols. to date (Baltimore: Johns Hopkins University Press, 1972 to date).

DocHistSupCt

Maeva Marcus et al., eds., *The Documentary History of the Supreme Court of the United States, 1789–1800,* 2 vols. to date (New York: Columbia University Press, 1985 to date).

Elliot, *Debates*

Jonathan Elliot, ed., *The Debates in the Several State Conventions on the Adoption of the Federal Constitution . . .,* 5 vols. (Philadelphia: Lippincott, 1836, 1845).

Evans, *American Bibliography*

Charles Evans, *American Bibliography: A Chronological Dictionary of All Books, Pamphlets and Periodical Publications . . . down to and including the Year 1820,* 14 vols. (Chicago: Blakely Press, 1903–59).

Farrand, *Records*

Max Farrand, ed., *The Records of the Federal Convention of 1787,* 4 vols., rev. ed. (New Haven: Yale University Press, 1937).

Fed. Cas.; F.2d

Two compilations of lower federal-court opinions ("Federal Cases"; "Federal Reporter, 2d Series"), as conventionally cited in legal materials. The first of these collects all lower federal-court cases appearing in any form before 1880. The second is the current reporter series for federal circuit court of appeals opinions.

The Federalist

There are numerous editions of this famous set of essays, so we have followed the standard legal practice of citing to the essay number. The author is indicated in parentheses.

Goebel, *History*

Julius Goebel, Jr., *History of the Supreme Court of the United States,* vol. 1, *Antecedents and Beginnings to 1801* (New York: Macmillan, 1971).

James, *Legal Treatises*

Eldon Revare James, "A List of Legal Treatises Printed in the British Colonies and the American States before 1801," in *Harvard Legal Essays Written in Honor of and Presented to Joseph Henry*

	Beale and Samuel Williston, ed. Roscoe Pound (Cambridge: Harvard University Press, 1934), 159–211.
JCC	Worthington C. Ford et al., eds., *Journals of the Continental Congress, 1774–1789,* 34 vols. (Washington D.C.: GPO, 1904–1937).
Letters of Louis D. Brandeis	Melvin I. Urofsky et al., eds., *Letters of Louis Dembitz Brandeis,* 5 vols. (Albany: State University of New York Press, 1971–79).
Letters of Paine Wingate	Charles Wingate, ed. *The Life and Letters of Paine Wingate,* 2 vols. (1930).
Life of James Iredell	Griffith J. McRee, ed., *Life and Correspondence of James Iredell . . .,* 2 vols. (New York: Appleton, 1857). No volume number is cited herein since all correspondence cited is found in volume 2.
Maclay, *Journal*	Edgar S. Maclay, ed., *The Journal of William Maclay, United States Senator from Pennsylvania, 1789–1791* (1890; reprint, New York: Boni, 1927).
Maclay, *Sketches*	William Maclay, *Sketches of Debate in the First Senate of the United States in 1789–90–91* (1880; reprint, New York: B. Franklin, 1969).
Papers of James Madison	William T. Hutchinson et al., eds., *The Papers of James Madison,* 15 vols. to date (Chicago: University of Chicago Press, 1962 to date).
Papers of Thomas Jefferson	Julian P. Boyd et al., eds., *The Papers of Thomas Jefferson,* 20 vols. to date (Princeton: Princeton University Press, 1950 to date).
Senate and *House Journals*	Cited by year. These are the official journals kept by the two houses of Congress. The original editions have been cited to herein.
Stat.	This is the conventional legal mode of citing to the volumes compiling the laws passed each session by Congress, technically entitled *The Public Statutes at Large . . .* Statutes are cited by date of passage, page, chapter, section, and volume of Stat.
Storing, *Anti-Federalist*	Herbert J. Storing, ed., *The Complete Anti-Federalist,* 7 vols. (Chicago: University of Chicago Press, 1981).

U.S.	The conventional legal citation form for *United States Reports,* in which are printed the opinions of the United States Supreme Court. The earliest volumes in this series are also identified by the abbreviated name of the court's reporter, within parentheses, for example: (4 Dall.) or (16 Pet.).
U.S.C.	The conventional legal citation for the *United States Code,* which is published in Washington, D.C., by the Government Printing Office.
Warren, *History*	Charles Warren, *The Supreme Court in United States History,* 2 vols., rev. ed. (Boston: Little Brown, 1926).
Warren, *New Light*	Charles Warren, "New Light on the History of the Federal Judiciary Act of 1789," 37 *Harvard Law Review* 49 (1923).
Wharton, *State Trials*	Francis Wharton, *State Trials of the United States during the Administration of Washington and Adams . . .* (Philadelphia: Corey and Hart, 1849).

Notes

We are extremely lucky that Professor Ritz left the notes in excellent shape, but there are lacunae in the typescript of the notes. We have tried to fill them in, but we have surely introduced technical errors that Professor Ritz would never have committed.

CHAPTER II

1. 34 *JCC* 520–21.
2. 1789 *Senate Journal* 6, and 1789 *House Journal* 6.
3. 1789 *Senate Journal* 9–10. The committee was Oliver Ellsworth of Connecticut, William Paterson of New Jersey, William Maclay of Pennsylvania, Caleb Strong of Massachusetts, Richard Henry Lee of Virginia, Richard Bassett of Delaware, William Few of Georgia, and Paine Wingate of New Hampshire.

On April 13, after they had appeared, Charles Carroll of Maryland and Ralph Izard of South Carolina were added to the committee. 1789 *Senate Journal* 11. Since the Senate finished its work on the Judiciary Bill on July 17, *id.* at 64.–65, and Rufus King, the first senator from New York to appear, took his seat on July 25, *id.* at 69, this completed the membership of the committee.

4. For the Crimes Committee, see n.37 *infra* and accompanying text.
5. Maclay, *Journal* 83.
6. *Id.* at 86.
7. See Goebel, *History* n.8 at 459.
8. Paine Wingate wrote to Timothy Pickering under date of April 27, saying, "Some general principles have been settled by a majority of the committee, but the system is yet immature." 2 *Letters of Paine Wingate* 299–300.

Oliver Ellsworth wrote to Richard Law under date of April 30, "The following are outlines of a judiciary system contemplating before a committee of the Senate." Wharton, *State Trials* 37.

See also Ralph Izard to Edward Rutledge, April 24, 1789, Ralph Izard Papers, South Caroliniana Library, University of South Carolina, Columbia, S.C.; David Sewall to Caleb Strong, May 2, 1789, Stephen Strong Collection, Forbes Library, Northampton, Mass. (reprinted in appendix 3); Caleb Strong to Ichabod Tucker, May 7, 1789, Tucker Family Papers, Essex Institute, Salem, Mass.
9. Maclay, *Journal* 29.
10. Maclay does not give the names of the members of the subcommittee. How-

ever, a letter from Fisher Ames to George Minot under date of July 8 says that these three "in particular have their fair share of this merit" for the bill. Seth Ames, ed., *Works of Fisher Ames,* vol. 1 (Boston: Little, Brown, 1854), 64. Furthermore, the manuscript of the bill is in the handwriting of Paterson, Ellsworth, and Strong.

11. Maclay, *Journal* 72.

12. *Ibid.*

13. 1789 *Senate Journal* 50.

14. Goebel, *History* 406.

15. See Appendix II, p. 184. The printer's account calls for 1,000 sheets to print 250 bills, so four forms were used to print this bill of sixteen pages. Similarly, 480 sheets were used for the subsequent June 21 printing of 120 more copies of the bill. Childs, *Senate Documents* 181.

16. In letters dated June 15, Ellsworth sent copies of the bill to Lieutenant Governor Oliver Wollcott, Lee-Kohns Collection, New York Public Library, New York; and to Richard Law, Ernst Law Manuscripts, Connecticut Historical Society.

17. Letter to John Dickinson, June 16, 1789, in *Correspondence of George Read* 481.

18. Childs, *Senate Documents* 181.

19. See list in Goebel, *History* n.29 at 467.

20. Maclay, *Journal* 98–99; Maclay, *Sketches* 97–98. This procedure appears to be that authorized by a rule adopted May 21. 1789 *Senate Journal* 39.

21. July 11, 1789, in 2 *Letters of Paine Wingate* 318.

22. Maclay, *Journal* 114.

23. *Id.* at 114–15; 1789 *Senate Journal* 64–65. Senators voting for the bill were Bassett, Carroll, Dalton, Ellsworth, Elmer, Few, Gunn, Henry, Johnson, Izard, Morris, Paterson, Read, and Strong. Senators against were Butler, Grayson, Langdon, Lee, Maclay, and Wingate. *Id.* at 64.

24. *Id.* at 61.

25. On June 25 a section of the bill dealing with Quakers was deleted. Maclay, *Journal* 87; Maclay, *Sketches* 87. Maclay reports an amendment of July 7 that appears in the final bill. Maclay, *Journal* 99; Maclay, *Sketches* 98. There is also a manuscript amendment that bears a notation showing that it was accepted on July 8. LC 43, amending p. 6, line 4. (The notation "LC" is explained in appendix 2.)

26. 1789 *Senate Journal* 64 (emphasis added).

27. 1789 *Senate Journal* 67; 1789 *House Journal* 78. The Senate had passed the bill too late on Friday, July 17, to carry it to the House on that date. The House did not meet on Saturday.

28. Childs, *House Documents* 212, quoting *New-York Journal.*

29. Letter from Thomas Hartley to Jasper Yeates, July 23, 1789, Yeates Papers, Historical Society of Pennsylvania, Philadelphia.

30. 1789 *House Journal* 142.

31. Letter from Roger Sherman to Samuel Huntington, Sept. 17, 1789, William Griswold Lane Collection, Yale University, New Haven, Conn.

32. Letter from Paine Wingate to John Langdon, Sept. 17, 1789, 2 *Letters of Paine Wingate* 334.

33. 1789 *Senate Journal* 139–40. The committee consisted of Ellsworth,

Paterson, and Senator Pierce Butler of South Carolina, an opponent of the measure. *Id.* at 81.

34. 1789 *House Journal* 145; 1789 *Senate Journal* 140.

35. Act of Sept. 24, 1789, ch. 20, 1 Stat. 73, commonly known as The Judiciary Act of 1789.

36. 1789 *Senate Journal* 33–34.

37. Thus the committee membership as originally established included William Samuel Johnson of Connecticut, George Read of Delaware, John Langdon of New Hampshire, Robert Morris of Pennsylvania, Tristam Dalton of Massachusetts, Jonathan Elmer of New Jersey, John Henry of Maryland, and James Gunn of Georgia. When he took his seat on May 21, William Grayson of Virginia was added to the committee. 1789 *Senate Journal* 39. On June 8, Pierce Butler of South Carolina took his seat. *Id.* at 46. On June 12 he was added to the committee. *Id.* at 51.

38. Sections 10 (dealing with national district courts) and 11 (dealing with national circuit courts) of the Judicial Bill as reported on June 12 contained the language quoted in the text. The deletion of this language was noted on Senator Wingate's copy of the June 12 printed bill, which, as is demonstrated elsewhere (see appendix 2), shows that the deletion was accomplished by a floor amendment—probably during the second or third readings of the Judicial Bill.

39. 1789 *Senate Journal* 77.

40. *Id.* at 82, 95, 107, 113; 1789 *House Journal* 119.

41. 1789 *Senate Journal* 138. The *House Journal* does not report the postponement of the Crimes Bill. 1789 *House Journal* 143–44.

42. 1789 *Senate Journal* 142.

43. Act of Apr. 30, 1790, ch. 9, 1 Stat. 112.

44. On January 19, 1790, in the second session of the First Congress, a motion was made to appoint a committee to report a crimes bill, 1790 *Senate Journal* 13, but action was postponed until the status of unfinished business could be established. It was resolved that unfinished business should be regarded as not passed upon by either house. 1790 *Senate Journal* 15; 1790 *House Journal* 20. A committee was appointed, and on the very same day it reported a bill, 1790 *Senate Journal* 17, which was the bill passed by the Senate the previous year, and the Senate passed it again. This time, the bill passed in the House. 1790 *House Journal* 77, 83.

45. Charles Warren comes to a similar conclusion concerning the deletion of the language "and defined by the laws of the same" from the Judicial Bill, although he does not see it as a temporary measure. Warren, *New Light* 73. Goebel sees the deletion as insignificant, merely the elimination of a redundancy. Goebel, *History* 496.

46. See, *e.g.,* "Brutus," Storing, *Anti-Federalist,* ¶¶ 2.9.172–79; 4 *Elliot* 136–39, 152–55, 163–65 (remarks of Spencer).

47. See, *e.g.,* Hamilton, *The Federalist,* no. 81; 3 Elliot, *Debates* 519–20 (remarks of Pendleton) (rebutting popular fears about loss of trial by jury); 3 *id.* 538 (remarks of Madison), 555, 561 (remarks of Marshall), 4 *id.* 150–51 (remarks of Johnston). All these concern regulation of the new judiciary by Congress.

48. Edward Dumbauld, *The Bill of Rights and What It Means Today* (Norman, Okla.: University of Oklahoma Press, 1957), 32–33.

49. See 2 *DocHistConst* 597–99, 623–25 (Pennsylvania); *Documents Illustrative of the Formation of the Union of the American States* 1019 (Massachusetts), 1024–26 (New Hampshire), 1027–34 (Virginia), 1034–38 (New York), and 1044–51 (North Carolina); 2 Elliot, *Debates* 550–51 (Maryland). See also Louise I. Trenholme, *Ratification of the Federal Constitution in North Carolina* (New York: Columbia University Press, 1932), 146–91.

50. 1789 *House Journal* 57; 1 *Annals* 440.

51. 1 *Annals* 452–3.

52. *Id.* at 458.

53. Small cases thus could not be appealed. To a modern eye, this may appear to be a discrimination against small cases, but in the context of the time, it was seen as a discrimination in favor of small cases.

54. The House defeated such a proposal on August 18, and the Senate defeated them on September 4 and 8. 1789 *House Journal* 104; 1789 *Senate Journal* 119, 126–27. The House also defeated on August 22 a proposal to amend Article I, Section 8, to limit Congress's power to create inferior national courts other than admiralty courts. 1789 *House Journal* 111. Although the House proposed an amendment that embodied an amount-in-controversy limitation for Supreme Court appeals, the Senate eliminated it on the ground that the Judicial Bill adequately provided for the same. See, *e.g.*, James Madison to Edmund Pendleton, Sept. 23, 1789, in 12 *Papers of James Madison* 418.

55. See the discussion in Drew L. Kershen, "Vicinage," 29 *Oklahoma Law Review* 801, esp. 844–60 (1976).

56. 1789 *House Journal* 36.

57. Warren, *New Light* 49.

CHAPTER III

1. Morton J. Horwitz, *The Transformation of American Law, 1780–1860* (Cambridge, Mass.: Harvard University Press, 1977), 28–29, 141–43, 228.

2. William E. Nelson, *Americanization of the Common Law* (Cambridge, Mass: Harvard University Press, 1975), 3–4, 28–30, 165–71, n.4 at 185, n.37 at 257.

3. *See also* Leonard W. Levy, *The Law of the Commonwealth and Chief Justice Shaw* (Cambridge, Mass: Harvard University Press, 1957), 290–95.

4. "A Declaration of Rights of the Inhabitants of the Commonwealth of Massachusetts, Article XXX of Part the First," 14 *Suffolk Law Review* 848 (1980).

5. Francis Newton Thorpe, comp., 1 *The Federal and State Constitutions . . .* (Washington, D.C.: Government Printing Office, 1909), 538.

6. Two examples of what can be done are: Herbert Alan Johnson, *Imported Eighteenth Century Law Treatises in American Libraries 1700–1799* (Knoxville: University of Tennessee Press, 1978) and William Hamilton Bryson, *Census of Law Books in Colonial Virginia* (Charlottesville: University Press of Virginia, 1978).

7. For an example, see Elizabeth Gaspar Brown, *British Statutes in American Law* (Ann Arbor: University of Michigan Law School, 1964).

8. The first edition was published in England in 1765–69. The first American edition was published in Philadelphia in 1771–72. Evans, *American Bibliography* 11996, 12327, 12328; James, *Legal Treatises* 31–33.

9. 3 Blackstone, *30–60.

10. *Id.* at *32–37.

11. *Id.* at *56: "the supreme court of judicature in the kingdom."

12. *Id.* at *37–57.

13. *Id.* at *41.

14. *Id.* at *46–50.

15. *Id.* at *55–56.

16. *Id.* at *56.

17. *Id.* at *56.

18. *Id.* at *61–70.

19. *Id.* at *71–85. Blackstone writes as though these special courts lay outside the hierarchical arrangement; examples are the forest courts, court of policies of assurance, the palace court at Westminster, the several courts in the city of London, the chancellor's courts in the two universities.

20. *Id.* at *66.

21. *Id.* at *68–69.

22. Robert Stevens, *Law and Politics: The House of Lords as a Judicial Body, 1800–1976* (Chapel Hill: University of North Carolina Press, 1978).

23. *Id.* at 4–5. Stevens says, "By the thirteenth century, the development of the common law had led to the delegation [by the sovereign] of judicial work at the trial level (and by the Tudor period even to the establishment of a hierarchy of judicial appeals), but the idea that a final appeal from the regular courts lay to Parliament was not seriously questioned after the fourteenth century." *Id.* at 6.

24. *Id.* at 6.

25. *Id.* at 26.

26. *Ibid.* Emphasis added.

27. *Id.* at 27.

28. *Id.* at 26.

29. Joseph H. Smith, *Appeals to the Privy Council from the American Plantations* (New York: Columbia University Press, 1950), 225–28.

30. 5th ed. (1979).

31. James Parker, comp., *The Conductor Generalis . . .* at 15 (Philadelphia: Robert Campbell, 1792).

32. Johnson defines "provocation" as "an appeal to a judge." Samuel Johnson, *A Dictionary of the English Language* (London: W. Strahan, 1755), s.v. "provocation."

33. *Id.,* s.v. "appeal." Johnson's *Dictionary* gives this as the only "common law" meaning.

34. 4 Blackstone *308.

35. L. Kinvin Wroth and Hiller B. Zobel, eds., 1 *Legal Papers of John Adams,* (Cambridge, Mass.: Belknap Press, 1965), xxxix.

36. *E.g.,* Va. Code § 16.1–92, 106, 113, 114, providing for "appeals," which are trials *de novo,* from district courts to circuit courts.

37. Erwin C. Surrency, "The Development of the Appellate Function: The Pennsylvania Experience," 20 *American Journal of Legal History* 173, 178–79 (1976).

38. Joseph Horrell, "George Mason and the Fairfax Court," 91 *Virginia Magazine of History and Biography* 418 (1983).

39. David Sewall was appointed to the Superior Court of Judicature in 1777, to

fill the vacancy caused by the resignation of John Adams as chief justice, and the elevation of William Cushing to the chief justiceship. He continued in this post until 1789 when he resigned upon his appointment to be United States district judge for the District of Maine. Massachusetts Bar Association, *The Supreme Judicial Court of Massachusetts 1692–1942* 42, 51 (1942).

40. Sewall to Strong, May 2, 1789, Strong Manuscripts, Forbes Public Library, Northampton, Mass. The letter is set forth in full in appendix 3, *supra*.

Cushing had been appointed in 1775, elevated to chief justice in 1777, and served on that court until he resigned in 1789 upon appointment to associate justice of the United States Supreme Court. *See* n.39 *supra*.

41. *Ibid*.

42. James Madison to George Eve, Jan. 2, 1789, 11 *Papers of James Madison* 403, 405. On January 13, he wrote in the same vein to Thomas Mann Randolph, 11 *Papers of James Madison* 415, 416–17.

43. This point is missed in A. G. Roeber, "'The Scrutiny of the Ill Natured Ignorant Vulgar,'" 91 *Virginia Magazine of History and Biography* 387 (1983). He calls attention to the statute, and the later changes, but has difficulty explaining its purpose.

44. Judiciary Act of 1789, §§ 10, 11, 25.

45. *Id.* at § 12.

46. Goebel, *History* 9–10.

47. Goebel recognizes that the superior courts of England were trial courts. *Id.* at 13–14. But in discussing appellate devices in England and American innovations, he writes as though the basic structure were one of appellate review. *Id.* at 19–35.

48. See the table below for statutory citations.

49. Carroll T. Bond, *The Court of Appeals in Maryland, A History* (Baltimore: Barton-Gillet, 1928), 22–57.

50. Constitution of 1776, Art. 6.

51. *Id.*, Art. 56.

52. Bond, *supra*. n.49 at 60–63.

53. *Id.* at 68.

54. *Id.* at 95–98.

55. 16 *JCC* 61–62.

56. *Id.* at 62–63.

57. The *Journals* are not explicit on this point, but the following Saturday was fixed for the election of judges. *Id.* at 64.

58. 30 *JCC* 356.

59. Goebel, *History* 458.

60. *Id.* at 468.

61. *Id.* n.31 at 468.

62. *Ibid*.

63. The inventories of law libraries set forth in the appendix to Paul M. Hamlin, *Legal Education in Colonial New York* (New York: New York University Law Quarterly Review, 1939), show that the library of James Alexander (1720) contained the Laws of Jamaica, Laws of New York, Laws of Massachusetts Bay, and Laws of New Jersey. Joseph Murray's library contained no identifiable state stat-

utes. John Chambers's library (1760) contained the Acts of Jamaica, Acts of Assembly, Acts of New York (2 vols.), Laws of New York (2 vols.), Acts of New Jersey, New Jersey Laws (3 vols.), and Laws of Nevis. Judge William Smith's library (1770) contained Connecticut Laws, Laws of Jamaica, New Jersey Laws, and Laws of New York (Bradford edition). No statute books were identified in the library of John Montgomerie (1730). *Id.* at 172, 180–81, 185, 188–89, 193–96. Even with most of these statutory compilations, there is no way to determine their dates of publication.

64. Following the ravages of the revolutionary war, the New York Society was trying to reestablish its library. On January 7, 1789, the Common Council of New York allowed the society to use a room in the city hall for its library, provided it should not be necessary for the accommodation of the "Genl Govt of the United States." On April 7, the society applied to Congress for use of the room, and although no action on this petition is recorded, it appears that it probably was favorably received, for the society conferred the privileges of membership in the society on the members of Congress. Austin Baxter Keep, *History of the New York Society Library* (New York: De Vinne Press, 1908), 208–10; William Dawson Johnston, *History of the Library of Congress* (Washington, D.C.: GPO, 1904), 17. Neither of these sources gives a citation for the statement that the society offered use of its library to Congress.

65. Evans, *American Bibliography* 22018.

66. *Catalogue,* text at n.65 *supra,* at 45. A *Continuation* of the *Catalogue,* published in 1791 (Evans, *American Bibliography* 23618), shows that the society by then had acquired the Laws of New-York (2 vols.) and Virginia laws. *Id.* at 93, 104. The Virginia laws are identified in *A Farther Continuation,* published in 1792 (Evans, *American Bibliography* 24610), as having been published in 1752.

67. Goebel, *History* n.31 at 468. Goebel used Hening for Virginia statutes and an 1801 edition for Massachusetts. Other statutes he used are identified by year of enactment, without any indication as to whether the statute would have been published and readily available in 1789. William W. Hening, *Statutes at Large . . . ,* 13 vols. (New York: Bartow, 1819–23).

68. The Continental Congress asked the states to send to it copies of their laws for two different, though related, purposes. It asked for copies of the acts adopted in accordance with the recommendations made by Congress for legislation. For example, on April 30, 1784, Congress recommended to the legislatures of the several states that Congress be given the power for a term of fifteen years to prohibit the import or export of goods in vessels controlled by powers with which the United States did not have treaties of commerce. The resolution required the assent of nine states to put it into effect. 26 *JCC* 317–22. The resolution was printed as a broadside and sent to the states. 26 *JCC,* bibliographical note 435,721. On August 29, 1784, the secretary wrote to the eight states that had not sent him copies of their acts adopted in pursuance of the resolution, pointing out that only five states had transmitted their laws to Congress, although it had been suggested that some other states had complied with the recommendation but had not forwarded their laws. E. Burnett, ed., 8 *Letters of Members of the Continental Congress* 204 (1936). The other type of request was embodied in a resolution adopted July 27, 1785, on the motion of Elbridge Gerry, which read:

Resolved, That the Secretary of Congress apply to the Executives of the several states for 13 copies of the legislative acts thereof, since the first of September 1774, inclusive: that one set of the said acts be retained for the use of Congress, and that he deliver to the delegates of each State one set (exclusive of its own Acts) for the use of the legislature thereof. And the Secretary is further directed to adopt a similar mode for procuring the acts which may hereafter by passed as aforesaid, to the end, that every state, being thus informed, may have the fullest confidence in the other states, and derive the advantages which may result from the joint wisdom of the whole.

29 *JCC* 582–83, and Bibliographical Note 488,925. It appears that the motion as presented by Gerry directed the commissioners of the continental loan offices to procure these acts and to draw on the Board of Treasury for payment, but that this language was stricken out before adoption. The text of Thomson's circular letter, dated July 28, 1785, is given in Burnett, *supra,* at 173. The circular letter to Pennsylvania along with the resolution of Congress, are published in Samuel Hazard, ed., 10 *Pennsylvania Archives* 488 (1854). On November 9, 1785, in another circular letter Charles Thomson reported that only Massachusetts and South Carolina had complied with the resolution of July 27 and that he had been informed by Connecticut that prior to the passing of the resolution it had sent copies of its acts to the legislatures of the several states. He concluded by saying, "I beg leave to request your attention to this matter." Burnett, *supra,* at 252.

Thomson noted in a letter dated October 5, 1785, addressed to the governor of South Carolina and acknowledging receipt of the South Carolina laws, that there was no need to apologize for their condition inasmuch as the set of Massachusetts acts that he had previously distributed "are in the same situation as yours, incompleat." Burnett, *supra,* at 226.

There was some later compliance. Thomson wrote the executive of North Carolina under date of June 14, 1786, that he had delivered to Colonel Blount, the state's delegate in Congress, bound volumes of the laws of Pennsylvania and New Jersey since the Declaration of Independence and a bound volume of at least some of the acts passed in Virginia beginning in 1783. Walter Clark, ed., 20 *State Records of North Carolina* (Raleigh: P. M. Hale, 1902), 651–52.

69. See *e.g.,* Charles M. Cook, *The American Codification Movement: A Study of Antebellum Legal Reform* (Westpoint, Conn: Greenwood Press, 1981), 6–8.

70. 1 Stat. 51, n.a.

71. C. E. Carter, ed., 2 *Territorial Papers of the United States* 207 (Washington, D.C.: Government Printing Office, 1934).

72. The Revolution's new state constitutions had spawned strong popularly elected legislatures. State courts attempted to check what some felt to be the excesses of democracy by finding some legislative action to violate those constitutions. See generally Edward S. Corwin, "The Establishment of Judicial Review" (parts I–II), 9 *Michigan Law Review* 102, 283, (1910, 1911); Gordon S. Wood, *The Creation of the American Republic, 1776–1787* (Chapel Hill: Univ. of North Carolina Press, 1969), 453–63.

CHAPTER IV

1. For some modern discussions, *see* Robert N. Clinton, "A Mandatory View of Federal Court Jurisdiction: A Guided Quest for the Original Understanding of

Article III," 132 *University of Pennsylvania Law Review* 741 (1984); and Akhil Reed Amar, "A Neo-Federalist View of Article III: Separating the Two Tiers of Federal Jurisdiction," 65 *Boston University Law Review* 205 (1985).

2. For a contemporaneous discussion of this problem, *see* "Brutus," Storing, *Anti-Federalist,* ¶¶ 2.9.137–138, 2.9.191–193. In ¶ 2.9.155, Brutus rephrases the judicial power precisely as has been done in the text, concluding also that the national judicial power was vast.

3. Warren, *New Light* 67.

4. Maclay, *Journal* 83.

5. Farrand, 1 and 2 *Records*. The manuscript of this motion is among those discovered by Warren, and its exact wording differs slightly from Maclay's quotation: "That no subordinate federal jurisdiction be established in any State, other than for Admiralty or Maritime causes, but that federal interference shall be limited to appeal[s] only from the state courts to the supreme federal courts of the U. States." Warren says that this manuscript "is not in Lee's handwriting" (*New Light* 67), but a comparison of it with letters signed by Lee quickly demonstrates that it is. Consequently, Warren's suggestion that Maclay might have erred in reporting that Lee made the motion is without foundation.

6. Warren, *New Light* 67–68.

7. [The editors disagree with Professor Ritz on this point. Richard Henry Lee was in the Senate precisely because of his Anti-Federalist suspicions of the power of the new central government. The last thing an Anti-Federalist would desire was the conversion of a state institution—particularly a state court—into a national institution. Nothing reported by Maclay indicates that Lee understood the constitutional grant in Article III to be mandatory, so that any court that exercised that power would be *ipso facto* a national court. Maclay said that "the effect of the [Lee] motion was to exclude the federal jurisdiction from each of the States except in admiralty and maritime cases." The editors think it likely that Lee intended to restrict national-court jurisdiction, at least to the extent of keeping most cases within the constitutional bounds of national-court jurisdiction out of all lower national courts. Maclay's further remarks indicate that Lee contemplated that state courts should handle these cases—as *state courts,* not as national ones. It is also open to doubt whether Lee agreed that the national Supreme Court was given at least a power to review all cases within the constitutional bounds of national-court jurisdiction by the word "shall" in Article III. Professor Ritz's belief that Article III was thought by the founders to be just as self-executing as Articles I and II is, however, peripheral to the primary arguments advanced in this book.]

8. Warren is thus incorrect in citing this debate for the proposition that Congress decided early that it had the power to "confine the Federal judicial power within narrow limits." Warren, *New Light* 62.

9. [The editors disagree with much of what follows in this section, to the extent that Professor Ritz argues that no important limitations or restrictions on national judicial power were placed into the Judiciary Act of 1789.

We believe, for example, that the First Congress intended for there to be in Section 11 a $500 amount-in-controversy prerequisite for the bringing of diversity and alienage cases in federal courts. We note, for another example, that Section 14 of the act expressly limits the issuance of national *habeas corpus* writs to applicants detained by national authority. We also believe that the silence in the act concerning "federal-question" jurisdiction, taken in conjunction with Section 25, which granted the Supreme Court power to hear appeals from state courts in the most important kinds of "federal-question" cases, and in conjunction with the frustration of the natural and contemporary expectation that "federal questions" would be heard in national courts by the absence of any mention of that jurisdiction in the act, was intended to communicate a denial of that jurisdiction to the national courts as a trial jurisdiction. The silence could, however, also be interpreted in an opposite manner, exemplifying the masterfully open-ended drafting that characterizes the act as a whole. These restrictions were necessary, as Professor Ritz implies, to placate those fearful of the potentially ravenous authority of the national courts.

We feel that the First Congress gave to the national courts the most important features of Article III jurisdiction. We agree with Professor Ritz that the First Congress never seems to have debated the question of the extent of any power it might have had to limit, or to grant, national-court jurisdiction. We further agree that the drafters of the act were uncomfortable with the limitations they did enact, that the limitations they enacted were consistent with promises made by supporters of the Constitution during the debates over ratification, and that the major "grants" of jurisdiction in Sections 9, 11, 12, 13, and 25 of the Judiciary Act do not purport expressly to limit or restrict national judicial authority, but seem only to regulate or channel that authority. Finally, we note the "loophole" of Section 14, granting in vague and open-ended terms broad powers to national courts to issue common-law writs.

We repeat that these deficiencies in Professor Ritz's argument deal with minor and peripheral matters; they in no way impede or dilute the major theses and insights of this book.]

10. [One of the editors has carefully examined the manuscript containing the earliest extant version of Section 11. Several changes in this section were made on the manuscript itself. When these changes are considered in the light of some contemporary letters that report the development of the resolutions from which the subcommittee drafted the bill, it becomes clear that the location of the semicolon is an accident. The argument will be set forth in detail in a separate publication.]

11. 1 *Annals* 452–53.

12. 1789 *House Journal* 105.

13. 1789 *Senate Journal* 130.

14. In the Judicial Bill as introduced into the Senate, the imposition of costs on a plaintiff or libellant recovering less than $500 or $300 respectively was made mandatory, but this was softened by the Senate.

15. Judiciary Act of 1789, § 21.

16. The last sentence of Section II provides that the circuit courts shall "also" have appellate jurisdiction over some unspecified cases. It is suggested below that this was intended to cover some unspecified appeals for trial, but that the provision was never implemented in practice. Ellsworth in drafting the "appeal" language of Section 20 may have had in mind the last sentence of Section 11—that in some instances a libellant in the district court would be permitted to "appeal" to the circuit court in the sense of having a trial there.

17. Article III, Section 2.

18. This letter is set forth and discussed in appendix 1.

19. Warren, *New Light* 62.

20. Warren, *New Light* 67. Warren quotes Ellsworth as chief justice in *Turner v. Bank of North America*, 4 U.S. (4 Dall.) 8 (1799), to the effect that the circuit courts had "cognizance, not of cases generally, but of a few specially circumstanced, amounting to a small proportion of the cases which an unlimited jurisdiction would embrace." Warren, *New Light* 69. In *Turner*, Ellsworth was considering whether the plaintiff had established that the case fell within the diversity jurisdiction. Of the total number of controversies, those between citizens of different states are but "a small proportion." There is no reason to think that Ellsworth meant anything other than that.

21. Act of Feb. 13, 1801, ch. 4, § 11, 2 Stat. 92.

22. Act of Mar. 8, 1802, ch. 8. § 2, 2 Stat. 132.

23. 41 U.S. (16 Pet.) 539 (1842).

24. Warren, *New Light* 71.

25. Act of Mar. 3, 1875, ch. 137, § 1, 18 Stat. 470.

26. Charles Alan Wright et al., 13 *Federal Practice and Procedure* § 3561, at 389 (St. Paul: West Publishing Co., 1975). At § 3503, n.10, Warren, *New Light*, is cited. [The editors note that Amar, *supra* n.1, takes the more sensible position that Section 25 of the Judiciary Act, granting to the Supreme Court appellate authority over state court decisions in most federal-question cases, fulfilled the expectations of most citizens that national jurisdiction would exist in federal-question cases.]

27. [The editors note that it was the customary practice in the early years of the Republic for substantive acts to include specific grants of jurisdiction. See, *e.g.*, Act of Feb. 21, 1793, ch. 11 §§ 5,6, 1 Stat. 322 (grant of national jurisdiction in patent act); Act of Apr. 4, 1800, ch. 19 § 58, 2 Stat. 35 (grant of national jurisdiction in bankruptcy act). Thus a general grant of federal-question jurisdiction was unnecessary.]

28. *DocHistSupCt* 171, 333.

29. Warren says: "It is a curious fact that the very first line in the official written minutes of the Court, kept by the clerk, contained an error. . . . The word 'Judicial' of course improperly appears in the official title of the Court, and was undoubtedly inserted by the Clerk (who was a Massachusetts man) because of the fact that in Massachusetts, the official title of the highest Court was the 'Supreme Judicial Court.'" Warren, 1 *History*, n.2 at 46. This judgment is repeated in *DocHistSupCt* n.1 at 171. Both, of course, assume that as of this date in 1790 the court had an official title and that it was "Supreme Court."

30. Beginning in Section 1 and continuing throughout the act, in the first official printing the words "supreme court" are in lowercase.

31. The use of uppercase type in the printing of the Judiciary Act of 1789 in *Statutes at Large* does not faithfully follow the official certified printed copies of that act.

32. *See* appendix 1.

33. Maclay, *Journal* 85–86.

34. Process Act of Sept. 29, 1789, ch. 21, § 1, 1 Stat. 93.

35. Pickering to Wingate, July 1, 1789, Emmet Collection, New York Public Library, New York.

36. It is puzzling why the provisions for review of decisions of the Maine district court are divided between Sections 10 (writ of error) and 21 (appeals).

37. Act of Feb. 13, 1801, ch. 4 § 21, 2 Stat. 96.

38. At least one minor exception exists today: the District of Wyoming includes those portions of Yellowstone National Park in Idaho and Montana. See 28 U.S.C. §§ 92, 106, 131 (1982).

39. The section was amended at least four times. There are three manuscript amendments. LC 38 adds a provision; LC 39 inserts a provision; and LC 42 inserts two provisions. (For the meaning of the designation "LC," see appendix 2.) Wingate's copy, while not showing these manuscript changes, does exhibit deletion of the language "and defined by the laws of the same."

40. This is very indirectly expressed in Section 11.

41. The language of the statute is "including all seizures under laws of impost, navigation or trade of the United States, where the seizures are made, on waters which are navigable from the sea by vessels of ten or more tons burthen, within their respective districts as well as upon the high seas." Warren thinks that this was an extraordinary provision, in light of the Anti-Federalist concern that the right to trial by jury not be impaired. He says that in England this type of case was tried in the common-law courts, and so to a jury. Warren, *New Light* 74. Goebel, however, sees nothing surprising in the provision, inasmuch as Connecticut, New York, and Virginia (where a noncitizen was a party) had adopted juryless procedures for the enforcement of their impost acts. Goebel, *History* 474.

42. The language of the statute is "and shall also have exclusive original cognizance of all seizures on land, or other waters than as aforesaid, made, and of all suits for penalties and forfeitures incurred, under the laws of the United States." Warren is somewhat misleading on this provision. He points out that the "Draft Bill did not vest jurisdiction in any federal court when made elsewhere than on the high seas," citing *The Sarah*, 21 U.S. (8 Wheat.) 391 (1823). Warren, *New Light* 35 and n.59. *The Sarah* involved the final act, not the draft bill.

43. The district court was given exclusive jurisdiction by Section 9 of all civil suits against consuls and vice-consuls, and of all criminal suits against the same within the limits of the criminal jurisdiction of the district courts previously set out in the section.

44. Judiciary Act of 1789, §§ 11, 19, 21 (requiring at least $300 in controversy for such appeals).

45. As introduced into the Senate, the Judicial Bill provided for concurrent national jurisdiction—either in the circuit courts or in the Supreme Court—of cases where the United States was plaintiff or petitioner. The grant of jurisdiction to the Supreme court was deleted before passage.

46. The circuit court would consist of two Supreme Court justices, as the district judge (as has been noted) would be disabled from reviewing his own decision. Section 21 gave no further review by the Supreme Court, but review was undertaken by the Court anyway. See below.

47. Judiciary Act of 1789, § 4.

48. See 5 *DocHistFirstFedCong* n.99 at 1185–86.

49. Madison to George Eve, Jan. 2, 1789; Madison to Thomas Mann Randolph, Jan. 13, 1789, 11 *Papers of James Madison* 403, 415.

50. Madison to Eve, *id.* n.49 at 403.

51. Madison to Randolph, *id.* n.49 at 416–17.

52. Goebel, *History* 478, says that the "petition in error" was "a method once used to secure review by the House of Lords in England, and still the method of

pursuing a supersedeas for review in Virginia." As authority for its use in England, Goebel cites only "Coke, Fourth Institute, 21." Coke's *Fourth Institute* at the page cited contains a discussion of "[t]he manner of bringing writs of Error in Parliament" (this is the heading in the index). All that the discussion says about a "petition in error" is the following: "If a judgment be given in the King's bench either upon a writ of error, or otherwise, the party grieved may upon a petition of right made to the King in English . . ." Edward Coke, *The Fourth Part of the Institutes of the Laws of England* *21 (London: W. Clarke & Sons, 1817), at 20. The rest of the discussion is devoted to procedure on writs of error, and there is no indication that England recognized anything called a "petition in error" as a distinctive judicial procedure.

As illustrative of Virginia usage, Goebel cites Virginia statutes that do not seem to have anything to do with appellate review. "Pursuing a supersedeas" is hardly the equivalent of seeking appellate review in the way the term is used in the Judicial Bill.

53. Act of May 1784.

54. There is no record of this amendment in either the *Senate Journal* or the manuscripts. However, Wingate noted the change on his printed bill, which shows that it was a floor amendment.

55. Sewall to Strong, May 2, 1789, Stephen Strong Manuscripts, Forbes Library, Northampton, Mass. (set forth in full in appendix 3).

56. The words "by appeal" in Section 22 must have been used in the sense of a transfer of a case for trial in a superior court either before or after trial in an inferior court. If this is not the meaning, there is considerable excess verbiage in the section. In Section 12 and again in this section it is made clear that diversity cases can be removed from state courts to the circuit courts only before trial, never after trial.

57. It is far from clear what "regulations and restrictions" were "herein after provided," pursuant to Section 22, if indeed there were any. The word "also" in Section 11 is quite important, for its omission would make it redundant of the other provisions for review. This part of Section 11 was misquoted in *Smith v. Jackson,* 1 Paine 453, 22 Fed. Cas. 13,064 (C.C.N.D. N.Y. 1825), by omitting "also."

58. Trials where states were defendants and private citizens were plaintiffs were mercifully terminated by passage of the Eleventh Amendment in 1798.

59. 3 U.S. (3 Dall.) 121 (1795).

60. 2 U.S. (2 Dall.) 409 (1792).

61. It was also used in *United States v. Judge Lawrence,* 3 U.S. (3 Dall.) 42 (1795).

62. Section 14 of the act, it must be noted, gave "all the before-mentioned courts of the United States" power to issue "all other writs not specially provided for by statute, which may be necessary for the exercise of their respective jurisdictions, and agreeable to the principles and usages of law."

63. It is clear that the Supreme Court permitted the use of fictions and other devices to give federal courts jurisdiction, contrary both to the language and a strict reading of the 1789 act and to the desires of Anti-Federalists, expressed for example in proposed constitutional amendments from the Maryland and New York ratification conventions. See, *e.g., Hylton v. United States,* 3 U.S. (3 Dall.) 54 (1795) (fictional ownership of 125 chariots attributed to Hylton in order to meet

the $2,000 jurisdictional amount necessary to give the Supreme Court jurisdiction upon writ of error). This practice was sharply cut back after the decision of the Court in *Bingham v. Cabot*, 3 U.S. (3 Dall.) 382 (1797), and the proclamation early in 1798 of the passage of the Eleventh Amendment.

64. 3 U.S. (3 Dall.) 6 (1794).

65. *Id.*, n.1 at 7.

66. 3 U.S. (3 Dall.) 121 (1795).

67. See *Penhallow v. Doane's Adm'rs*, 3 U.S. (3 Dall.) 54 (1795); *Talbot v. Jansen*, 3 U.S. (3 Dall.) 133 (1795); *Geyer v. Michel and the Ship Den Onzekeren*, 3 U.S. (3 Dall.) 285 (1796); *United States v. La Vengeance*, 3 U.S. (3 Dall.) 297 (1796); *Moodie v. The Ship Phoebe Anne*, 3 U.S. (3 Dall.) 319 (1796).

68. *M'Donough v. Dannery and the Ship Mary Ford*, 3 U.S. (3 Dall.) 186 (1796).

69. 3 U.S. (3 Dall.) 321 (1796).

70. Emphasis has been added to the statutory language.

71. This point will be made at length in the next chapter.

72. 3 U.S. at 328.

73. 5 U.S. (1 Cranch) 137 (1803).

74. Bedford to Read, June 24, 1789, in *Correspondence of George Read* 482–83.

75. Bradford to Boudinot, June 28, 1789, Wallace Collection, Historical Society of Pennsylvania, Philadelphia. Bradford noted that his opinion had also been solicited by Senator Robert Morris, and that he had sent his comments also to Morris.

76. Shippen to Morris, July 13, 1789, Autograph Collection, Historical Society of Pennsylvania, Philadelphia.

77. Goebel, *History* n.152 at 502.

78. Parker to Lee, July 6, 1789, Lee Family Manuscripts, University of Virginia, Charlottesville, Va.

79. Maclay, *Journal* 93–94.

80. *Id.* at 92–106.

81. 2 *Letters of Paine Wingate* 339.

82. Pinckney to Madison, Mar. 28, 1789, in 12 *Papers of James Madison* 34–35.

83. [The editors are of opinion that Pinckney was probably referring to questions of debts, both those incurred by colonists before 1776 and still owing to British creditors, and especially those incurred by states in financing the Revolution and owed to individuals.]

84. 1 Stat. 50, n.a. at 51–53; C. E. Carter, ed., 2 *Territorial Papers of the United States* 39–50 (1934).

85. 26 *JCC* 274–79; 6 *Papers of Thomas Jefferson* 571–80.

86. 1 Stat. 51, n.a.

87. 32 *JCC* 253.

88. 1 Stat. 51, n.a.

89. 2 *Territorial Papers, supra* n. 85, at 207.

CHAPTER V

1. For example, Oliver Ellsworth never refers to the "courts of the United States." Instead, in Section 11, when he refers to both circuit and district court, he speaks of "either of said courts." On the other hand, Caleb Strong, who probably

drafted the later sections of the act, frequently uses the term, "courts of the United States," and does not use "either of said courts." The usage begins with Section 26, known to have been drafted by Caleb Strong, because the manuscript exists in his handwriting, and continues throughout the remaining sections of the act. In Section 34, Ellsworth picks up the same usage. The reason is of course speculative: to make Section 34 consistent with the sections in which it was placed; because Ellsworth decided the phraseology was preferable; or even that Ellsworth was not conscious of the change.

Similarly, in Section 26, Caleb Strong introduces unnecessary detail that is not to be found in the sections drafted by Ellsworth. In proceedings for forfeitures, etc., this section provides that "where the forfeiture, breach or non-performance shall appear, by the default or confession of the defendant, or upon demurrer, the court before whom the action is, shall render judgment therein for the plaintiff to recover so much as is due according to equity." Ellsworth very well may have considered this section unnecessary, since it adds nothing to what otherwise would have been understood.

2. Irving Brant, 1 *James Madison* 456 (Indianapolis: Bobbs-Merrill, 1941).

3. The Declaration of Independence refers to "these United Colonies," but in referring to the body agreeing to the declaration, the language is, "the representatives of the united States of America, in General Congress, Assembled."

4. However, in the engrossed bill, the Supreme Court is referred to by use of the uppercase, and the other courts by capitalizing only the word "Court," as "circuit Court" and "district Court."

5. See n.1 *supra*.

6. Paul M. Hamlin and Charles E. Baker, *Supreme Court of Judicature of the Province of New York 1691–1704* (New York: New York Historical Society, 1952), 52. Emphasis to phrases using "respective" and "several" throughout this chapter has been added by the author.

7. The meaning could be better conveyed by referring to the justices going on circuit in the *several* counties and being assisted by the justices of the peace of each of the *respective* counties.

8. Joseph H. Smith et al., eds., *Court Records of Prince Georges County, Maryland 1696–1699* 429 (Washington, D.C.: American Historical Association, 1964).

9. 9 *JCC* 777–78.

10. 20 *JCC* 501.

11. 29 *JCC* 804.

12. 29 *JCC* 798–804.

13. 29 *JCC* 801.

14. "A Committee of the Massachusetts Legislature on Additional Amendments to the Federal Constitution, 1790," 2 *American Historical Review* 99, 104 (1896).

15. 6 *Diaries of George Washington* 165 and n.1 (1979).

16. "An Act, Supplementary to an act, entitled 'An act to establish an uniform and more convenient system of Judicature,'" 49 *Acts and Resolutions of the General Assembly of South Carolina, Passed in December 1799* 53 (1800).

17. Cong. Globe, 42d Cong., 1st Sess., 653, quoted in *Allen v. McCurry,* 449 U.S. 90, 98 (1980).

18. Crosskey, *Politics and the Constitution* 50–53.

19. Quoted in *Documentary History of the Constitution of the United States of America* (Washington, D.C.: Department of State, 1894), 1–2.

20. Article I, Section 7, paragraph 2 refers to making an entry "on the Journal of each House respectively." Since different entries will be made (of members who vote for or against an override of a veto) the more appropriate word is "respectively," although the word "several" would not be inappropriate.

21. Art. I, § 8; Art. IV, § 1 and § 2.

22. Art. I, § 10; Art. IV, § 1 and §2.

23. § 5: "That the first session of the said circuit court in the *several* districts shall commence at the times following . . . and the subsequent sessions in the *respective* districts on the like days of every sixth calendar month afterwards."

§ 7: "That the Supreme Court, and the district courts shall have power to appoint clerks for their *respective* courts. . . . And the said clerks shall also *severally* give bond."

Inasmuch as the date for commencing the circuit courts was different in the different districts, and the amount of bonds given by the clerks was likewise different, a better usage would have been to use the word "respective."

24. § 9.

25. §§ 10, 32, 35.

26. §§ 15, 32.

27. § 29.

28. § 28.

29. § 29.

30. §§ 9, 11, 13, 22.

31. Goebel, *History* 12.

32. *Id.* at 35–49.

33. *Id.* at 486.

34. *Id.* at 478.

35. *Ibid.*

36. *Ibid.*

37. The resolution referred by the convention to the Committee of Detail apparently simply said: "That the Jurisdiction of the national Judiciary shall extend to cases arising under the Laws passed by the general Legislature, and to such other Questions as involve the national Peace and Harmony." 2 Farrand, *Records* 132–33. It is of high significance that the word "cases" is also used to define the areas in which the legislature is to be authorized to legislate. *Id.* at 131–32.

A distinction in usage begins to appear in a draft in the handwriting of Edmund Randolph, with emendations by John Rutledge. See *id.* at 137 for "cases" and at 147 for "disputes," a forerunner of "controversies."

James Wilson in his drafts used the words "cases" and "controversies." *Id.* at 157 and 162–63. In what appears to be very nearly a final draft of the report of the Committee of Detail, the distinction is drawn very much as in the final Constitution. *Id.* at 172–73.

38. Wilfred J. Ritz, *American Judicial Proceedings First Printed Before 1801* 41 (Westport, Conn.: Greenwood Press, 1984).

39. *Ibid.*

40. Ch. 11, §§ 2,3, 1 Stat. 244.

41. Warren, *History* 69–83.

42. Such a reading of the Constitution has potentialities not limited to imposing nonjudicial duties on the courts. It can also be used to support the courts in "making law," that is, in engaging in judicial legislation. The courts do this on the theory that it is an appropriate part of deciding controversies. The language of the Constitution, if the word "case" is given this broader meaning, is broad enough to authorize this activity, whether it is tied to litigation between parties or not.

43. The 1780 constitution is reprinted in 14 *Suffolk Law Review* 841–72 (1980); the cited passage is at 848.

44. §§ 9, 11; § 9 as to district courts; § 11 as to circuit courts.

45. In the manuscript, the phrase "of a civil nature" is underlined, after the word "suits," perhaps by someone other than Ellsworth.

46. The Eleventh Amendment does not affect this grant of jurisdiction.

47. § 21. See also § 19, "in causes in equity and of admiralty and maritime jurisdiction" and §§ 9 and 30, "all causes except civil causes of admiralty and maritime jurisdiction."

48. § 29.

49. § 28.

50. § 30.

51. § 32.

52. The word "cause" is also used in the act as a general word to refer to a judicial proceeding, whatever its nature. For example, Section 25 provides, "instead of remanding the cause" and "if the cause shall have been once remanded."

53. § 11: "of all suits of a civil nature at common law or in equity."
§ 25: "That a final judgment or decree in any suit, in the highest court of law or equity."

54. § 10.

55. *See* 3 Blackstone, *288.

56. § 13.

57. § 15.

58. § 18.

59. § 20.

60. § 5.

61. § 14.

62. § 29.

63. § 33.

64. § 9.

65. In context, the word "trial" can sometimes be construed as referring to the whole proceeding, but the emphasis seems to be on the fact-finding process. Examples of this possibility are found in Section 11, providing, "But no person shall be arrested in one district for trial in another, in any civil action" and in Section 15, providing for discovery proceedings in the "trial of actions at law."

66. LC 16 Back.

67. *Ibid.*

CHAPTER VI

1. *See* Morton J. Horwitz, *The Transformation of American Law, 1780–1860* (Cambridge, Mass.: Harvard University Press, 1977), 9–16; Kathryn Preyer, "Jurisdiction to Punish: Federal Authority and the Criminal Law," 4 *Law and History*

Review 223 (1986); Robert C. Palmer, "The Federal Common Law of Crime," 4 *id.* 267 (1986); Stephen B. Presser, "The Supra-Constitution, the Courts and the Federal Common Law of Crimes: A Comment on Palmer and Preyer," 4 *id.* 325 (1986); Stewart Jay, "Origins of Federal Common Law" (Pts. 1–2), 133 *University of Pennsylvania Law Review* 1003, 1231 (1985); Wythe Holt, "The First Federal Question Case," 3 *Law and History Review* 169 (1985); Stephen B. Presser, "A Tale of Two Judges: Richard Peters, Samuel Chase, and the Broken Promise of Federalist Jurisprudence," 73 *Northwestern University Law Review* 26 (1978).

2. Warren *New Light* 73. See also Warren, 1 *History* 437–38.

3. 19 *JCC* 217.

4. *Id.* at 234.

5. *Id.* at 274.

6. *Id.* at 354, emphasis added. Inasmuch as in my transcription of the ordinance, which does not have sections, I have considerably rearranged the order of the provisions, the careful reader will surely desire to compare my transcription, following, with the original text.

Ordinance of April 5, 1781, For Establishing Courts For the Trial of Piracies and Felonies Committed on The High Seas

Whereas by the ninth article of the confederation and perpetual union of the thirteen United States of America, it is agreed, that the United States in Congress assembled, shall have the sole and exclusive right and power (inter alia) of appointing courts for the trial of piracies and felonies committed on the high seas. And whereas it is expedient that such courts should be speedily erected, and it is reasonable that the same mode of trial should be adopted for offenders of this kind on the high seas as is used for offenders of the like sort upon the land,

Be it therefore ordained, and it is hereby ordained by the United States of America in Congress assembled, and by the authority of the same, that all and every person and persons who heretofore have committed, or who hereafter shall commit, any piracy or felony upon the high seas, or who shall be charged as accessories to the same, either before or after the fact, may and shall be enquired of, tried and judged by grand and petit juries, according to the course of the common law, in like manner as if the piracy or felony were committed upon the land, and within some county, district or precinct in one of these United States. And the justices of the supreme or superior courts of judicature, and judge of the Court of Admiralty of the several and respective states, or any two or more of them, are hereby constituted and appointed judges for hearing and trying such offenders.

And be it further ordained, that if any person or persons shall be indicted for any piracy or felony done, or hereafter to be done, upon the high seas, or as accessories before or after the fact, either on the land or upon the seas, by a grand jury for any county, district, or precinct within any of these United States, before the justices of the supreme or superior court and judge of the admiralty, or any two of them, that then such order, process, judgment and execution shall be used, had, done and made to and against every such person and persons, so being indicted, as against robbers, murderers, or other felons for robbery, murder, or other felony done upon the land within such county, district, or precinct, as by the laws of the said State is accustomed; and the trial of such offence or offences, if it be denied by the offender or offenders, shall be had by twelve lawful men of the said county, district, or precinct; and such as shall be convicted of any such offence or offences by verdict, confession, or otherwise, in the said court, shall have and suffer such pains of death, losses of lands, goods and chattels, or other punishment, and by the same authority as if they had been convicted and attainted of any robbery, felony or other the said offences done upon the land; and shall be utterly excluded the benefit of clergy where the same is taken away or not admitted for such like offences committed within the body of a county, or on land where such trial shall be had.

And be it further ordained, that if there shall be more than one judge of the admiralty in any of the United States, that then, and in such case, the supreme executive power of such State may and shall commissionate one of them exclusively to join in performing the duties required by this ordinance.

And be it further ordained, that all losses and forfeitures of lands, goods and chattels, incurred upon any such conviction and attainder, shall go and belong to the State in which the said conviction and attainder shall be had.

7. Crosskey discusses at length the reason that the Constitutional Convention thought it necessary or desirable to give Congress an express power "to define and punish piracies and felonies on the high seas," since under Crosskey's thesis this was but one example of a much larger power of Congress to legislate—but he never mentions this ordinance. Crosskey, *Politics and the Constitution* 443–67. Goebel devotes one paragraph to the whole subject of the trial of piracies and felonies committed on the high seas (Goebel, *History* 173), but neither he nor Henry J. Bourguignon (*The First Federal Court: The Federal Appellate Prize Court of the American Revolution 1775–1787* [Philadelphia: American Philosophical Society, 1977]) appears to discuss the ordinance either.

8. The language of the ordinance was unclear as to whether it was necessary to include the judge of the court of admiralty in the panel that actually tried a case or whether two or more justices of the superior trial court were sufficient. Although not referring to the ordinance, New Jersey, on December 18, 1781, as a part of legislation regulating and establishing an admiralty jurisdiction, made explicit provision for the mode of trying pirates. N.J. *Acts* 1781, ch. 6. It provided that the court should consist of the "Justices of the Supreme Court or any two of them, and the Judge of the Admiralty." *Id.* at § 15. It referred to the trial of pirates in the late British colonies as having been "heretofore without a Jury, and in a Method much conformed to the Civil Law, the Exercise of which Jurisdiction in Criminal Cases was contrary to the Spirit of the Common Law," and noted that in England itself this mode of procedure had been changed. The act directed that the offense "shall be enquired of, tried and judged by Grand and Pettit Juries, according to the Course of the Common Law, in like Manner as if the Treason, felony or Crime were committed within one of the Counties of this State." *Id.* A convicted offender was to "have and suffer such Punishment and Forfeitures as Pirates, Felony and Robbers upon the Seas ought to have and suffer." *Id.,* § 16.

On February 16, 1783, Massachusetts adopted "An Act for carrying into Execution an Ordinance of Congress for establishing Courts for the Trial of Felonies and Piracies committed on the High Seas." Massachusetts *Acts and Laws, 1783,* ch. 10. In the preamble the legislature paraphrased the language of the Confederation Ordinance, that "the Justices of the Supreme Judicial Court and the Judge of Admiralty of this Commonwealth, or any two of them" were appointed judges to try persons charged with piracy, but made no attempt to interpret this language so as to make specific provision as to whether a judge of admiralty had to be included. The legislation does declare that the "Judges of the Maritime Courts" shall be deemed judges of the Court of Admiralty until such time as judges "expressly by that name" shall be nominated, commissioned, and sworn. *Id.*

The Continental Congress by an amendment of March 4, 1783, made clear that the panel must include the judge of admiralty. 24 *JCC* 164.

South Carolina by an act of February 27, 1788, referred to the ordinance of April 5, 1781 and the later amendment, but the legislation provided only that the "grand and petit jurors for the district of Charlestown" should try pirates. *Acts and Ordinances of the General Assembly of the State of South Carolina, Passed in February, 1788* (Act of Feb. 27) (Charleston 1788).

There seems to be an absence of reports of cases arising under the ordinance, although J. C. Bancroft Davis implies that there were such cases. 131 U.S., appendix, xiv (1889). On May 22, 1781, Pennsylvania sent a letter to the Continental Congress stating the proceedings in the Pennsylvania Court of Admiralty in the trial of a person for piracy, under the ninth Article of Confederation, and expressing certain doubts concerning the power of executing, reprieving, and pardoning criminals in such cases. The committee to which the letter was referred reported on June 14:

> That they have conferred with the said Governor Reed in Council, and the facts in the present case, being as stated in the said letter, the said Governor and Council were of opinion with your Committee, that *the tryal was not legal* for want of a competent Court, and therefore that the criminal should be reprieved.
>
> Your Committee farther Report that the question about the powers of executing, reprieving or pardoning in such cases, that may happen hereafter, seems to require the *determination of Congress* which is submitted.

This report, in the writing of Samuel Livermore of New Hampshire, is endorsed, "Debated July 26, 1781. Nothing concluded," and was postponed. 20 *JCC* 644.

The reason for the doubt of the competency of the court is that the trial was had solely before the judge of the Court of Admiralty, whereas the ordinance (as amended) required that he be joined by at least one judge of a superior trial court.

9. 19 *JCC* 374–75.

10. *Id.* at 375.

11. 20 *JCC* 496–97.

12. *Id.* at 599.

13. *Id.* at 695.

14. See chapter 4.

15. The editors of Madison's papers read this motion as being ambiguous, either as providing for appeals to the Confederation Court of Appeals in Cases of Capture from the state courts for the trials of piracies, or as giving the Court of

Appeals in Cases of Capture original rather than appellate jurisdiction over cases involving felonies and piracies on the high seas—but this latter "seems very unlikely" to the editors. 3 *Papers of James Madison* n.5. at 67. Similarly, Goebel, who thinks of "appeal" in the modern sense of appellate review, finds Madison's motion "inexplicable." Goebel, *History* 173.

16. 17 *JCC* 468–69.

17. 19 *JCC* 40.

18. *Id.* at 155.

19. 20 *JCC* 547–48. The committee report was written by Robert Morris of Pennsylvania.

20. [The editors disagree with Professor Ritz on this minor point. While with Professor Ritz they agree that the national criminal jurisdiction probably lies within the constitutional "arising-under" language of Article III, Section 2, they disagree that to place the national criminal jurisdiction under the language concerning "controversies to which the United States shall be a party" would be unreasonable.]

21. St. George Tucker, ed., 1 *Blackstone's Commentaries,* part I (1803), 420. Tucker did not even refer to a national criminal jurisdiction beyond those for which some express authority could be found in the Constitution—the seat of government; forts, magazines, arsenals, and dockyards; treason; piracies and felonies committed upon the high seas; offenses against the law of nations—with one exception, offenses "against the revenue laws of the U.S." *Ibid.*

22. 5 *JCC* 475.

23. Farrand, 2 *Records* 144.

24. The full text of Section 2 of Article VII is as follows:

Sect. 2. Treason against the United States shall consist only in levying war against the United States, or any of them; and in adhering to the enemies of the United States, or any of them. The Legislature of the United States shall have power to declare the punishment of treason. No person shall be convicted of treason, unless on the testimony of two witnesses. No attainder of treason shall work corruption of blood, nor forfeiture, except during the life of the person attainted.

Farrand, 2 *Records* 182 (misnumbered Article VI).

25. For the debate discussed in this and the following two paragraphs, *see* Farrand, 2 *Records* 345–50.

26. *Id.* at 601.

27. *Id.* at 182.

28. *Id.* at 312 (Journal), 317 (Madison).

29. *Id.* at 316.

30. *Id.* at 610.

31. Farrand, 3 *Records* 587.

32. The journal of the convention shows only that there was a motion to reconsider this clause, and that upon reconsideration the word "punish" was struck out. Some members, on their copies of the report of the Committee of Style, inserted the words "to punish" and then crossed them out. Farrand, 2 *Records* 611. Madison inserted the word "punish" before "offences against the law of nations,"

crossed it out, and, probably later in life, noted that it was a "typographical omission." *Id.* at 595.

33. See Farrand, 4 *Records* 114–15 (listing the pages in Farrand upon which these clauses were considered).

34. 13 *DocHistConst* 387–88. The writer was responding to James Wilson's speech of October 6 in which he had said, in explaining the omission of a guarantee of trial by jury in civil cases, that "the oppression of government is effectually barred, by declaring that in all criminal cases the trial by jury shall be preserved." 2 *DocHistConst* 169.

35. *Id.* at 515.

36. 3 *DocHistConst* 525 (emphasis added).

37. 13 *DocHistConst* 349–50 (George Mason's objections); 14 *DocHistConst* 151 ("George Mason's Objections," *Massachusetts Centinel*, Nov. 21, 1787); *id.* at 7 (Brutus, Junior, *New York Journal*, Nov. 8, 1787); *id.* at 154 (B. Brutus on Mason's Objections, *Virginia Journal*, Nov. 22, 1787); *id.* at 292 (Luther Martin's Speech, Nov. 29, 1787); 15 *DocHistConst* (Luther Martin's "Genuine Information IX," Baltimore *Maryland Gazette* Jan. 29, 1788); *id.* at 30 (Dissent of Minority of Pennsylvania Convention, *Pennsylvania Packet*, Dec. 18, 1787); *id.* at 134 (Edmund Randolph's letter to the Virginia House of Delegates).

38. 13 *DocHistConst* 431–32. The editors identify the writer as having been Tench Coxe.

39. Farrand, 2 *Records* 334 (Journal), 342–42 (Madison).

40. *Id.* at 631–40.

41. Storing, 3 *Anti-Federalist* ¶ 3.11.13.

42. Storing, 2 *Anti-Federalist* ¶ 2.9.170.

43. *Id.* at ¶ 2.9.172.

44. Storing, 5 *Anti-Federalist* ¶ 5.14.10.

45. *Id.* at ¶ 5.16.36. [The editors note that Patrick Henry may have had in mind the "necessary-and-proper" clause of Article I, Section 8 when he spoke of "their general powers."]

46. 4 Storing, *Anti-Federalist* ¶ 4.6.20.

47. *Id.,* ¶ 4.6.21.

48. Wharton, *State Trials* n.1 at 38.

49. 1789 *Senate Journal* 34.

50. See chapter 2.

51. 1789 *Senate Journal* 50.

52. *Id.* at 64.

53. *Id.* at 67.

54. *Id.* at 77.

55. On his copy of the Judicial Bill, Senator Paine Wingate showed this amendment by drawing a line through these words. He did so only in the circuit court provision, but Wingate did not mark down all changes made by the Senate. For a discussion of the importance of Wingate's copy of the bill, see appendix 2.

56. 1789 *Senate Journal* 82.

57. *Id.* at 85.

58. *Id.* at 107.

59. 1789 *House Journal* 119.

60. *Id.* at 79.
61. *Id.* at 113.
62. *Id.* at 142.
63. 1789 *Senate Journal* 138.
64. 1789 *House Journal* 143.
65. 1789 *Senate Journal* 138.
66. *Id.* at 142.
67. *Id.* at 161.
68. Ch. 5, 1 Stat. 29.
69. Ch. 11, 1 Stat. 55. The Coasting Act was amended and explained by an Act of Sept. 29, 1789, ch. 22, 1 Stat. 94.
70. The person giving or offering the bribe was subjected to the same forfeiture, but without being barred from office.
71. Ch. 5, § 35, 1 Stat. 47.
72. Ch. 5, § 34, 1 Stat. 46.
73. Ch. 11, § 35, 1 Stat. 65.
74. Judiciary Act of 1789, § 9.
75. *Id.* at § 11.
76. *Id.* at § 5.
77. *Id.* at § 14.
78. *Id.* at § 29.
79. *Id.* at § 33.
80. *Id.* at § 35.
81. Ch. 5, § 35, 1 Stat. 46–47.
82. Ch. 5, § 34, 1 Stat. 46.
83. Ch. 11, § 36, 1 Stat. 65.
84. Resolution 2, 1 Stat. 96–97.
85. Resolution (unnumbered), 1 Stat. 97–98.
86. Resolution 3, 1 Stat. 97.
87. 4 Blackstone, *136–37.
88. 1789 *Senate Journal* 163.
89. Nathaniel Chipman, *A Dissertation on the Act Adopting the Common and Statute Laws of England* (Rutland, Vermont: Anthony Haswell, 1793), *130.
90. *Id.* at *133.
91. *Id.* at *135–136.
92. Nathaniel Pendleton, who became district judge for Georgia, had been appointed a Georgia delegate to the convention, but he never attended.
93. Act of Sept. 15, 1789, ch. 14, § 2, 1 Stat. 68. The law made no provision for copies for the judges.
94. Guilds and Swaine printed both the *Laws of the United States* and the *Journals of the House of Representatives,* while Thomas Greenleaf printed the *Journal of the Senate,* all in New York City in 1789.
95. Judiciary Act of 1789, § 3.
96. For a discussion of Francis Hopkinson's law-writing activities, see Wilfred J. Ritz, "The Francis Hopkinson Law Reports," 74 *Law Library Journal* 298 (1981).
97. *Massachusetts Centinel,* Dec. 9, 1789.
98. Goebel, *History* 557.
99. *DocHistSupCt* 60–68.

100. Samuel Johnston to James Iredell, Mar. 18, 1790, *Life of James Iredell* 285.

101. "I understand that you set off immediately for your Southern Circuit." Samuel Ashe to Iredell, April 10, 1790, *Life of James Iredell* 287.

102. A fifteen-page pamphlet containing the charge, delivered at all of Jay's stops on the first Eastern Circuit, was issued in Portsmouth, New Hampshire (Ritz, *supra.* n.96, 4.20 [1]; Evans, *American Bibliography* 22587). It was also printed in several newspapers. *Boston Independent Chronicle,* May 27, 1790; *New Hampshire Gazette,* June 3, 1790; *American Museum,* Oct. 1790, appendix pp. 57–60. All of the extant grand-jury charges made by the Supreme Court judges on circuit in the 1790s will be published in the second and third volumes of *Documentary History of the Supreme Court.*

103. *New York Gazette of the United States,* Apr. 6, 1790.

104. *United States v. Hopkins and Brown,* Ms. Minutes, Circuit Court for New York District 1790–1808, Apr. 13–14, 1790, Federal Archives National Records Center, Bayonne, N.J.; Goebel, *History* 622–23.

105. *Ibid.; Boston, Massachusetts Centinel,* May 5, 1790.

106. *Philadelphia Pennsylvania Gazette,* Apr. 14, Apr. 20, 1790; *Boston, Massachusetts Centinel,* May 1, 1790.

107. 1 Stat. 112.

108. Maclay, *Journal* 133.

109. *Id.* at 135.

110. 1790 *Senate Journal* 13; see also Maclay, *Journal* 175.

111. 1790 *Senate Journal* 16.

112. *Id.* at 17–18.

113. Maclay, *Journal* 182.

114. *Id.* at 183.

115. *Ibid.*

116. 1790 *Senate Journal* 17–18.

117. *Id.* at 18.

118. 1789 *Senate Journal* 15.

CHAPTER VII

1. See chapter 2.

2. Maclay, *Journal* 72.

3. See n.13 of chapter 2.

4. The printer, it is fair to say, probably made the following changes in setting the manuscript in type:

a. *till,* LC 4 Back, line 6 from bottom, changed to "until," printed bill p. 3, line 31;

b. *forreigner,* LC 7 Back, line 8 from bottom, and other subsequent locations, changed to "foreigner," printed bill, p. 5, line 10, and all other locations;

c. *barr,* LC 8 Back, line 14, changed to "bar," printed bill p. 6, line 9;

d. *publick,* LC 9, lines 15 and 20, changed to "public," printed bill p. 6, lines 31 and 36; and

e. *domestick(s),* LC 9, lines 16 and 37, changed to "domestic(s)," printed bill p. 6, lines 33 and 37.

This does not account for all the changes and discrepancies, however. *See* Goebel, *History* n.27 at 465–66.

5. These technical designations of the manuscript bill are explained in appendix 2.

6. Maclay, *Journal* 87; Maclay, *Sketches* 89.

7. For example, the equity section was number 16 in the original bill. On third reading, it is referred to as Section 15, both when it was deleted, and again when it was restored. 1789 *Senate Journal* 62 and 63. A new section was inserted between Sections 17 and 18, 1789 *Senate Journal* 61, which sections had been 18 and 19 in the bill as introduced.

8. *See* appendix 1.

9. Unfortunately, Senator Paine Wingate's numbering on his annotated copy of the printed bill neither supports nor undercuts the conclusions in this paragraph. It would appear that Senator Wingate numbered the sections in the printed bill as introduced, when the bill still had thirty-three sections, but he erroneously numbered two sections as being Section 29 so as to arrive at a total of thirty-two sections. Later he altered the numbers on the sections he had previously numbered 24 through the first 29, leaving the last four numbers unchanged, for a total of thirty-two; since he took no note of the addition of a new section, number 19 of the final bill, his total is incorrect.

10. See chapter 3.

11. See chapter 4.

12. 2 *Letters of Paine Wingate* 318 (1930). The letter is cited in Goebel, *History* n.114 at 496, and n.155 at 503.

13. He did not record the amendment made on July 11 that became Section 19 of the final bill, nor did he record two amendments made on July 13 to Section 22, which relates to supersedeas. While these amendments might be considered legalistic and so not of interest to a nonlawyer like Wingate, he did take note of some that were equally legalistic, or even more so.

14. There are three amendments reported in the *Journal* that also exist in manuscript. These are LC 22, 24 and 35, the first two being amendments reported in the *Journal* as agreed to on July 11, and the last one agreed to on July 13. Wingate's annotated bill does not reflect the July 11 amendment represented in LC 22, but it does reflect the other two amendments, LC 24 and LC35. (See appendix 2 for an explanation of the designation "LC".)

15. LC 41, 37, and 34, amending Section 6; LC 22 amending Section 12; LC 36 amending Section 15; and LC 40 amending Section 33.

16. LC 33a and 33, amending Section 4; LC 31 amending Section 7; LC 42, 38, and 39, amending Section 9 (of final bill); LC 32 and 43 amending Section 11; LC 46 amending Section 13; and LC 45 amending Section 34.

17. LC 32 changing Section 11.

18. For example, Senator Wingate's copy of the Judicial Bill shows only one change in what became Section 9. He shows that the original language, which read "And the trial of facts in both cases last mentioned shall be by jury," was changed to, "And the trial of issues in fact in the three cases last mentioned shall be by jury." But it is difficult to determine from the language which were the "both cases last mentioned" and so which case was added by the amendment. The lan-

guage of the engrossed bill has been adjusted so as to make the subject clear. The text of this adjustment appears on LC 42 in the handwriting of Ellsworth, but it is a change that does not exactly fit into the printed bill, raising the inference that it was made by the subcommittee after the Judicial Bill had been recommitted.

19. 1789 *Senate Journal* 14.

20. Some of the manuscript amendments have dates written on them, but these appear to be written in a modern hand.

21. 41 U.S. (16 Pet.) 1 (1842).

22. Warren, *New Light* 86.

23. *Black & White Taxicab & Transfer Co. v. Brown & Yellow Taxicab & Transfer Co.,* 276 U.S. 518, 535 (1928).

24. 39 *New York University Law Review* 383 (1964).

25. *Id.* at 390.

26. Crosskey, *Politics and the Constitution* 626–28, 866–71.

27. It is doubtful that Ellsworth either intended to put the phrase in every section or intended to leave it out of every section, inasmuch as on a single page he deletes the phrase in one section and leaves it in another.

28. The phrase, "And be it further enacted" is also omitted in Section 27. Paine Wingate's copy shows the section was amended by the Senate to incorporate the phrase.

29. 1789 *Senate Journal* 61. The language of the *Journal* that states that the phrase is to be struck where redundant implies that there are sections where it is not redundant. Even so, the phrase was struck out in all of the sections.

30. This apparently is the view of the editors of the *Statutes at Large,* who have bracketed a "further" into these two sections, 7 and 31.

31. Emphases added by author. [The editors note that the force of this argument is weakened by the fact that there are other sections that are applicable to all of the courts of the United States, such as Section 15 authorizing all the said courts to grant motions for new trials in the trial of actions at law. The same sort of argument could be made about Sections 14–17, 26, and 29–30.]

32. Warren, *New Light* 108.

33. *Id.* at n.135. Query: If Warren did not know about the printed bill, why does he refer to the "manuscript" draft bill, as though he were distinguishing it from some other draft bill?

34. The notation, "page 15th," on the manuscript of section 34 is a notation by a clerk, not by Ellsworth.

35. This situation is different from that which prevailed at the Constitutional Convention of 1787, when there was no provision made for paying the expenses of the convention, such as for printing. Even so, the convention eventually resorted to the printing press to aid its deliberations by printing reports of the Committee of Detail and Committee of Style. The Continental Congress used the printing press extensively throughout its existence.

36. See appendix 2.

37. Maclay, *Sketches* 78. Warren refers to the *Sketches* as one of his sources and cites it frequently. *E.g.,* Warren, *New Light* n.32 at 63.

38. Warren, *New Light* n.63 at 76, citing Worthington Chaucey Ford, III, *Writings of John Quincy Adams,* vol. 1 (New York: Macmillan, 1913–17) no p.

39. This is Warren's language. Warren, *New Light* n.36 at 64, citing 2 *Life of James Iredell,* no p.

40. This work is cited by Warren in *New Light* n.9 at 52. In volume 1 at 167, its editor quotes a paragraph from a letter from William Grayson to Patrick Henry in which Grayson comments on the Judicial Bill and says, "as soon as it is printed I will send you a copy." 1 *Life of James Iredell* 167.

41. The confusion begins at least as early as 1912, when Evans listed as printed in the year 1788, as a twelve-page folio, "An Act to establish the Judicial Courts of the United States. New-York: Printed by Thomas Greenleaf." Evans, *American Bibliography,* no.21,511. Besides the erroneous dating, the Senate bill has sixteen pages and not twelve. The bill as it passed the Senate was printed as a House bill of twelve pages, but it does not bear the name of any printer.

The Senate bill is now listed in Bristol, *Supplement to Evans' American Bibliography* as B7153; the House bill is listed by Bristol as B7155. Roger P. Bristol, *Supplement to Evans' American Bibliography* (Charlottesville, Va.: University Press of Virginia, 1970–1971).

42. 1789 *Senate Journal* 61.

43. LC 37, amending Section 6; LC 41 Front, amending Section 5 and bearing a reference to line 25. Warren, *New Light* 72.

44. LC 29, amending Section 12, and bearing a reference to page 6, line 9. Warren, *New Light* n.97 at 92.

45. LC40, amending Section 33, and bearing a page 15 notation. Warren, *New Light* n.132 at 107.

46. LC 32, amending Section 11, and bearing a notation of page 6, line 9. Warren, *New Light* n.69 at 79. LC 39, amending Section 9, and bearing a notation of page 6, line 2. *Id.* n.57 at 74. LC 43, amending Section 12, and bearing a notation of page 6, line 4. *Id.* n.91 at 91. And LC 46, amending Section 13 and bearing a notation of page 6 and lines 25 to 14 from the bottom. *Id.* n.98 at 93.

47. See appendix 1.

48. Goebel, *History* 463–65.

49. In referring to the printed bill, Goebel goes no further than to say, "Three known copies of this print exist. Whether or not it has hitherto been used for historical purposes we do not know." *Id.* at 465.

50. *Id.* at 466.

51. *Id.* at 502.

52. *Id.* at n.149 at 502.

53. See chapter 5.

54. Act of Sept. 29, 1789, ch. 21, § 2, 1 Stat. 93. In the manuscript of Ellsworth's draft, the language states that process "shall be . . . the same, as near as may be, in the *respective* States where the proceedings shall be had, as in similar, or the most analogous cases, now is used or accustomed in the *respective* courts of such States" (emphasis added).

55. By 1789 the United States had entered into treaties with five nations: France, Great Britain, Morocco, the Netherlands, and Sweden. See Charles I. Bevans, comp., *Treaties and Other International Agreements of America 1776– 1949,* 12 vols. (Washington, D.C.: Government Printing Office, 1968–76); William M. Malloy, comp., *Treaties, Conventions, International Acts, Protocols and*

Agreements between the United States of America and Other Powers 1776–1909, 2 vols. (Washington, D.C.: Government Printing Office, 1910).

Article XI of the 1788 Convention with France provided for the procedure to be followed when a crew member of a vessel committed a crime and then withdrew to the vessel. Bevans, 7 *supra* 799; Malloy, 1 *supra* 495.

56. This same treaty with France in Article XII provided that differences and suits between subjects of France who were in the United States or citizens of the United States who were in France should be determined by the consuls and vice-consuls of the country of their nationality. Such suits are outside the jurisdiction of the national courts, and if brought in this country would have been brought in the state courts. Malloy, 1 *supra* n.55 at 495; Bevans, 7 *supra* n.55 at 799.

57. 3 Dallas (3 U.S.) 386 (1798).

58. *Id.* at 397.

59. William W. Hening, *Statutes at Large . . .* , 13 vols. (New York: Bartow, 1819–23), IX, 127.

60. LC 32. This manuscript is in the handwriting of a scribe.

61. The "s" on "trials" has the same squiggle as the "s" on "laws" in the manuscript Section 34, a squiggle that indicates a different way of writing the final "s" than seems to have been Ellsworth's practice.

62. See appendix 1 for a discussion of some mistakes that Charles Warren makes on this topic.

63. 28 Hen. 8, ch. 15, preamble.

64. 28 Hen. 8, ch. 15, § 1.

65. 1 Wm. 3, ch. 7, § 1. The preamble says that under 28 Hen. 8, ch. 15, it was necessary to bring pirates to England for trial, and this statute was passed to remedy that defect.

66. Carl Ubbelohde, *The Vice-Admiralty Courts and the American Revolution* (Chapel Hill: University of North Carolina Press, 1960), mentions the trial of pirates at only two points, and then without any supporting authority. He says that pirates were either sent to England for trial in the High Court of Admiralty's Court of Oyer and Terminer or tried by special courts of admiralty in the colonies, and under either procedure the trial was by jury. *Id.* n.18 at 17. He also says that Judge Jared Ingersoll of the Pennsylvania Vice-Court of Admiralty defended himself against critics in 1774 by saying that his commission did not extend to trial of felonies, including piracy, and so he, as a judge who sat without a jury, had no jurisdiction to try persons for offenses for which death could be imposed as punishment. *Id.* at 185.

On the other hand, a manuscript found among the papers of the Pennsylvania Admiralty Court, titled "The Form & Manner of Proceedings to be observed by the Register of the Court of Admiralty for the Tryal of Pyrates," describes the procedure set forth in the 1700 statute, concluding with the statement, "A true Copy taken from that which accompanied the Commission. Nov. 20th, 1729. Pat. Baird Reg." This would indicate that pirates were still being tried in America without juries even after the 1700 statute had expired. This manuscript is reprinted, "The Procedure for the Trial of a Pirate," 1 *American Journal of Legal History* 251–56 (1957).

67. Pa. Acts 1778, ch. 74, §§ 13–15; Pa. Acts 1780, ch. 152, §§ 18–20; N.J. Acts 1781, ch. 6, §15.

68. Act of Apr. 30, 1790, ch. 9, § 8, 1 Stat. 113–14.

69. The special problem posed by crimes on the high seas was noted in a letter written by William Smith of South Carolina to Edward Rutledge of the same state, under date of August 9, 1789. But since Section 34 was already in the bill, it is significant only as showing what lawyers were thinking about. Smith wrote:

> I have read your observations on the Judicial with attention & having some-what more time than I thought I should have had at the outset of this letter will briefly acquaint you what impression they have made on my mind.
>
> 1. Objection to the District Judge holding special Courts Ans—occa-sions may occur when they be very necessary—the seizure of goods—a ship—which it may be proper & expedient to condemn forthwith—a crime committed on the High Seas—& the witnesses, who are sailors, about to de-part—you recollect that the District Court is a crt of Adm.

Smith to Rutledge, Aug. 9, 1789, in "The Letters of William Loughton Smith to Edward Rutledge . . . ," ed. George C. Rogers, 69 *South Carolina Historical Magazine* 1 (1968), at 21.

Charles Pinckney made a motion in the Continental Congress on September 6, 1785, directing the secretary of foreign affairs to report the draft of an ordinance for instituting a court for the trial and punishment of piracies and felonies com-mitted on the high seas in the same manner in all the states. Pickney said that the Ordinance of April 1781, then in effect, "has a different operation in some of the States." 29 *JCC* 682. On October 3, the secretary reported an ordinance. *Id.* at 797.

The ordinance provided for trial of persons charged with piracy or felony on the high seas in the place "where the Witnesses and Proofs of such Piracy or Felony may more easily and expeditiously be had." *Id.* at 799. The ordinance provided that "the whole Trial shall be conducted according to the Course of the common Law." *Id.* at 801. It provided that all accessories to piracy should be considered principals, but that accessories to felonies committed on the high seas should be treated "as they are considered by the Laws of the State, in which the Offenders shall be tried." *Id.* at 804. The report was printed. *Id.* at 928. But it was never acted upon. *Id.* at 805.

70. See authorities cited in n.1, *supra*.

71. Warren, *New Light* 73; see also Warren, 1 *History* 437–38.

72. Goebel says, "There was at the moment expectation that the Senate would have before it a bill defining crimes against the United States." Goebel, *History* 496. It is entirely possible, however, that by the time the words were expunged, a decision had been made that the Senate would not "define" crimes but only deter-mine the punishment, which is the language used when the committee did report on July 28.

CHAPTER VIII

1. Report of the Attorney-General, read in the House of Representatives, De-cember 31, 1790. The colophon reads "Printed by Francis Childs and John Swaine." This thirty-six-page imprint (thirty-four numbered pages) is Evans, *American Bibliography* 23908.

A second edition was published by the same printer and presumably in the same year, which differs only in that it has thirty-two instead of thirty-four numbered pages. The lines in the notes are set longer so as to accomplish this reduction in number of pages. This is Evans, *American Bibliography* 23909. The text of the two publications appears to be exactly the same.

The report was reprinted in *American State Papers,* 1 *Miscellaneous* 21–36 (1834).

This report is hereinafter cited as *1790 Report.*

2. *But see* Moncure Daniel Conway, *Omitted Chapters of History Disclosed in the Life and Papers of Edmund Randolph,* 2d ed. (New York: G. P. Putnam's Sons, 1889), 142–44, where the author reports that Associate Justice Stanley Matthews of the United States Supreme Court said the report showed "an accurate and perspicuous analysis of the judicial power."

Randolph's substance and style may also be examined in Edmund Randolph, *History of Virginia,* edited by Arthur H. Shaffer, (Charlottesville: University Press of Virginia, 1970), a manuscript prepared by Randolph that was printed in 1970 by the Virginia Historical Society.

3. *1790 Report* 11.

4. *Id.* at 28.

5. *Id.* at 33–34.

6. Conway, *supra* n.2 at 144.

7. *1790 Report* 28.

8. *Id.* at 33.

9. Warren, *New Light* 88. Warren was relying upon Randolph's explanatory note 26 for his conclusion.

10. *1790 Report* 10. This statement is made in the first part of Randolph's *Report,* in which he outlines what he considers to be the principal defects of the Judiciary Act.

11. *Id.* at 33.

12. Under date of August 5, 1790, Randolph wrote James Wilson proposing that the two of them should join in giving a series of law lectures at the Collegee of Philadelphia. At the time, James Wilson was being considered for a law professorship. The letter is quoted in part in Charles Page Smith, *James Wilson, Founding Father, 1742–1798* (Chapel Hill: University of North Carolina Press, 1956), 309. Smith cites his source as being the William L. Clements Library, Ann Arbor, Mich. According to the library, however, the manuscript appears not to be among its collections.

13. Act of Feb. 13, 1801, ch. 4, § 2, 2 Stat. 89.

14. *Henfield's Case,* Wharton, *State Trials* 49 (1849); 11 Fed. Cas. No. 6,360 (C.C.D.Pa. 1793). There was no contemporary report of *Henfield's Case,* other than some newspaper accounts. Wharton's report is based on the papers of counsel. The report consists of a grand-jury charge by Jay at Richmond on May 22, 1793; a grand-jury charge by Wilson at Philadelphia on July 22, 1793; the indictment; points made by District Attorney Rawle in his argument for the prosecution; a short summary of the arguments for the defense; the charge to the jury; a report on the jury verdict of acquittal; and a few other papers. It does not contain any report on the argument of Randolph nor does it show any citation to Section 34.

15. Randolph's letter was apparently written in response to a series of questions

relating to *Henfield's Case* that had been posed by Madison. It is published in Conway, *Omitted Chapters, supra* n.2 at 184.–86.

16. The citation is to volume 1 of the two-volume Folwell edition printed in 1796. Evans, *American Bibliography* 31356. George A. Strait, Harvard Law School Library, assisted in confirming that Section 34 does appear on page 74.

17. 4 U.S. (4 Dall.) xxvi (1807).

18. *Id.* at xxxi. Dallas was apparently a nonbeliever in his own argument; he made a point of noting that he considered it "his duty, as counsel for the defendant, (without declaring his own opinion) to bring it before the Court." *Id.* at xxvi.

19. This trial was not reported, except by newspapers, until 1804. Ralph R. Shaw and Richard H. Shoemaker, *American Bibliography, A Preliminary Checklist for 1804* (New York: Scarecrow Press, 1958), nos. 5972, 5973, and 7638. It seems doubtful if there were three distinct printings issued in 1804. Wharton used this report, together with some other materials in developing his report in Wharton, *State Trials* 688 (1849), 25 Fed. Cas. No. 14,709 (C.C.D. Va. 1800).

20. *Id.* at 709. The report does not contain a reference to the section by number.

21. 1 *Trial of Samuel Chase* 7 (Washington, D.C.: S. H. Smith 1805).

22. Testimony of Mr. Hay, *id.* at 177; Testimony of Mr. Nicholas, *id.* at 191.

23. *Id.* at 489–90 (1805).

24. See remarks made in 1809 by Samuel Dana of Connecticut, 20 *Annals* 208. However, Dana never expressly refers to an application of Section 34 in this proceeding, although Professor Crosskey interprets the remarks as referring to it. Crosskey, *Politics and the Constitution* 774.

25. Act of Apr. 29, 1802, ch. 31, § 6, 1 Stat. 156.

26. 53 U.S. (12 How.) 361 (1852).

27. *Id.* at 363.

28. *Id.* at 366. This rule, unsatisfactory at the time, became increasingly so with the passage of time, and was interpreted out of existence in *Funk v. United States,* 290 U.S. 371 (1933), and *Wolfle v. United States,* 291 U.S. 7 (1934).

29. Act of Feb. 6, 1889, ch. 113, § 3, 25 Stat. 655.

30. 3 U.S. (3 Dall.) 344 (1797).

31. *Id.* at 356.

32. *Ibid.*

33. *Robinson v. Campbell,* 16 U.S. (3 Wheat.) 212 (1818); *Hawkins and May v. Barney's Lessee,* 30 U.S. (5 Pet.) 464 (1831).

34. *Bank of Hamilton v. Lessee of Dudley,* 27 U.S. (2 Pet.) 525 (1829).

35. *United States v. Hoar,* 2 Mason's Repr. 311, 26 Fed. Cas. No. 15,373 (C.C.D. Mass. 1821).

36. *M'Cluny v. Silliman,* 28 U.S. (3 Pet.) 270 (1930).

37. *Wayman v. Southard,* 23 U.S. (10 Wheat.) 311 (1825).

38. 37 U.S. (12 Pet.) 86 (1838).

39. 41 U.S. (16 Pet.) 1 (1842).

40. A recent study of this case is: Tony Allan Freyer, *Harmony and Dissonance: The Swift & Erie Cases in American Federalism* (New York: New York University Press, 1981). See pp. 1–43 for an explanation of why the commercial law issues were the most important issues in the case for Story and his contemporaries.

41. 41 U.S. at 18–19.

42. [Professor Ritz has assumed that an endorsee's rights are determined by the law of the locale where the instrument was at the time of the endorsement. This rule became the law during the course of the nineteenth century; see *Restatement, Conflicts of Law,* 1st ed. (St. Paul: American Law Institute Publishers, 1934), § 349. However, Story apparently differs. "[T]he law of the place of the negotiation . . . [should not] govern; for the transfer is not, as to the acceptor or maker, a new contract; but it is under, and a part of, the original contract, and springs up from the law of the place where that contract was made." Joseph Story, *Commentaries on the Conflicts of Laws* (Boston: Hilliard, Gray, and Company, 1834),§ 317 at 264. Isaac Redfield's edition of Story repeats this language exactly, (Boston: Little, Brown, and Company, 6th ed., 1865), § 317 at 421.]

43. *United States v. Reid,* 53 U.S. (12 How.) 361 (1852), discussed in the text at n.26, *supra.*

44. (Boston: Little, Brown, and Company, 1899).

45. (New York: Columbia University Press, 1909).

46. *Id.* § 534 at 236.

47. 215 U.S. 349 (1910).

48. *Id.* at 351.

49. *Id.* at 370.

50. *Id.* at 370–71.

51. *Id.* at 372.

52. 276 U.S. 518 (1928).

53. *Id.* at 533.

54. *Id.* at 535: "An examination of the original document by a most competent hand has shown that Mr. Justice Story probably was wrong if anyone is interested to inquire what the framers of the instrument meant. 37 Harvard Law Review 49, at pp. 81–88."

55. Felix Frankfurter and James Landis, *The Business of the Supreme Court* (New York: Macmillan, 1928).

56. See Felix Frankfurter, "Distribution of Judicial Power between United States and State Courts," 13 *Cornell Law Quarterly* 499, esp. 520–30 (1928).

57. David W. Levy and Bruce Allen Murphy, "Preserving the Progressive Spirit in a Conservative Time: The Joint Reform Efforts of Justice Brandeis and Professor Frankfurter, 1916–1933," 78 *Michigan Law Review* 1252, 1290–91 (1980); Bruce Allen Murphy, "Elements of Extrajudicial Strategy: A Look at the Political Roles of Justices Brandeis and Frankfurter," 69 *Georgetown Law Journal* 101, 123–28 (1980).

58. 304 U.S. 64 (1938).

59. *Tompkins v. Erie Railroad Co.,* 90 F.2d 603 (2d Cir. 1937).

60. *Id.* at 604.

61. Irving Younger, "What Happened in *Erie,*" 56 *Texas Law Review* 1011, 1025–26 (1978); Frederick C. Hicks, *Materials and Methods of Legal Research,* 3d ed. (Rochester, N.Y.: Lawyers Cooperative Pub. Co. 1942), 376–77.

62. Merlo John Pusey, 2 *Charles Evans Hughes* (New York: Macmillan, 1951), 710, citing in n.22 the author's interview with Hughes on June 4, 1947.

63. *Ibid.*

64. Although Brandeis is known for the fact-packed Brandeis brief, he appar-

ently did not let "the facts" interfere with reaching the result that he wanted to reach. Chaim Weizmann says of him, comparing him with Woodrow Wilson, that "he was apt to evolve theories, based on the highest principles, from his inner consciousness, and then expect the facts to fit in with them. If the facts failed to oblige, so much the worse for the facts." Chaim Weizmann, *Trial and Error* (New York: Harper, 1949), 248.

In his *Erie* opinion, to reach the overruling result, Brandeis also had to abandon some of his previously held principles: "He has always maintained that the Court should not decide issues that were not before it. He had also said that constitutional issues should be avoided altogether if another ground was available to justify a result." Lewis J. Paper, *Brandeis* (Englewood Cliffs, N.J.: Prentice-Hall, 1983), 383. In *Erie* neither party presented the issue to the court for decision, and it was unnecessary to give the decision constitutional overtones. But the latter was done, presumably, to bar Congress from overturning the decision by legislation.

APPENDIX I

1. Warren, *New Light*.

2. Warren, *History*. Although the title page of the first edition bears the date 1923, the following page says that the book was copyrighted and published in 1922.

3. 1 *id.* at 31–33.

4. 41 U.S. (16 Pet.) 1 (1842).

5. Warren, 2 *History* 89. See also *id.* at 698.

6. 1 *Letters of Louis D. Brandeis* n.3 at 177 refers to a letter written by Brandeis to Warren on December 1, 1901, regarding some Massachusetts legislation. See also 3 *id.* at 63–64 setting forth another letter Brandeis wrote to Warren on April 14, 1913, commenting favorably on the latter's writings and asking him to discuss *Adair v. United States,* 208 U.S. 161 (1908).

7. 5 *Letters of Louis D. Brandeis* 54. On June 16, 1922, Brandeis had written Felix Frankfurter, "Charles Warren's USSC. in History of U.S. interests me intensely." *Id.* at 52.

8. Henry Flanders, 2 *The Lives and Times of the Chief Justices of the Supreme Court of the United States* (Philadelphia: Lippincott, Granebo, 1855–1858), 159. Warren cites this work in Warren, 1 *History* n.2 at 149, and in *New Light* n.3 at 50. William Garrott Brown in his *Life of Oliver Ellsworth* (1905; reprint, New York: Da Capo Press, 1970), n.1 at 186, repeats Flanders's statement and adds, "but he gives no reference and does not state that he himself had seen the document." H. L. Carson repeats Flanders's statement without citation of authority. Hampton L. Carson, *Supreme Court of the United States,* 2d ed. (Philadelphia: A. R. Keller, 1892), 129.

9. On October 24, 1924, Brandeis again wrote Warren a congratulatory letter, this time concerning Warren's lectures at Princeton, and added, "So I venture to express again the hope that your studies for the history of the lower federal courts are progressing." 5 *Letters of Louis D. Brandeis* 54 (1978). While this letter does not refer to the *New Light* article, it is worded in terms of a continuing study by Warren of the lower federal courts. The editors of Brandeis's letters, however, read the letter as showing that Warren never took up Brandeis's suggestion about a study of the lower court system. *Id.* n.2 at 54.

10. David W. Levy and Bruce Allen Murphy, "Preserving the Progressive Spirit in a Conservative Time: The Joint Reform Efforts of Justice Brandeis and Professor Frankfurter, 1916–1933," 78 *Michigan Law Review* 1252, 1275–91 (1980); Murphy, "Elements of Extrajudicial Strategy: A Look at the Political Roles of Justices Brandeis and Frankfurter," 69 *Georgetown Law Journal* 101, 123–26 (1980); Bruce Allen Murphy, *The Brandeis/Frankfurter Connection* 84–86 (New York: Oxford University Press, 1982).

11. The marginal notation on the back of LC 11, which is marked for insertion into the text, is counted by Warren as an amendment made by the Senate restricting the appellate jurisdiction of the Supreme Court. Warren, *New Light* 102. (The designation "LC" is explained in appendix 2.)

12. Warren, *New Light* n.5 at 50. The history of the care of the Senate files is seet forth in 1 *DocHistFirstFedCong* ix–x, but without taking note of the Warren article or of the temporary separation of the Judicial Bill manuscripts from the other files, detailed *infra*.

13. There is no other "Bill as passed by the Senate" except the House-printed version, and Warren's description does not seem to relate to a "printed" bill as passed by the Senate. The engrossed bill either was never removed from the Senate files or else it was returned to the Senate while the rest of the manuscripts were retained in the Library of Congress. In 1956 it was in the National Archives, not with the other manuscripts in the Library of Congress.

14. In 1956 when I sought to examine these manuscripts, I wrote a letter to the clerk of the Senate, inquiring whether the documents were still in the Senate files, and whether they could be examined there. The clerk replied that the archives of the Senate had been transferred to the Library of Congress. On a visit that summer to the Manuscripts Division of the Library, I was told that under the division of responsibility between the library and the National Archives, government documents such as these would be kept in the National Archives. When I went to the archives I was told that the manuscripts were not in its possession, although they were supposed to be; if anywhere, they must be in the Library of Congress. After returning to the library, and repeating a request to see the manuscripts, I was referred to Mr. Powell, head of the division. Mr. Powell said that he thought perhaps they were in the library and that he would check the shelf list. In a few minutes he returned, with the news that the manuscripts were in the vault, and when I filled out the proper request slip, I would be able to examine them. When the attendant at the desk returned with a large manila envelope, he showed it to his colleague, pointed to the writing on the envelope, and commented to the effect, "A lot of people would be surprised at what all is in that vault!"

I was handed a large, ragged, dusty manila envelope, across which had been written in a large hand in blue crayon:

Judiciary Act
of 1789
A Bill to establish the Judicial Courts of the U.S.

Beneath this, the following was written with an ordinary pencil, and circled with the same blue crayon:

246

Judiciary Act, 1789

Mar. 23 To be arranged, repaired
mounted and (perhaps) bound.
And returned to Senate files.

The documents at that date had been repaired and mounted, and arranged to the extent that each leaf bore a separate stamped number.

When I next examined the documents, on July 15, 1958, they were still at the Library of Congress, but the manila envelope had been discarded, and the manuscripts were in a more suitable folder.

Beginning on May 11, 1964, I tried to obtain from the Library of Congress photographic reproductions of these manuscripts, along with other materials relating to the First Congress. It took until July 10 to receive a response, which came from the National Archives, not the library, stating that the manuscripts were located among the records of the United States Senate (RG 46). Without being privy to the internal workings of the federal government, one might presume that this request for photoreproductions triggered a transfer of the manuscripts from the Library of Congress to the National Archives.

15. Warren, *New Light* 50–51.

16. *Id.* at 51.

17. *Id.* n.6 at 51, quoting from Madison to Joseph Wood (Ellsworth's son-in-law), Feb. 27, 1836, in Philip R. Fendall, ed., *Letters and Other Writings of James Madison,* vol. 4 (Philadelphia: Lippincott 1865), 427–28. Warren also cites Brown, *Ellsworth, supra* n.8, at 186: "There is enough in the Journals of the two Houses and in the debates of the House of Representatives to sustain Madison's impression that it went through without any radical change." Referring to this statement, Warren says, "The new facts disprove the statement." Warren, *New Light* n.6 at 51.

18. *Id.* at 60–61.

19. *Id.* at 61.

20. Some have read Warren's discussion of the early development of the Judicial Bill as though he were discussing only changes made by the Senate during stage four, that is, in the reported bill. See *e.g.,* James H. Chadbourn and A. Leo Levin, "Original Jurisdiction of Federal Questions," 90 *University of Pennsylvania Law Review* 639, n.9 at 641 (1942).

21. Warren, *New Light* 61–62.

22. *Id.* at 60–61, citing as the source Wharton, *State Trials* 37, 38 note. This quotation follows the text in Wharton except that Wharton also places a comma after "in controversies between foreigners and citizens." The presence or absence of this comma affects the meaning. Is the comma after "equity" being used to punctuate a series or as the beginning of an appositional or parenthetical phrase? That is, did Ellsworth mean by "original jurisdiction in law and equity" the same thing as "arising under this constitution, the laws of the United States"—the federal-question jurisdiction—or is this simply a descriptive statement of diversity suits, which can be brought either in law or equity? The Constitution says, "in law and equity, arising under this constitution, the laws of the United States." If Ellsworth was referring to this provision, it seems a little odd that he would not have referred to the more significant part of the clause, "arising under" rather than the part that

does not really define the grant of jurisdiction. Be that as it may, the language of this letter as misquoted by Warren does not unambiguously state that the committee was making an express grant of "federal-question" jurisdiction to the national courts.

23. Warren, *New Light* n.29 at 61.

24. *Id.* at 62.

25. *Id.* at 51.

26. 11 U.S. (7 Cranch) 32 (1812).

27. 14 U.S. (1 Wheat.) 415 (1814).

28. 41 U.S. (16 Pet.) 1 (1842).

29. Warren, *New Light* 85.

30. *Id.* at 79.

31. *Id.* at 99.

32. *Id.* n.14 at 79.

33. 1789 *Senate Journal* 61.

34. Warren discusses the first part of the amendment in *New Light* 99, citing the *Senate Journal* in footnote 133. He discusses the second part of the amendment at page 78 without citing the *Senate Journal*.

35. Alongside the margin, after one false start, which has been crossed out, he wrote as an additional sentence to this section: "And the mode of giving testimony in suits in equity & in causes of admiralty & maritime jurisdiction shall be the same as in trials at common law, or as is herein after specially provided." However, this last sentence, which is not crossed out, does not appear in the printed bill.

At the end of the line, he added (writing smaller apparently in order to fit his words into the available space): "Nor shall depositions be admitted in either of said courts in cases in equity." This was then crossed out. The smaller handwriting perhaps leads to the inference that this phrase was added and then deleted at a later time.

36. Maclay, *Sketches* 93. Read and Paterson, who favored equity, spoke against the clause. Maclay, who was against equity, favored the clause. *Id.* at 93–94.

37. 1789 *Senate Journal* 61–62.

38. Maclay, *Sketches* 101.

39. The quotes and discussion in this and the following paragraph are from *id.* at 102–4.

40. In light of this misreading, Warren says that LC 36, Paterson's motion to delete the section, was made on July 1 and was lost. It would appear that this motion was made on July 11, although the manuscript bears no date so this cannot be determined with certainty. The opposition to the clause arose first on July 1, on which date, Maclay reports, "Dr. Johnson rose first against the clause." Maclay, *Sketches* 93. The oppostion lost and the section was retained.

41. Vigorous objection was raised by Maclay and others to a provision in the draft bill of final Section 15 extending chancery methods of discovery to common-law cases. On this issue Ellsworth was on the opposite side to Maclay, who extensively reports both the debate and that he was successful in getting the offending provision stricken from the bill. See *id.* at 91–93. While Warren correctly reports this debate and the result, he misquotes the language that was stricken, quoting considerably more of the statute than was in fact eliminated. Warren, *New Light* n.103 at 96.

42. *Id.* at 96.

43. 5 U.S. (1 Cranch) 137, 174 (1803).

44. Warren, *New Light* 57. However, Warren errs in his listing of the members, claiming that Paine Wingate was a member of the convention (he was not) and omitting Richard Bassett (he was). Goebel, *History* n.8 at 459, calls attention to the error.

45. Warren, *New Light* n.21 at 57.

46. Warren's discussion of Section 13 is pretty much of a hodgepodge. He says that the Senate "inserted a limitation on the Court's jurisdiction over controversies 'where a State is a party,' by inserting the words 'except between a State and its citizens.' The fear had been expressed in many of the State Conventions that the language of the Constitution authorized a suit between a sovereign State by its citizens, in the Supreme Court, and the change from the Draft Bill was evidently made to allay this fear." Warren, *New Light* 93.

This limitation barring the national courts from jurisdiction in controversies "between a State and its citizens" was in both the manuscript and in the printed bills. Any efforts to allay the fears Warren refers to were made in the committee, not by action on the floor of the Senate.

47. 1 Warren, *History* 242.

48. Maclay, *Journal* 92, reports: "Mr. Lee moved that the postponed clause about the ambassadors, consuls, &c., should be taken up." Section 13 is the only section in the bill to which this description can refer.

49. Section 9 was amended to give the district courts jurisdiction exclusive of the state courts over suits against consuls or vice-consuls, "except for offences above the description aforesaid."

50. Maclay, *Sketches* 93, says the clause was taken up on July 1; Wingate noted this change on his copy of the bill. The inference therefore is that the action was taken on July 1.

51. LC 46. Warren, *New Light* n.98 at 93, cites and quotes this manuscript amendment, and in doing so ignores the page and line notations on the manuscript since those notations when related to the manuscript bill would have resulted in meaninglessness.

APPENDIX II

1. James H. Hutson, "The Creation of the Constitution: The Integrity of the Documentary Record," 65 *Texas Law Review* 1 (1986).

2. See, *e.g.,* Warren, *New Light* nn.60, 61 at 75.

3. See, *e.g.,* Goebel, *History* n.127 at 498.

4. This manuscript was found in the National Archives file relating to the Penal Bill. It was offered and agreed to by the Senate on April 14, 1790. *1790 Senate Journal* 59.

5. See chapter 2 and chapter 4.

6. Maclay, *Journal* 83.

7. James B. Childs, "The Story of the United States Senate Documents, 1st Congress, 1st Session, New York 1789," 56 *Papers of the Bibliographical Society* 175–94 (1962).

8. *Id.* at 183–84.

9. Ellsworth to Law, June 15, 1789, Ernst Law Manuscripts, Connecticut Historical Society, Hartford, Conn.

10. Ellsworth to Wolcott, June 15, 1789, Lee-Kohns Collection, New York Public Library, New York.

11. Read to Dickinson, June 16, 1789, in *Correspondence of George Read* 481.

12. Maclay, *Journal* 78. Maclay and Morris jointly sent a copy to President Mifflin of Pennsylvania. 11 *Pennsylvania Archives* 590–91 (1855).

13. Goebel, *History* 466. Goebel thinks that the "compositors had before them a manuscript copy of a bill of a later recension than the manuscript in the National Archives." He also thinks that there was "a later printing of the bill with amendments, no copy of which has been found." *Id.* n.120 at 497. He draws this conclusion, at least in part, from a notation on manuscript amendment LC 46 reading "amended in print." This reference is more logically interpreted as simply a reference to the printed copy of the bill being used by the Senate. While there was a second printing of the bill, about June 23, the date at which this printing was done strongly indicates it was simply the running off of additional copies of the June 16 print of the bill. There was no action taken between the dates that would have necessitated running off a new and different printing of the bill.

14. See Rollo G. Silver, *The American Printer 1787–1825* (Charlottesville: University Press of Virginia, 1967), 9, 93.

15. Spelling changes are detailed in chapter 7, n.4.

16. [This note was left blank by Professor Ritz. The editors have chosen not to speculate about the nature of these discrepancies. See the next note.]

17. Substantive discrepancies are pointed out and discussed in Goebel, *History* n.27 at 465–66.

18. Maclay, *Journal* 72; Maclay, *Sketches* 78.

19. The *Journal* does not list the members present at each day's session, but generally simply says, "Present as yesterday." The *Journal* for June 3 shows that Wingate was present to take the oath of office. 1789 *Senate Journal* 44–45. Thereafter there is no indication that he was absent from any session, and his name is quite frequently mentioned in connection with some specific action taken by the Senate.

20. 1789 *Senate Journal* 63. This amendment inserted the words "issues in" in the last line of Section 9.

21. For example, he makes no note of the Senate action of July 11, inserting a new section (19 of the final bill) between Sections 17 and 18 of the "renumbered" printed bill.

22. Goebel, *History* n.27 at 465. Goebel's source for this information says there are three copies, one in the Library of Congress, one in the New York Public Library, and one in the Chapin Library at Williams College, Williamstown, Mass. Childs, *Senate Documents* 183–84. Goebel used the New York Public Library copy.

23. *Id.* at 181.

24. *Id.* at 184.

25. 1789 *Senate Journal* 59–63.

26. Even if we assume that June 23 is the date of delivery, and it could have been earlier, and even if the order could have been placed after the second reading

began on June 22 so as to make possible delivery on June 23, nothing happened at the beginning of the second reading to have made a reprinting worthwhile. Maclay reports that on June 22 there was much discourse about the mode of doing business, much wrangling about words, and extended debate on Lee's motion to limit the federal courts to an admiralty and maritime jurisdiction, but without a vote's being taken. Maclay, *Journal* 85.

27. Read to Dickinson, *supra* n.11.

28. 5 *DocHistFirstFedCong* 1212 n.

29. 58 *Papers of the Bibliographical Society of America* 91–132 (1964). Childs expresses doubt about this bill being the House bill because, as he says, "it would be the only House Bill printed by Thomas Greenleaf thus far located." *Id.* at 112–13. However, there is another such bill in the Library of Congress, "An Act to establish an Executive Department to be denominated the Department of War," reproduced as Broadside no. 69 in *Broadsides Relating to the Ratification of the Constitution* issued by the Sesquicentennial Commission in 1927.

30. *New-York Journal,* July 20, 1789.

31. Hartley to Yeates, July 23, 1789, Yeates Papers, Historical Society of Pennsylvania, Philadelphia.

32. Childs, *House Documents* 112–13. Childs recognizes that upon passage by one house a bill becomes an "act" of that house, but when it reaches the other house it is still only a "bill" insofar as that house is concerned. Childs's reluctance to identify this bill misled the editors of *Short-title Evans* to be mp. 5,683.

33. Act of Sept. 15, 1789, ch. 14, § 2, 1 Stat. 68.

34. A copy is in the New York Public Library. *Checklist of Additions to Evans' American Bibliography in the Rare Book Division of the New York Public Library,* no. 945(23) (1960). This imprint and related ones are discussed in Childs, *House Documents* 125–32. Another copy is in the Chapin Library of Williams College, Williamstown, Mass. On October 8, 1789, George Washington sent a copy to Beverly Randolph, governor of Virginia. 5 *Calendar of State Papers* 19 (1885).

35. Childs, *House Documents* 130. A copy is known from a sale catalog, C. F. Heartman, Oct. 1, 1932. *Id.* While no complete set of these printings, on ordinary paper and not certified, is known, there are copies of some of the other acts in the New York Public Library, the American Antiquarian Society, Worcester, Mass., and the National Archives. *Id.*

36. Childs, *House Documents* 129, reports finding the same broken letter "t" in the officially certified copy as is found in a known Childs and Swaine imprint.

37. Bristol B7,185, mp. 45707 reads as follows: "Congress of the United States . . . An act to establish the judicial courts . . . Approved, September the 24th, 1789. [New York, F. Childs, 1789] 12 p. 34 cm. New York Public 945(23) MWiW-C; NN."

This description and the citation to "New York Public 945(23)" indicate that this is the certified copy in the New York Public Library, except that Bristol fails to state in his description that the imprint has a "Printed certificate signed in ms. by Samuel A. Otis and John Beckley," which information is provided for twenty-eight of the thirty-one entries made by Bristol for the certified copies in the New York Public Library. Without the additional descriptive line, the entry describes an imprint published on ordinary paper for distribution to members of Congress.

Such a copy of another act is in the New York Public Library and adequately described by Bristol in entry B7174. On the whole though, it seems most probable that Bristol intended the entry to be for the certified copy, and the failure to so describe it was only an oversight. Microcard mp. 45707 has not yet been issued, and so it cannot be determined how the Early American *Imprints* Project will handle the entry. *Short-title Evans* apparently treats it as one of the certified copies.

38. This is Bristol B7197, mp. 45179. Only one copy is known. It is at the University of Virginia and is reproduced on the microcard.

39. 5 *Diaries of George Washington* 452 (1979).

40. Childs, *House Documents* 129–30. These may have been copies over and above the ones necessary to fill the government's order for copies for members of Congress.

41. Evans, *American Bibliography* 21511 lists "An Act to establish the judicial courts of the United States. New York: Printed by Thomas Greenleaf. [1788] pp. 12. fol." Obviously, the dating is wrong. But beyond that is also the problem of the printer. Thomas Greenleaf printed "bills" but is not known to have printed a copy of the Judicial Bill titled "An Act." On the other hand, the "Act" in the sense of a law was printed by Childs, and the "Act" that was the law did have twelve pages. Microcard Evans 21511 says the entry is "Apparently a ghost of a later Federal Act."

42. Again bibliographical confusion enters the picture. It is Evans, *American Bibliography* 22949, erroneously dated 1790 instead of 1789. See Childs, *House Documents* 126.

43. 1789 *Senate Journal* 38–39.

44. Childs, *House Documents* 96–97.

45. The publication of these separate pamphlets is also referred to in letters that James Madison wrote to Wilson Cary Nicholas. On July 18, Madison began a letter to Nicholas by saying, "I enclose herewith the only printed addition which has been made to the sheets of the Journal forwarded by Mr. Hopkins." 12 *Papers of James Madison* 294. This was followed by another letter dated August 2, "My last enclosed a continuation of the printed Journals of the H. of Reps. I now add two sheets more. They are not otherwise valuable than as they serve to make up an entire sett." 12 *Papers of James Madison* 320.

There has been some confusion about this August 2 letter. Thomas Jefferson is named as the recipient and it is published in 15 *Papers of Thomas Jefferson* 324–25. The editors of the Madison Papers say that the evidence favors Nicholas as the recipient. This is confirmed by Madison's reference to an earlier letter, and there was such a letter to Nicholas written on July 18, as we have just seen, while there is no known similar letter to Jefferson. Childs, *House Documents,* relies on and quotes from the letter as published in *Papers of Thomas Jefferson,* but erroneously gives the date as "4 Aug." and reads the word "valuable" as "available."

46. Childs, *Senate Documents* n.3 at 178, says "some copies of the legislative journal seem to have been issued in blue-gray covers in at least the following parts": pp. 1–68 (through July 22), 69–100 (July 23–Aug. 20), 101–72 (through Sept. 29). Childs does not give the basis for his information, nor whether any copies are known. He does say there is a memorandum accompanying Greenleaf's account, showing that various quantities of these parts "up to a total of 700 copies were delivered at different times in each month, from 21 July to 9 Oct." *Ibid.*

47. "Thomas Lloyd's Reports of the First Federal Congress," 18 *William and Mary Quarterly* (3d Ser.) 519, 530 (1961).

48. *Id.* at 531.

49. *Id.* at 520. This publication is usually cited as *Annals of Congress* or simply as *Annals.* It was published with two numbered columns to the page and thus is usually cited by column, not page.

50. See William R. Casto, "The First Congress's Understanding of Its Authority over the Federal Courts' Jurisdiction," 26 *Boston College Law Review* 1101, 1127–41 (1985).

51. *See* Warren, *New Light* n.32 at 63.

52. *See* Goebel, *History* 831.

53. In *Nixon v. Fitzgerald,* 457 U.S. 731 (1982), the justices of the Supreme Court used different editions of Maclay, but this created no problem as both editions are complete on the subject involved. Justice Powell used the 1890 *Journal.* *Id.* n.31 at 750–51. Justice White used the 1969 reprint of the 1880 *Sketches. Id.* n.18 at 776.

54. In the preface to the 1890 edition, Edgar S. Maclay wrote that, in the 1880 edition, "Many passages . . . were suppressed, as being too caustic in their strictures on eminent personages whom we are accustomed to regard with the highest veneration." Maclay, *Journal* vi.

55. Warren, *New Light* n.100 at 98.

56. Goebel, *History* 498.

57. Warren, *New Light* 49.

58. Goebel, *History* 494.

59. We should be grateful to Maclay for what he did leave in the way of information about the First Congress instead of harping about what he did not report. After all, he is the only senator, so far as is now known, who kept a journal during the First Congress, or at least the only one whose journal has survived.

60. Childs, *House Documents;* Childs, *Senate Documents.*

61. 1789 *Senate Journal* 10.

62. *Id.* at 14.

63. 1 *Documentary History of the First Federal Congress* x–xi.

64. 3 *id.* xiv–xvi.

65. 1 *Journal of the House of Representatives,* publisher's note (Wilmington, Del.: Michael Glazier, Inc., 1977), [ii].

66. Joseph Gales, comp. (Washington, D.C., Government Printing Office, 1834).

Index

Brown and White Taxicab (continued)
Co. v. Brown and Yellow Taxicab
and Transfer Co.:* 160
Black's Law Dictionary: 38
Blackstone, William: 32–33, 39, 115,
217 nn.19, 34
Blair, John: 117, 119
Boston Gazette: 191
Boudinot, Elias: 73
Bowling, Kenneth: 193
Bradford, William, Jr.: 73, 76,
226 n.75
Brandeis, Louis: 9, 25, 79, 160–63,
166, 244 nn.57, 64, 245 nn.64, 6, 7,
9; *see also* Section 34, Judiciary Act
of 1789
Brearley, David: 117–18
Bribery, penalty for: 113, 235 n.70
Bristol, Roger P.: 196
Britain: *see* England, eighteenth-
century law in
Broughman, Lord: 34
Brown (mutineer): 119
Brown v. Van Braam: 156
Bruntjen, Carol and Scott: 196
"Brutus": 109
Butler, Pierce: 15, 62, 162, 163, 191,
214 n.23, 215 nn.33, 37

Calder v. Bull: 142
Callender, James Thompson: 154–55
Capital punishment: 122
Cardozo, Benjamin: 163
Carroll, Charles: 213 n.3, 214 n.23
Carter, Howard M.: 159
Carter, John: 90
Case: and controversy contrasted, 89–
92, 146, 228 n.37, 229 n.42; and
cause contrasted, 93
*Catalogue of the Books belonging to the
said Library* (New York Society): 50
Cause: 93–94, 96, 229 nn.47, 52; and
case contrasted, 93
Certiorari, writ of: 39, 67, 70; in *Erie
Railroad Co. v. Tompkins,* 162
Chancery: *see* Court of Chancery
Chase, Samuel: 154–55, 157
Checklist of American Imprints, A: 196

Childs, Francis: 188, 190, 197
Childs, James B.: 183, 186, 187, 196,
251 nn.29, 32, 34–36, 252 nn.40–
42, 44–46
Chipman, Nathaniel: 116–17
Choice of law: 12
Circuit courts: 23; jurisdiction of,
56–57, 59, 69, 114 (*see also* Judi-
ciary Act of 1789, Section 11); and
district courts contrasted, 64–66;
first session of, 119–20; makeup of,
224 n.46
Civil actions: 71
Clements (Virginia defendant):
155–56
Coasting Act: 113, 115, 235 n.69
Coke, Edward: 36
Collateral estoppel: 28
Collection Act: 113, 115
Commentaries (Blackstone): 32
Common law: 7, 73–74; English, 32,
33, 116–17, 217 nn.23, 33; in
Northwest Territory, 78; trials at,
97, 142–44; of crimes, 98, 116,
146–48; federal, 98; Section 34
and, 142–45; writs of, 222 n.9
Commonwealth v. Schaffer: 154
Conductor Generalis: 38
Confederation: 98–102; trials for mari-
time crimes under, 99–101, 105
Congress, First U.S.: 3–5, 8–21, 40;
and state-law data, 49–50; and Article III, 54–56, 72–79; and criminal jurisdiction, 111–17; second
session of, 120–25; surviving manuscripts of, 180–90; *see also* House of
Representatives, First U.S.; Senate,
First U.S.
Congress, U.S.: criminal powers of,
99, 105–106, 108; *see also* Congress, First U.S.; Continental Congress; Senate, U.S.
Congressional Register: 190
Connecticut: separation of powers in,
31; appellate-review apparatus of,
42
Constitution, U.S.: Article III of, 4–7,
11, 14, 21, 22, 40, 51, 53–56, 58,